A People
Highly Favoured
of God

A People Highly Favoured of God

*The Nova Scotia Yankees
and the American Revolution*

*GORDON STEWART
and GEORGE RAWLYK*

Macmillan of Canada / Toronto

ISBN 7705-0866-9

Library of Congress Catalogue Card No. 70-178199

Printed in Canada for the
Macmillan Company of Canada Limited
70 Bond St., Toronto

Contents

PART TWO:

*Henry Alline and the Great
Awakening in Nova Scotia*

"Curse ye Meroz, said the Angel of the Lord, curse ye bitterly the Inhabitants thereof; because they came not to the Help of the Lord against the Mighty." *Judges*, 5, 23

"[The Inhabitants of Meroz] did not assist their Brethren. They Attended their Business at Home and would not fight, though the Safety of their Country, and Recovery of their Liberty, called them to the Field . . . they stood NEUTERS while their Nation was engaged in war."

Samuel Finley, *The Curse of Meroz; or the Danger of Neutrality in the Cause of God and our Country*

"CHRIST has declared there is no such Thing as a Neuter; neither in his Kingdom nor his Enemies for if they are not engaged in His Cause they be in the Cause of Anti-Christ."

Henry Alline, *Two Mites on Some of the Most Important and Much Disputed Points of Divinity*

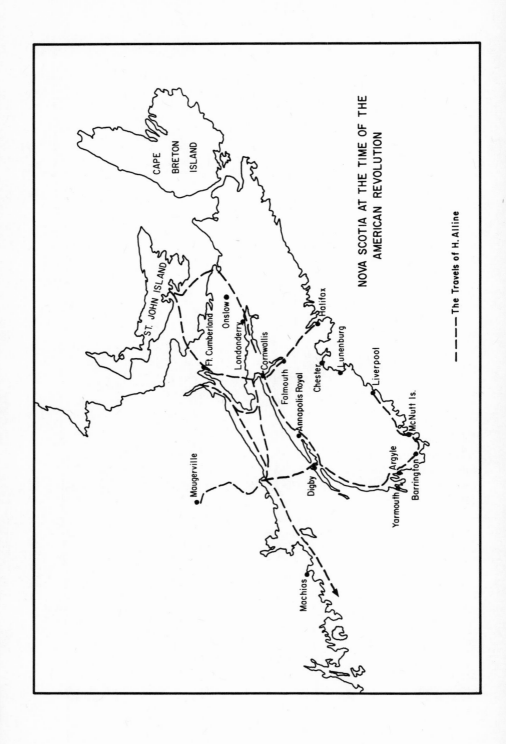

NOVA SCOTIA AT THE TIME OF THE
AMERICAN REVOLUTION

------ The Travels of H. Alline

CAPE
BRETON
ISLAND

ST. JOHN ISLAND

Ft. Cumberland
Onslow
Londonderry
Cornwallis
Falmouth
Annapolis Royal
Chester
Lunenburg
Halifax
Liverpool
McNutt Is.
Argyle
Barrington
Yarmouth
Digby
Maugerville
Machias

Preface

In analysing and describing the response of Nova Scotia to the American Revolution this study concentrates on intellectual history, particularly on the influence of religious ideas. This does not stem from a belief that such an approach provides the magic key to a complete understanding of Nova Scotian behaviour or that such an approach is somehow more enlightening than a socio-economic investigation. Quite simply, most of the evidence to be found is in the form of petitions, memorials and sermons and is, therefore, amenable to this type of examination. In spite of, or more probably, because of its small, scattered and recently settled population there is little evidence in the form of probate records, assessment lists or tax returns to give a comprehensive picture of the colony's socio-economic structure in the pre-revolutionary period. There is, on the other hand, some evidence concerning the reaction of many of the people to the outbreak of the revolutionary war and adequate evidence on the great religious revival that spread through most of the colony from 1776 to 1783. The primary purpose of this book is to analyse the religious ideology produced during this revival and to assess its effect on the attitudes of recent New England immigrants in Nova Scotia towards the Revolution.

This is, however, not the same type of intellectual study as that produced, for instance, by Professor Bernard Bailyn in his seminal *Ideological Origins of the American Revolution*, but merely written on a more restricted scale commensurate with Nova Scotia's relative backwardness and the limitations of the authors. It is a fundamentally different level of approach since it does not deal, at any stage, with the opinions and writings of traditional elite groups. The leader of the revival, Henry Alline, the self-taught son of a small farmer, openly acknowledged his limited education and despised those who obtained learning "merely to attain the Name of a Collegian."[1] His major opponent, Jonathan Scott, who conducted a futile campaign against the revival, was a one-time apprentice shoemaker and fisherman who had trained himself as a minister and who, even after his ordination, still made his living from farming. Neither of these two men had seen the insides of Harvard or Yale or had attended any educational establishment, however modest, since their childhood days. This approach is not, therefore, open to the criticism that because it deals with ideas it ignores the views of ordinary people. This is an intellectual history of a people "at the bottom" who read but little and whose major preoccupations in life were tilling fields and catching fish.

But, in this context, it must be emphasized "intellectual history" is probably too pretentious a term to use. Because this book deals with the value system of inarticulate, largely uneducated farmers and fishermen living in isolated settlements, there is none of the richness and sophistication in the ideas under investigation that American scholars have discovered in revolutionary pamphlets and other sources. The ideology propagated by Alline during the Great Awakening in Nova Scotia was simple, confined to one track and repetitive. Rather than being intellectual history it is more accurate to regard this volume as an attempt to describe the effect of widely held religious values on a particular society at a critical period in its development. But while recognizing these limitations in the ideas under investigation it is worth noting the unusual opportunities offered by this type of evidence. It is usually extremely difficult to discover the values and ideas held by the inarticulate masses in the American colonies. Yet in the Nova Scotian outsettlements there was no superstructure of lawyers and merchants to monopolize public communication within the social system and to smother, by their superior talents, the efforts of the less articulate to express themselves. In the Nova Scotian outsettlements these top layers of society were peeled off, as it were, and the farmers and fishermen exposed and left to formulate their own responses to the crises they faced.

It is essential, in this connexion, to clarify which people in Nova Scotia this study deals with. It is, quite specifically, restricted to an investigation of the so-called Nova Scotia "Yankees" who lived in townships scattered through the back country of the colony. In 1758 and 1759, Governor Charles Lawrence of Nova Scotia had issued two proclamations encouraging New Englanders to come to the northern colony.[2] He wished to settle English-speaking Protestants on lands from which most of the Acadians had been expelled in 1755 and also in 1758. In the second of these proclamations, made public in January of 1759, Lawrence emphasized that "the quantities of land granted will be in proportion to the abilities of the planter to settle, cultivate and enclose the same" and that quit-rents would not be collected by the crown until ten years after the issuing of the grant. After asserting that no one person would be granted more than one thousand acres, Lawrence assured all potential emigrants that they would feel at home in Nova Scotia. The government, both at the local township and provincial level as well as the courts of justice, was "constituted in like manner with those of Massachusetts, Connecticut and the other Northern Colonies." And as far as religious freedom was concerned "full liberty of conscience . . . Papists excluded" was promised.

The generous terms offered by Lawrence were, without question, far more attractive than those being circulated at the same time, about their New England holdings, by various land-speculators and proprietors. The Nova Scotia governor could not have selected a more propitious time to recruit settlers in Massachusetts, Connecticut and Rhode Island.[3] There were hundreds of farmers looking for cheap yet good arable land to cultivate and there were also hundreds of fishermen wanting the chance to move to the southern tip of Nova Scotia where they could "carry on the fishery to greater advantage."[4]

From 1759 to the end of 1763, when the emigration movement lost much of its original momentum, approximately five thousand Yankees had settled in Nova Scotia.[5] The vast majority of these people, whether farmers or fishermen, came from that relatively small corner of New England created when a line is drawn from New London, Connecticut, northwards to Brookfield, Massachusetts, and then eastwards to Plymouth. This was the area where, in 1759 and 1760, there was considerable tension and controversy between the "Proprietors" and others over the right to common lands as well as over the high prices being charged by the former for farming land. This was also the region which had been profoundly affected by the Great Awakening — the religious revival that had swept the colonies in the early 1740s.

To leave the relative security of settled New England to become uprooted immigrants on the distant Nova Scotia frontier was not an easy decision for anyone to make and indicates something of the extent of the existing discontent with the economic and social status quo. Those who were farmers pushed into the vacated Acadian lands on the south shore of the Minas Basin and around Cobequid Bay, in the vicinity of Annapolis Royal, and the Isthmus of Chignecto. A few others, from Essex County north of Boston, moved up the St. John River to Maugerville, near present-day Fredericton. The fishermen, on the other hand, settled at Yarmouth, Barrington, Liverpool and Chester, that region of Nova Scotia that had since the middle of the seventeenth century been regarded as a strategically located outpost of the New England fishery. By the outbreak of the Revolution there were living in the isolated New England outsettlements of Nova Scotia 12,000 Yankees, out of a total population of some 20,000 inhabitants.

This book is a revised version of Gordon Stewart's doctoral dissertation, "Religion and the Yankee Mind of Nova Scotia during the American Revolution" (completed in August 1971 at Queen's University), where the specialist reader can find fuller documentation for the case presented here.

A study of the Nova Scotia Yankees under stress during the American Revolution and of the impact Henry Alline had upon the colony, it is an attempt to place Nova Scotia's response to the

Revolution in the larger context of North American, and especially New England, development, and also within the framework of recent American historiography.

We are especially indebted to various librarians and archivists in the United States and in Canada who have made much of our research both possible and enjoyable. In particular, the staffs of the following institutions have been most helpful: the Public Archives of Canada, the Public Archives of Nova Scotia, the Acadia University Archives, the Massachusetts State Archives, the Massachusetts Historical Society, the Rhode Island Historical Society, the Connecticut Historical Society and the Douglas Library at Queen's University. We also owe a great deal to the generous financial assistance provided by the Canada Council and by Queen's University. Most graduate students in the History 823 seminar at Queen's University from 1969 to 1970 have helped in some way to clarify our thinking about revolutionary Nova Scotia and we acknowledge their contributions. Professor Carl Berger of the History Department, University of Toronto, and Professor S. F. Wise of the History Department, Carleton University, and Director of the Canadian Armed Forces Directorate of History carefully read an earlier draft of the manuscript and suggested a number of ways in which the study could be improved. We have implemented many of their suggestions. In conclusion, we would like to express our thanks to Mrs. Diane Mew of the Macmillan Company of Canada for her assistance in the writing of the book. She has been both a patient editor and a sensitive critic.

May, 1971
East Lansing, Michigan   GORDON STEWART
Kingston, Ontario   GEORGE RAWLYK

A People
Highly Favoured
of God

Introduction

In recent interpretations of the American Revolution, many historians have focused their attention on ideological factors. In particular, the work of Bernard Bailyn has, in a masterly manner, illuminated the process by which traditional colonial political, legal and religious values and attitudes were, in the late 1760s and 1770s, transformed into a revolutionary ideology that propelled many colonists to fight for American independence. During these years the "views men held towards the relationships that bound them to each other — the discipline and pattern of society" moved in a fundamentally different direction. As far as Bailyn is concerned the "right, the need, the absolute obligation to disobey legally constituted authority" became the "universal cry" of the Patriots as they attempted to obtain liberty during the decade following the Stamp Act Crisis.[1]

In a less convincing study, Professor Alan Heimert has attempted to explain the influence of evangelical religion in the formation of the American revolutionary mind. For him, evangelical Calvinism "provided pre-Revolutionary America with a radical, even democratic, social and political ideology" and "embodied, and inspired, a thrust toward American nationalism."[2] While Heimert's analysis has been received with some misgivings, mainly on the grounds that he has read too much into post-1740 sermon literature, the interpretation advanced by

Bailyn has been widely accepted by other scholars working in the field. According to this version, the Revolution was essentially an affair of the mind, a growing awareness during the late 1760s and 1770s of the uniqueness of "American" political, social and religious values that were being threatened by an imagined British conspiracy. Such an analysis implies, as Professor Robert E. Brown had earlier argued in the case of Massachusetts, that the American colonies were relatively democratic with no deep and permanent class divisions and that the Revolution was directed specifically against the "new" British colonial policy.[3] The underlying implication of such an interpretation of the Revolution is that a virtual consensus united most colonists around certain American values.

One of the most frequent criticisms levelled against this consensus interpretation of the Revolution is that, since it relies principally on an approach through the history of ideas, it deals only with élite groups in the American colonies and fails to explain what motivated the great mass of the people to participate in a struggle for political liberty. The Bailyn method, relying on the written words of articulate, educated, well-connected men is, therefore, characterized by some critics as élitist history which, at best, can only partially explain the forces behind the Revolution. Even in the case of Heimert, who deals in detail with the evangelical movement that affected many of the poorer areas of the colonies, there is a tendency, when seeking to estimate the relationship of revivalism to political issues of the time, to turn to the writings of educated ministers and preachers. Professor Jessie Lemisch, perhaps the most persistent critic of the consensus approach, has argued that the time has come to shift the focus of analysis and begin writing the history of the Revolution from the perspective of the revolutionary mobs. In spite of the great difficulties in obtaining evidence about such people, Lemisch maintains that there is a great deal that can be discovered about the distinctive forces of change generated by the inarticulate masses in the colonies.[4]

The debate generated by Bailyn's study is the latest stage of two decades of revisionist writing on the revolutionary period, but in the case of Nova Scotia's response to the Revolution no new interpretations have appeared in the past thirty years.

Since the publication in 1937 of J.B. Brebner's influential and groundbreaking study, *The Neutral Yankees of Nova Scotia*, it has been generally accepted that the Nova Scotia Yankees during the revolutionary war, like their Acadian predecessors during periods of Anglo-French conflict, resolved to walk the knife-edge of neutrality.[5] Even though he warned his readers of the great danger of relying "on a single explanation for Nova Scotian behaviour" Brebner nevertheless concluded that the colony's "insulation from the rest of North America" provided the "principal clue" to Nova Scotia's pragmatic response to the Revolution. Brebner thus emphasized what he perceived to be a striking theme of continuity in Nova Scotia's eighteenth-century experience. The Yankees, in spite of their New England origins and ties, were forced into the same frustrating predicament as their predecessors, the neutral French-speaking Acadians. When war came to the northeastern extremity of the Thirteen Colonies, whether it was the imperial struggle between France and Britain or the Revolutionary War between Britain and America, it seemed, for Brebner, "naturally and almost inevitably" that the residents of Nova Scotia had no capacity for any independent action. Barely fifteen years out of New England, the Nova Scotia Yankees had been transformed, in a sense, by the forces of geography, into "Acadian Neutrals."

Locked into his "neutrality paradigm," Brebner probably placed far too much stress on the strikingly similar response of the Acadians in 1755 and the Yankees in 1776. In Nova Scotia, the Yankees, as Brebner correctly pointed out, were certainly affected by many of the same strategic and geographical considerations that had impinged upon the Acadians two decades earlier. But the Yankee society was grounded upon radically different beliefs and attitudes and it was by no means almost inevitable that the New England settlers would respond to these pressures in the same way. Impressed by the thread of continuity he had discovered in *New England's Outpost* (1927), his history of the Acadians, Brebner was tempted to impose this environmental deterministic framework on his account of the Nova Scotia Yankees during the revolutionary period.

A further weakness in Brebner's study is his almost total neglect of the religious revival that profoundly affected most of the outsettlements during the Revolution. The revival, "The Great Awakening of Nova Scotia," was led by the charismatic Henry Alline, who was one Nova Scotian able to perceive a special purpose for his fellow colonists in the midst of the confused revolutionary situation. Since Brebner was writing in the 1930s when religious history had not achieved the importance it is now accorded by many American and European scholars, this omission is understandable. But his failure to give sufficient attention to such a major social occurrence in the outsettlements in the war years was also determined to some extent by his tendency to concentrate on the situation in Halifax. He undertook a thorough description of the outsettlements but always through the perspective of an observer in Halifax. Brebner himself was well aware that events proceeded in the capital quite independently of events in the outsettlements, but he failed to give the same detailed attention to the latter sequence of events as he did to affairs in Halifax. He gives a first-class analysis of Halifax from the inside but his approach to the outsettlements is usually from an outside point of view. In this manner Brebner not only failed to appreciate the possible significance of the religious revival but he missed many of the nuances and subtleties of the Yankee predicament during the revolutionary period.

Since the publication of Brebner's book two scholars have attempted to examine more fully the effect of the revival on the Nova Scotia Yankees. But in both cases the general framework of the neutrality thesis has not been questioned. Professor Maurice W. Armstrong in 1946 argued that the religious enthusiasm was primarily an aspect of the Yankee neutrality complex. Armstrong concluded that "the Great Awakening itself may be considered to have been a retreat from the grim realities of the world to the safety and pleasantly exciting warmth of the revival meeting."[6] This explanation of the revival was simply an extended footnote to the Brebner thesis, for the religious movement appeared to be merely one way in which the Yankees could make neutrality more tolerable. Their attention was turned to religious issues and in the revival meetings they could forget about the war. A more recent analysis of the revival, by Professor S. D. Clark, also reaffirmed a faith in the neutrality thesis. According to Clark "the forces at work in 1776 were essentially the same forces which earlier had led the Acadians to seek a position of neutrality."[7]

Both Armstrong and Clark discovered that during the revival the Yankees were beginning to formulate a new value system that they hoped would provide them with a new collective identity. Yet Armstrong and Clark acknowledged the appropriateness of the neutrality thesis to characterize Yankee behaviour during the war. They seemed reluctant to investigate the possibility that since the Yankees, according to their own analyses, were pursuing an "independent" course, the whole neutrality concept might be inadequate. In spite of the way their evidence was pushing them, Armstrong and Clark could not free themselves from the neutrality strait-jacket Brebner had thrown over the historical problem.

This is not, however, to argue that the neutrality thesis is completely irrelevant but simply that it is too limited to account for all the forces operating in Yankee society. Some Yankees during the first year of the war did sign petitions in which they requested the status of neutrals. But such memorials were restricted to that short period. There is little evidence to indicate that this quest for neutrality persisted for the following six years of war. Brebner, placing a great deal of emphasis on parallels with the Acadians, concluded that these petitions represented the typical or dominating characteristic of Yankee society not only during 1775 and 1776 but also throughout the entire revolutionary war. The implication of his neutrality thesis was that the Yankees possessed a clear view of their predicament, made a calculated assessment of the options open to them and embarked, like the Acadians, on a deliberate campaign to be recognized as neutrals. But this is too simple and too static a concept to apply to the Nova Scotia Yankees. Neutrality was only one part of their response to events and even then it was confined to the critical opening months of the revolutionary war. Neutrality was not a persistent characteristic of Yankee society.

If neutrality pleas are kept in proper perspective other factors may be more clearly discerned and a quite different picture emerges. The situation in the outsettlements appears much more fluid and unstable; far from being pragmatically certain of what course they ought to follow, the Yankees may be seen as a people confused by the repercussions of the war between Britain and the colonies they had recently left. The war precipitated an acute disorientation in the traditional loyalties and value systems of the Yankees in Nova Scotia. It was in these disturbed conditions that the revival, led by Henry Alline, extended its influence throughout most of the outsettlements. If the revival is seen against this background of socio-psychological unrest its importance and impact on that society comes into clearer focus.

Once the "neutral Yankee" concept is placed in its proper context it may be seen that the revival was not a sudden emotional explosion unrelated to the previous history of the Nova Scotia Yankees. In order to come to grips with the complex impact of the revival, it is necessary to examine the essential nature and development of Yankee society in the colony from the early 1760s. Related in this way to recent Yankee history, it may become much more evident why the Great Awakening was so relevant for the Yankees in terms of the political and military crises they faced from 1776 to 1783.

The Nova Scotia Yankees did not turn to the revival simply as a second-best alternative to participating, with their former colonies, in the Revolution. Nor was it basically a revolt of the outsettlements against Halifax or an irrational outburst against all forms of traditionalism and authority. The Great Awakening of Nova Scotia may be viewed instead as an attempt by many inhabitants to appropriate a sense of identity — an awareness of being Nova Scotian. The Nova Scotia Yankees needed a new ideology to understand and cope with contemporary issues and events. They were a people holding many New England values; they still possessed an attachment to their New England homeland. Yet during the war they were trapped in the British-controlled northern colony. This situation precipitated a crisis in their value system and patterns of loyalty. It was during this time of acute disorientation that the revival achieved its greatest popularity. Religious enthusiasm then in this context, a social movement of profound consequence, was symptomatic of a collective identity crisis as well as a searching for an acceptable and meaningful ideology. Resolution of this crisis came not only when people were converted but also when they accepted Alline's analysis of contemporary events.

Part I

"The Whole Province is in Confusion, Trouble and Anguish"

1

The
Missing Decade

As Britain persisted in the years after 1763 in her attempts to tax the Thirteen Colonies and to bring her American possessions under tighter control, the New England colonists organized political resistance and carefully defined the legally limited dependence they believed the colonies were subject to. As John Adams explained many years later, it was in those ten years of political debate that many Americans, fearing what the Patriots believed was a British "conspiracy" to destroy American "liberty," began to discard their loyalty to Britain. "The real American Revolution" occurred in the decade preceding the military events of 1775-76 and, observed Adams, consisted in the "radical change in the principles, opinions, sentiments and affections of the people."[1]

Those thousands of Yankees who had emigrated to Nova Scotia in the early 1760s did not, however, undergo this radical change. The colonists who remained in New England, in contrast, experienced "in the intense political heat after 1763" a new awareness of certain American practices and values that they felt had to be protected even if this entailed independence from Britain. By 1776 the revolutionary ideology had produced a "comprehensive view, unique in its moral and intellectual appeal, about the world and America's place in it."[2] During this

3

decade of transformation in New England and most of the Thirteen Colonies, the Yankees in Nova Scotia remained remarkably untouched by these contemporary currents of opinion that were radically changing America's view of the relationship with Britain.

Nova Scotia's response to this decade of radical change was an exception to the general pattern of political transformation that affected New Englanders in the 1760s and 1770s. This is not to argue, however, that there were no controversial issues in Nova Scotia during this period. There were, but the configuration of attitudes produced by them remained in the form of a non-revolutionary ideology. The failure of colonial revolutionary ideas to take root in Nova Scotia was not simply the result of remoteness, sparseness of settlement and the lack of homogeneity in the population, although these were important background factors. What primarily decided that the Nova Scotia Yankees would not conform to the general American pattern was that the form of government and the nature of society precluded the development of what some historians have described as the necessary "general enlightenment" of key sections of the population. Some of the rhetoric of protest may have appeared to be the same but in Nova Scotia it always tended to be hedged with limitations and weakened by self-doubt. The Nova Scotia Yankees were, throughout these years, an isolated group of colonists whose traditional values and assumptions failed to transcend their traditionality and become the foundation for novel revolutionary opinions.

One thing which tended to set Nova Scotia apart from the New England colonies, especially, was that the methods adopted for its settlement had been unique. And in the eyes of some influential Americans in the 1760s this fact had been disastrous for the future political and constitutional development of "New England's Outpost." The first serious attempt by the British authorities to control the whole of peninsular Nova Scotia occurred in 1749 when Governor Edward Cornwallis arrived at Halifax, the new capital. The settlement of Halifax was primarily a military venture designed to create a strong British counterpoise to Louisbourg, the French "Gibraltar of North America." For the next ten years Nova Scotia was governed by military officials from the new fortress-capital. By 1758, a House of Assembly had been finally set up by the reluctant Lawrence. But the aura of suspicion created by the ten years of tight military rule was never completely cleared from the minds of many American colonists, particularly in New England, which region had, since the middle of the seventeenth century, been closely involved in Nova Scotia affairs.

In spite of Governor Charles Lawrence's assurance made to potential New England emigrants in 1759 that the form of government in Nova Scotia would be similar to that of the New England colonies, there were several fundamental differences which ensured that the northern colony would be kept under strict British control and would consequently develop quite differently. With the convening of the Assembly in October 1758 Nova Scotia possessed a governmental structure consisting of a governor, a Council and a House of Assembly, but in contrast to Massachusetts there was no charter to limit the powers of the executive branch. Throughout the period from 1758 to 1776 the Council was composed of men nominated by the governors in Nova Scotia or by the Board of Trade in London. The appointments were made to the Council with the explicit criterion in mind that the candidate be well disposed to the administration. Those who served on the Council invariably either held official positions in the colony or were in some way dependent on the government for patronage. Throughout the 1760s and early 1770s these appointed Councils, as one contemporary critic put it, "brandished the shield of Prerogative." In Massachusetts, prior to 1774, the governors had been forced to deal with strong political opposition from within the elected Council. In Nova Scotia the Council usually provided unquestioning support for the administration.[3]

The position of the governor was made even more secure from potential opposition because most of the government's income was independent of local control. Beginning with the establishment of Halifax in 1749 the British authorities, through Parliament, supplied most of the money required to run the colony. Between 1748 and 1752, for example, over £300,000 was spent on Nova Scotia and this policy of annual appropriations continued through the 1760s and 1770s. The only other sources of revenue apart from these parliamentary grants were returns from certain imposts and an excise on such items as spirituous beverages. But from 1758 to 1767 these sources brought in about £2,250 annually while parliamentary grants averaged £9,000 per annum. These circumstances meant that in Nova Scotia control of the purse was simply not an issue on which constitutional debate between governor and Assembly could focus. The governor, supported by an appointed Council, was subjected to very little pressure by the representatives of the people. The Assembly itself functioned differently from its counterpart in Massachusetts. Throughout the period from 1758 to 1776, the Nova Scotian Assembly did not reflect the views of the areas outside Halifax. The effective majority in the House was made up of Halifax men who generally were attached to the office-holding, patronage-seeking circles in the capital.[4]

Nova Scotians living in the outsettlements were never able to shake themselves entirely free from the control of the Halifax officials. In sharp contrast, many residents of New England, with varying degrees of assertiveness and clarity, maintained that they were living in "lands of liberty" where royal authority was strictly limited. During the 1760s they defined and defended those ancient rights and privileges they believed were inalienably theirs. The Nova Scotia Yankees, however, found it difficult to share this perception of their colony's past. Nova Scotia had never been a "land of liberty" either under the weak government at Annapolis Royal from 1710 to 1749, when the population had been overwhelmingly Roman Catholic and French-speaking, or when under the military control of Halifax from 1749 to 1758.

During the decade of military rule, some Yankee settlers in Halifax had emphasized the arbitrary nature of the Nova Scotian government and this criticism must have significantly influenced the prevailing stereotype of the colony in New England. There was no doubt, wrote one Halifax merchant back to Boston in 1757, that arbitrary and bad government was undermining the development of Nova Scotia. As a result the New England immigrants were "determined to fly from such illegal, high and arbitrary Measures to take their flight and return to a

Land of Liberty where their Fortunes and Persons would not be exposed to the Prejudice and Caprice of men so contrary to them in Circumstances and Principles."[5] Early in the following year these same people complained that they were "the shameful and Contemptible By-Word of America; The Slaves of Nova Scotia, the Creatures of Military Govrs; whose will, is our Law, and whose Person, is our God."[6] Judged by the standards then current in the New England colonies, the government in Halifax was tyrannical and Nova Scotia was not a land of liberty. The Yankee immigrants were very conscious of being confronted by a system quite alien to New England political and constitutional traditions.

Involved as they were in the Seven Years' War, most New Englanders regarded Nova Scotia and its problems as being of little consequence. Nevertheless, a few American observers, even before the war had ended, began to consider the implications for all the Thirteen Colonies of British policy in Nova Scotia. Writing in 1759 from London where he was in contact with the men who made British colonial policy, Benjamin Franklin, a native of Massachusetts, maintained that the British planned to extend the type of administration they had set up in Nova Scotia to all of the Thirteen Colonies. The attitude of the British government towards the colonies, as Franklin saw it, was "that the Colonies have too many and too great Privileges; and that it is not only the Interest of the Crown but of the Nation to reduce them." As for particular ministers, the Earl of Halifax, who "governs all" at the Board of Trade, had revealed his remedy — his Nova Scotia design — for the malady of colonial independence. According to Franklin, "the fruitless experiment he has try'd at the nations cost of a military Government for a colony sufficiently shows what he thinks would be best for us."[7] For Franklin, what had happened in Nova Scotia since 1749 was a clear warning to the Thirteen Colonies that a more rigorous assertion of ministerial control would probably follow the signing of a peace treaty with France.

Events in the 1760s seemed to prove the accuracy of Franklin's prediction regarding the new British colonial policy and Nova Scotia's special role in ministerial plans. In 1763, as part of his attempt to exercise stricter control over the colonies, George

Grenville, Chancellor of the Exchequer, arranged for an order-in-council to establish a new Vice-Admiralty Court in Halifax with original jurisdiction over all cases arising from evasion of the terms of the Navigation Acts. Halifax was deliberately chosen because it was free of any of the insidious influence of the "mobbish inhabitants" who made the British position so weak in Boston and other American ports. Even though, in the four years of its existence from 1764 to 1768, little business was done by the Halifax Court, it became a symbol of the new departure in British colonial policy. It was obvious why Halifax had been selected; Nova Scotia was the only colony where the British government could be certain that there would be no opposition to "the cornerstone in the new imperial rule."[8]

By 1764 then, it seemed obvious in New England that Nova Scotia was being turned into a British power base in North America from which British officials could force their will on the other colonies. Nova Scotia was increasingly regarded not as a recently settled colony similar to the other colonies but as simply a tool of scheming British ministers. Writing in 1765 on the rights of the colonies, Stephen Hopkins, governor of Rhode Island, pointed out that the British entrenchment in Nova Scotia enabled customs officers "to make a seizure in Georgia, of goods ever so legally imported, and carry the trial to Halifax, at fifteen hundred miles distance" where the owner would be forced to defend his case "among total strangers."[9] Hopkins felt that the uncontested British hold on Nova Scotia encouraged the ministers to proceed with their arbitrary measures, convinced that this was one certain way of overcoming the stubborn resistance they might expect in the other colonies. The possession of Nova Scotia did not, of course, incline Britain to embark on these new policies. Nevertheless the northern colony was a useful base, uncontaminated with the "democratic" tendencies that gave officials a difficult time in other colonies. The American colonists who thought about imperial affairs came, therefore, to resent even more the manner in which Britain had, since 1749, used Nova Scotia to further her own imperial aims.

This resentment came to the surface during a pamphlet controversy in the mid-1760s, sparked off by Hopkins' essay on the rights of the colonies. In reply to Hopkins' defence of colonial rights "a Gentleman at Halifax" published in Newport, Rhode Island, two pieces in which he vigorously defended parliamentary supremacy. These attempts to disprove the case against Britain produced a furious reaction in New England, particularly in Rhode Island. And James Otis, the Boston lawyer, politician, and anti-British pamphleteer, felt compelled to join the battle of words and rebut the arguments of the "Halifax Gentleman." Nova Scotia, as such, was not directly involved in this heated controversy but the manner in which the history of the northern colony and its image were used by both sides in the debate reveals the sort of language used when Nova Scotia was discussed in the 1760s.

Martin Howard, the "Halifax Gentleman," began his criticism of Hopkins' assertions by insisting that the colonies were "dependent upon" Britain and that the ministry would, therefore, not be "patiently dictated to." Parliament had absolute authority over the colonies — it might abuse this authority and give cause for complaint but it was impossible for the colonists to deny that this authority existed. Quite simply, the "jurisdiction of parliament" was "transcendant and entire" and ministers might "levy internal taxes as well as regulate trade." The stamp duty could be regarded as iniquitous, and the Halifax writer did not wish to see the tax laid upon the colonies, but he saw no way to avoid a harsh but legitimate exercise of power.[10] The publication of such a forthright defence of unchecked parliamentary supremacy roused intense feelings in those colonies where the pamphlet was read. The Providence newspapers printed fourteen rebuttals and the Rhode Island Assembly had difficulty in restraining some of its members from ordering the "libel" to be burned by the public hangman. Martin Howard was ridiculed as "a petty tyrant" and a former "hireling scribbler for the custom house."[11]

As well as encouraging the persistence of the poor image the colonists had of Nova Scotia since 1749, Howard's letter touched colonial nerves in one particular respect that opened up old resentments and grievances about the northern colony. In his second pamphlet, Howard had reminded New Englanders of the indispensable role played by Commodore Peter Warren and his British warships in the taking of Louisbourg in 1745 and in

the critical period following the fall of that fortress when the
Duc d'Anville was heading for North America with a formid-
able fleet intent on devastating the English colonies.[12] This argument, designed to instil into the colonies a gratitude for the
expensive military protection rendered them by Britain in the
recent wars, was particularly galling to New Englanders, using
as it did the case of Louisbourg and involving Nova Scotia. In
1745 it had been mainly New England troops who had captured
Louisbourg yet, with the Treaty of Aix-la-Chapelle of 1748,
this major prize of colonial arms was returned by the British
negotiators to France. In 1749 the expensive alternative was
adopted of constructing a completely new military and naval
base at Halifax. In addition to this, in 1755, when New England
provincial troops had played the dominant role in defeating the
French at Fort Beauséjour in the Chignecto neck of Nova
Scotia, the British had ignored the colonial contribution and had
omitted to mention them in despatches. This left bitter feelings
in New England, particularly in Massachusetts.[13] Nova Scotia
was an area of North America that New England had played an
important role in conquering and pacifying only to see, from
1749 onwards, the British take the credit and monopolize the
fruits of victory.

The way in which Britain had used New England for her own
imperial ends in Nova Scotia clearly still rankled in 1765. Some
of the deep undercurrents of resentment can be seen rising to the
surface of public consciousness as Otis made free use of geographical locations as terms of abuse. The designation of Howard as the "Halifax Tartar" or the "Halifax genius" or simply
as the "Halifaxian" seemed sufficiently venomous phrases of
contempt as Otis sneered them out in his pamphlet. Halifax had
figured so prominently in British double-dealing in the north
that its mere mention seemed enough to conjure up in New England bitter memories of British arrogance.[14]

That James Otis' picture of Nova Scotia as a refuge for ultra-
royalists and as a colony taken over by Britain for her own
purposes was not merely a figment of his spiteful imagination
may be seen from the more sober writings of John Adams. On
2 January, 1766, commenting on the effect of the repeal of the
Stamp Act in the colonies, Adams was jubilant. "The spirit of

Liberty," he rejoiced, is triumphant everywhere and "such an Union was never known before in America." The only exceptions to the "Union" were Quebec and Nova Scotia. Adams, however, found no difficulty in explaining one of these anomalies. Halifax consisted "of a sett of Fugitives and Vagabonds, who are also kept in fear by a Fleet and an Army."[15] Thus, even in 1766, eight years after a House of Assembly had been established in Nova Scotia and three or four years after several thousand New England farmers and fishermen had moved to the northern colony, John Adams still saw Nova Scotia as dominated by British military power and devoid of the local protest movements that had achieved such widespread popularity and success in other colonies.

It is hardly surprising that in the mid-1760s, in the midst of the Stamp Act troubles and with the presence from 1764 to 1768 of the new Vice-Admiralty Court in Halifax, Nova Scotia should be subjected to criticism and rejected as one of their number by the other American colonies. What is important to note, however, is the ease with which colonists could push Nova Scotia out of their thinking. There was simply nothing in the history of the colony that showed in a favourable light. There are, moreover, signs that the unfavourable image of Nova Scotia was never updated. Those colonists who read an account of Nova Scotia reprinted in 1770 were informed still of the old story of Nova Scotia's poor beginnings. British money was spent in organizing the colony from 1749 on but "the success . . . in no way answered this Expense except so far as it respects the particular Service of the Navy."[16] This particular writer attributed Nova Scotia's difficulties more to Indian danger than to official mismanagement. But whatever the reasons there was no getting round the fact that it was a colony whose development had proceeded on quite different lines from the New England colonies.

A more informed and sweeping indictment was published in 1773 or 1774 by a member of the Nova Scotia House of Assembly in a pamphlet circulated in New England.[17] The anonymous author of this pamphlet reviewed the whole course of Nova Scotia's development from 1749 down to the early 1770s. According to this writer, the government of Nova Scotia was nothing more than "a Junto of cunning and wicked Men; whose Views extend no farther than their own private Emolument, and who further the Distresses of the Community in order to promote a slavish Dependence on themselves." The root of the problem lay in the form of government which had, in 1749, been set up like that of "Garrison Towns out of England." Although the establishment of an Assembly had changed the outward form of government, the Legislature spent most of its time bickering and gave neither time nor attention to the establishment of "some Method or Order in the Detail of Government." By the 1770s there was no visible improvement. A governor like Lord William Campbell, who ruled from October 1767 to October 1773 and who had "great Interest[s] and Family Connections," easily cowed and dominated the submissive politicians of "so poor a Country" as Nova Scotia. Both the Council and the Assembly were "principally made up of officers of Government." It seemed then that colonial critics were correct; the establishment of an Assembly had done little to alter Nova Scotia's corrupt and dependent status.

Even the features of Nova Scotia which held out hope that the colony would begin to move towards the more independent and democratic pattern of the colonies to the south had failed to change its character. Writing in the winter of 1773-74, the same period as the pamphlet on Nova Scotia was printed, John Adams noted that in a colony where the "Governor was entirely dependent on the Crown and the Council in danger of becoming so [and] if the Judges were made so too, the Liberties of the Country would be totally lost."[18] Adams' remarks were entirely directed towards the situation in Massachusetts and had nothing to do with whatever knowledge he may have possessed about Nova Scotia. What is clear, however, is that judged by the political and constitutional doctrines that were forming the rationale for rebellion in the Thirteen Colonies, Nova Scotia was a colony where liberty was "totally lost." After fifteen years of Assembly politics, little progress had been made from the arbitrary, military regime of 1749-58. Indeed it seemed that Nova Scotia had at least been efficient then, but by the 1770s was corrupt as well as dependent. Nova Scotia was a colony where the governor, backed by British power, held virtually undisputed sway. In

1758, Nova Scotia had been "the shamefull and Contemptible By-Word of America"; in 1766, Adams had referred to the colony as "a sett of Fugitives and Vagabonds"; as the Revolution approached the image of Nova Scotia as a hopelessly backward colony, politically and constitutionally, persisted.

These assessments by other colonists of the course of Nova Scotia's history may not be very informative concerning actual developments in the northern colony. There was clearly a widespread ignorance of Nova Scotian affairs although this did not prevent one holding decided views on the subject. American colonists were not surprised that Nova Scotia had not joined the "Union" of 1765 and thereafter they never seemed to expect that the colony would become one of them in the struggle against British policies. Nova Scotia was not, and never had been, a land of liberty and there seemed to be no possibility of changing that characteristic. But why was this negative attitude so persistent in the colonies? Nova Scotia had, after all, been granted an Assembly in 1758 and over the next few years there had been an influx of several thousand New Englanders with experience of local autonomy and practice in self-government. Why did no one take seriously the possibility that these settlers could push Nova Scotia in the direction taken by the other colonies? Part of the answer lies in the fact of colonial ignorance of Nova Scotia; Americans stuck closely to the old version of Nova Scotia's dependency on Britain as if this somehow reassured them of the bad intentions of Britain. But more important than this, the Yankee settlers themselves in Nova Scotia confirmed and acknowledged the great difficulty in changing the nature of government in the colony. The limited extent to which the rhetoric of resistance could be applied in the Nova Scotia context manifested itself in the various tortuous attempts of the Nova Scotia Yankees in the 1760s and early 1770s to construct a viable basis from which they could pressure the authorities.

As always, the manner in which Nova Scotia differed from the other colonies played a decisive role in smothering the growth of reasoned protest based on ascertainable rights and well-known precedents. A fundamental point in the American case against Britain was that the colonists by their own efforts had settled and civilized the eastern parts of a savage and wild continent. Britain was quite mistaken in expecting the colonies to view the mother country as the source of all improvement in North America. As Benjamin Franklin put it, the colonists "by planting and improving a Wilderness, far distant from their Mother Country, at a vast Expence and the Risque of many lives from the savage Inhabitants" had thereby "greatly increased the Trade and Commerce of the Nation and added a large tract of improved Country to the Crown." All this, emphasized Franklin, had been accomplished "without any Aid from or Expence to Great Britain."[19] Nova Scotia could not be fitted into this version of colonial history. The land in Nova Scotia belonged to the crown by right of conquest and treaty obligations long before the New England emigrants arrived. Halifax, the largest settlement and seat of government, had been established at British expense and with British troops in 1749; parliamentary grants were provided throughout the first decade of military rule. Foreign Protestants from the interior of Europe had been transported to Lunenburg, south of Halifax, in the 1750s, the Acadian settlers had been expelled at British expense in 1755 and 1758; and, finally, in the early years of New England settlement the British organized the distribution of foodstuffs to help the Yankee immigrants through a difficult period. It was well known that Nova Scotia did not conform to the general historical development of the other colonies and Franklin, anxious to make the colonial case clear, pointed this out in 1766. Nova Scotia, quite specifically, was an exception to the rule that the colonies had not been settled by "any money granted by parliament."

Another basic belief of the colonists, particularly the New England ones, was that in their charters they had been given certain rights which could not be rescinded by the crown or usurped by Parliament. In 1766, John Adams succinctly explained the importance attached by the colonists to these charters. Adopting the same approach as Franklin was urging on the British at this time, Adams argued that the

> first Settlement [of the colonies] certainly was not a national Act, i.e., not an Act of the People nor the Parliament. Nor

was it a national Expence. Neither the People of England,
nor their Representatives contributed anything towards it.
Nor was the Settlement made on a Territory belonging to
the People nor the Crown of England.[20]

Here again, it is clear that once the colonists began articulating
their view of their past history in order to press their case against
Britain, Nova Scotia had to be left out of the picture.

Adams proceeded to describe the relationship that did exist
between Britain and the colonies as a result of this distinctive
method of settlement. The settlers in the seventeenth century
had been "driven by oppression from the Realm" and were
thereby "dismembered from the Dominion, till at last they
offered to make a Contract with the Nation, or the Crown, and
to become subject to the Crown upon certain conditions, which
Contract Subordination and Conditions were wrought into their
Charters."[21] The charters were a vital source and safeguard of
colonial liberty. The rights possessed by the colonies were not
dependent upon the crown's pleasure but were irrevocably written into the charters which laid down that the king should gov-
ern the colonies upon certain conditions. The contract was a
mutual agreement; the ministry could not break the British side
without permitting the colonists to dissolve their obligations of
dependence.

The settlers who had moved from New England to Nova
Scotia in the early 1760s possessed no charter of mutual obligation. They had removed themselves to a colony ruled by un-
adulterated royal authority. Certain promises had been made to
them in the two proclamations issued by Governor Lawrence.
He had, apparently, also made persuasive verbal commitments
that the royal government would not interfere in the running of
local affairs.[22] The second proclamation has erroneously been
described as the "Charter of Nova Scotia."[23] But this proclamation, as the settlers themselves soon realized, possessed none of
the vital characteristics of the New England charters and provided them with no continuing guarantee of its promises. Moving north at a time of imperial cooperation and of relative
harmony between the colonies and Britain, the New Englanders
had been inclined, perhaps, to trust the promises made in the

proclamation. But within a short period of time, few of the Nova Scotia Yankees questioned the uselessness of a governor's proclamation in guaranteeing similar constitutional rights and political liberties as those possessed by New Englanders. The Yankees had attached the greatest importance to the new provisions of the second proclamation. These assurances of the "Civil and Religious Rights and Liberties as we enjoyed them in the Governments from whence we came" had constituted their "principal Inducement" to move to Nova Scotia.[24]

In the early stages of settlement the people regarded the second proclamation as sufficient defence of their political rights. In the summer months of 1760 the Liverpool settlers were apparently "in high spirits and extremely well pleased" with the way things were going in their township.[25] In the Minas Basin townships, the new inhabitants regarded this initial period as a time when they were governed by "a just and upright Administration." But this happy state of affairs did not last long.[26] In October 1760, Governor Lawrence, the strong man behind the expulsion of the Acadians and the drafter of the proclamation, died. It is not possible to establish how sincere Lawrence was in making the promises of 1759 to the New Englanders. At the time the Acadians were being shipped out of the colony he had held back inviting English-speaking settlers until the terms could be "deliberately formed," which suggests that Lawrence hoped to retain careful control over the prospective population.[27] The fact that the October 1758 proclamation contained no reference to the form of government further indicates that, as governor, Lawrence intended, if he could get away with it, to settle the colony with people who would be amenable to direct royal government. Once he saw that New England farmers and fishermen would not budge until clear statements on this subject had been made, he issued the January 1759 proclamation containing the fine-sounding, but general, promises that Nova Scotia was no different from Massachusetts. This, to say the least, seems most disingenuous on Lawrence's part, since he must have known that the firmly established position of the Halifax authorities would make it extremely difficult for poor farmers in the outsettlements to participate in the type of political activity that limited the governor's position in Massachusetts. It has been

suggested that there was a combination of genuine misunder-
standing on the part of Lawrence with an oversanguine expectation on the part of the new settlers — that Lawrence probably
did not realize what the settlers had in mind when they insisted
on the New England forms of government.[28] Whatever Lawrence's motives were, his death prevented the settlers from
discovering any duplicity and they continued to regard his
proclamation and promises as the only guarantees located in
Nova Scotia of their rights and liberties. Whether Lawrence
would have stuck to the terms of the proclamation, as defined
by the New England settlers, is a matter of speculation, although
it seems unlikely he would have. But what is certain is that his
successors ignored the document on which the settlers had pinned
so much faith.

By 1761 the Council in Halifax was granting lands in the
new townships, thereby undermining the position and function
of the proprietors and depriving the settlers of the mechanism
by which they had hoped to build communities composed of their
"own Countrymen." In 1762, the proprietors of the township of
Liverpool protested against the appointment by the Council of
a committee to make new grants of land in the township. By
1765 the last hopes of retaining the degree of local autonomy
possessed by New England townships disappeared. In an act
passed in that year it was stipulated that the Grand Jury of each
county was to nominate two or more persons for each township
office and from these the Court of Quarter Sessions, controlled
by Halifax, was to choose and appoint the officials. In 1767 the
Halifax government gained complete control over the townships
when an act was passed which ruled that a writ was required for
the distribution of separate lots in the townships. The acts of
1765 and 1767 were the culmination of a trend begun as early as
1761 to go back on the promises made by Lawrence.[29]

When the Nova Scotia Yankees attempted to formulate
reasoned opposition to these and other actions of the Halifax
government, the full ambiguity, even weakness, of their position
was brought home to them. Unlike the other Americans who
could use the history of their colonies and remind the English
of their long held rights, the Yankees in Nova Scotia found it
difficult to support their claims against the royal government in

Halifax. The petition from Liverpool in July 1762 clearly indicates the ideological tangle in which they found themselves. In protesting against the Council-appointed committee to bring new settlers into the township, the Liverpool petitioners insisted that the privilege of admitting new settlers to the township belonged "to no body of people but ourselves." The only written source to which they could appeal was, of course, the proclamation of 1759. Aware, however, of their inability to do anything more than lamely charge the present governnment with breaking the promises of a dead governor, they attempted to broaden the base of their protest by making explicit references to their New England background. They claimed their rights as "free men . . . not only by his Majesty's Proclamation but because [they] were born in a Country of Liberty in a Land that belongs to the Crown of England."[30] The petitioners realized the inadequacy of appealing merely to the proclamation and hoped to bring the traditional rights and liberties of New England colonies to support their tenuous legal position in Nova Scotia. They realized that they were not living in a "Country of Liberty" but in a colony in which they only possessed the easily revocable rights contained in a proclamation. This petition of 1762 reveals the major obstacles confronting the Nova Scotia Yankees in their efforts to arrive at a coherent defence of their rights in the new colony. They were not at all sure that their case built upon the promise of 1759 was strong, so they attempted to transfer the rights possessed by the New England colonies into Nova Scotia. In the strictly Nova Scotian context, they had a very weak case.

In the 1760s, while the other American colonists were insisting that their traditional rights, liberties and practices could not be violated by the British government, the Nova Scotia Yankees were still at the stage of asking that privileges and rights be granted to them by the imperial representatives in Halifax. The result was that they were always dubious about their actual rights in the new colony. Thus the Liverpool proprietors did not assert but only "conceived" they had "right of authority vested in ourselves . . . to nominate and appoint men among us to be our Committee and to do other Offices that the Town may event." Additional doubt came to the surface when the petitioners added weakly that "at least, we pray we may [have the right]." Further confirming an underlying feeling that the rights they "conceived" they possessed were actually not as certain as they claimed, the petitioners ended up by requesting of the Council that "we may have the privilege to choose our own Committee."[31] As Nova Scotians, the people realized they had no rights to which they could unequivocally appeal and use as a rallying point. They had taken a risk by agreeing to settle under the promises made in the 1759 proclamation and although they could complain of the non-fulfillment of its terms they could not argue that the government was depriving them of ancient rights sanctified by decades of usage. The New England colonies did possess such rights and were determined to retain them in the face of British opposition, but the Yankees in Nova Scotia had not even reached the stage of having any privileges. All they could do was to try to make the government transform promises into privileges. To force the well-entrenched royal government in Halifax into such concessions was well beyond the political strength possessed by the scattered Yankee townships of Nova Scotia.

About the same time as the Liverpool petition, a memorial was sent to the Lords of Trade and Plantations by several townships in the Minas Basin area on the other side of peninsular Nova Scotia.[32] This memorial is interesting in that it attempts to play down the role of the English authorities in settling the Yankees in the area around Minas Basin. The memorialists conveniently forgot that the English authorities had cleared the Acadian farmers off the land, had placed the settlers on crown land and had even supplied some food in the early days. They ignored all this and simply totted up their own expenses. They had brought with them livestock to the value of "at least £12,000" and the dilapidated condition of houses, fences and dykes on their arrival necessitated an expenditure of "at least £30,000" in rebuilding and repairs. They were looking for a usable past. But the fact that there were houses, dykes and fences, even though not in the best condition, made the point much less convincing than it was in the other colonies where virgin land had been improved and eventually "civilized."

The memorialists went on to complain that they were now

"wholly deprived of those Rights and Priviledges" that they had enjoyed in "the Governments from whence we came." Again the line of argument adopted is revealing. These rights and privileges were due to them not as Nova Scotians but as New Englanders and all they could do was to urge on the government that the 1759 proclamation had been designed to transfer such rights from New England to Nova Scotia. The whole case as presented by the settlers in the Minas Basin townships rested on their interpretation of Lawrence's promises. On the issue that had aroused Liverpool, the admission of new settlers by a non-elected committee, the memorial appealed to "the Promise given us by the late Governor Lawrence" that they "should have the Privilege of Naming and admitting Settlers of our own Countrymen to the Several Townships in this country." The lieutenant-governor, Jonathan Belcher, charged the memorialists, had "set on foot and supported" the "uncommon and Tyrannical conduct" that had been meted out to the Minas Basin settlers. Yet after this heated denunciation of the authorities, the memorialists had to draw back because all they had to rely on were the promises of Lawrence which now depended for their implementation entirely on Belcher or his successor. In the end they could only plead with the Lords of Trade and Plantations that "we may be indulged with the same Privileges that all his Majesty's Subjects Enjoy in the other Governments on the Continent and that all the Engagements made to us by the late Governor Lawrence may be fulfilled." As in the case of the Liverpool petition, so in this memorial the rhetoric of protest, at times most assertive in tone, gave way to a request that Nova Scotia be granted the same rights as the other New England colonies had possessed since the seventeenth century.

What the Nova Scotia Yankees were attempting to accomplish with these petitions was to make the 1759 proclamation perform the functions that the charter did in some of the New England colonies, that is to define the limits and to restrict the powers of royal government. They persistently linked Lawrence's promises with the right enjoyed in the New England colonies in the hope that the British authorities would accept the identification as legitimate. But the British officials in Halifax were determined to retain all their prerogatives and allow none of the concessions which they believed had seriously weakened royal government in the other American colonies. Having witnessed the growing inability of governors to resist local political pressures in the charter colonies, the royal officials in Halifax were acutely aware of the importance of the issue and were prepared at all costs to avoid a repetition of the mistakes of conceding too many privileges. Such concessions, they felt, were the root cause of Britain's inability to control the colonies.

In December 1763, for instance, Lieutenant-Governor Belcher, in describing the role the Church of England was to play in Nova Scotia, stressed the dangerous consequences of allowing the settlers to introduce "the Ecclesiastical Plans and Constitutions of a Neighbouring Charter Government (from whence this Province is chiefly settled)." It was essential, urged Belcher, that such attempts to duplicate New England institutions and practices be "early Suppressed, since, if they gain ground by Time and Usage, it will be almost impracticible to change the Model." The independent course taken by the American colonies was proof, argued Belcher, of what could happen in Nova Scotia if the claims of the settlers were admitted. It was the task of the authorities, while the settlers were still struggling economically, and were politically weak and disorganized and somewhat doubtful of their constitutional position in Nova Scotia, to insist that none of the characteristics of the charter governments would be introduced into Nova Scotia.[33] The 1759 proclamation was simply ignored by the royal officials. By the mid-1760s it was evident that the Yankee settlers had failed in their attempts to loosen the tight British hold on Nova Scotia. The 1759 proclamation was not "the Charter of Nova Scotia" and the New England settlers had to accommodate themselves to this fact of political and constitutional life in the new colony.

It is important for understanding the development of Nova Scotia in the 1760s to appreciate the subtle but fundamental difference of Nova Scotian political protest from that of the other American colonies. The Nova Scotia Yankees found themselves in a unique predicament. All they could rely on to press their demands for the basic rights they had formerly possessed in New England was the proclamation of 1759. The settlers were, however, aware of the limited extent to which they could appeal to these retractable promises. The one way they hoped to present the Halifax authorities with powerful arguments was to intro-

duce the fact that they had come from the New England colonies. They hoped in this way to transfer somehow the historical
rights of the charter colonies into Nova Scotia. That they were
forced to adopt this approach confirmed the unlikelihood of the
local Nova Scotian situation producing from its own circumstances the rhetoric of resistance which emerged naturally and
easily in the colonies to the south. Even in 1771 the Nova Scotia
Yankees had not advanced beyond the stage of asking that privileges be bestowed on them by the English government. In the
spring of that year "the Freeholders" of Cornwallis held a meeting at which they chose a committee "to treat with Colo'l
Elaxander McNutt in the matter of applying to his Majesty
for a Charter of Privileges Both Sivil and Relidgeous etc."[34]
These years were a crucial period in moulding revolutionary
sentiment in the other seaboard colonies. Contemporary trends
seen against a certain interpretation of past history convinced
many colonists that a ministerial plot was designed to enslave
them.[35] But the restricted and dependent nature of their constitutional and political position and their lack of a usable past
forced the Nova Scotia Yankees to adopt a much more equivocal
and a much less hostile attitude towards Britain and British
authority in their colony. Nova Scotia, even with its Yankee
population in the outsettlements, continued to diverge from the
general trends operating in American colonial society.

That they were, in 1771, still making exactly the same appeals
to authority as they had been making in 1762 certainly suggests
that the Yankees had made little progress in terms of political
thinking. Since the petitions of the early 1760s made so much of
the fact that most of the settlers had come from the New
England colonies, it might have been expected that the following years would have seen the reliance on this New England
heritage develop into a search for ideological aid from the more
politically mature and articulate colonies. The constitutional
predicament in which they found themselves in Nova Scotia was,
of course, different from that in the New England colonies and
the rhetoric would necessarily have had to be amended to cor-
respond to the nature of the struggle for liberty in the northern
colony. And the increasing assertiveness of the colonies seemed
a natural source of assistance. Yet nothing like this occurred. No

appeals for help were made to the New England colonies, nor any parallels sought in the contemporary New England political struggle against Britain. Yet this was not because Nova Scotia was isolated from the rest of the American continent. There were a considerable number of contacts between Nova Scotia and New England and channels of communication for political ends did exist, but no attempt was made to tap this rich heritage of political and legal knowledge. On the contrary, the contacts made with New England tended to be almost entirely non-political in nature.

2

Religious Ties
and the
Missing Decade

During the pre-revolutionary period and especially in the 1760s some New Englanders dis-
played a keen interest in the religious life of Nova Scotia. And
this concern, among other things, underlined the fact that the
northern colony had not experienced the critical decade of political and religious development which had prepared the way for
revolution in the Thirteen Colonies. Nova Scotia was viewed
as a frontier mission field — remote and backward but, nevertheless, New England's special spiritual responsibility. The Nova
Scotia Yankees accepted this perception of their backwardness
and dependence. And this perception, together with the hard
realities of the Nova Scotia situation, helps to explain why their
intense religious life was not channelled along the same politico-
religious path as that of the New Englanders. As in the political
and ideological sphere, the Nova Scotia Yankees, even in the
realm of religion, had missed a decade of American transformation.

While no writings still exist to indicate that New Englanders
had anything favourable to say about the Nova Scotia govern-

ment, there is evidence that some of the New England colonists were anxious to influence the religious character of that new area of Yankee settlement. The most comprehensive explanation of the nature of this interest, and of the intentions of those New Englanders who displayed such concern, was given in a sermon delivered in 1768 at Hingham, Massachusetts, by the Reverend Ebenezer Gay.[1] The occasion of the sermon was the ordination of Caleb Gannett who was about to proceed to Cumberland in Nova Scotia as the first settled minister of that township. In selecting a title for his sermon, Gay revealed the general belief that Nova Scotia was on the fringe of colonial civilization; like Macedonia in the New Testament, it was a remote and backward province. Yet Gay insisted that Nova Scotia had a significant role to play in the North American world. Nova Scotia's remote position did not mean that the New England colonies should ignore her but rather that they should regard the settlement of Nova Scotia by the Yankees as the most recent step in the mission of New England to civilize and Christianize the wild continent. Gannett's imminent departure for Nova Scotia was part of God's cosmic plan for the American scene. It was, according to Gay, "the doing of the Lord," for the Protestant settlement of Nova Scotia was a further stage in the "spread of the Glorious Gospel, which our Fathers, not yet a century and a half ago, brought with them into this land, then a howling wilderness of savages, a wide extended region of darkness." Nova Scotia might be "one of the remotest and most uncultivated parts of our colonies" but the settlers in Cumberland were none the less taking part in the "enlargement of the Redeemer's kingdom."

Viewed strictly in this light, Nova Scotia possessed few of the poor connotations that it had in the general political context. Gannett, a Harvard graduate, had been to Nova Scotia and had, according to Gay, brought back no "such report of it as should dishearten his brethren, the sons of New England and of Harvard from endeavouring when they may be called, to go over and help the people there." While those colonists engaged in the political struggle against Britain saw little point, and much difficulty, in bringing Nova Scotia into active participation in the general resistance movement in the colonies, Gay perceived the 1760s as the time for Nova Scotia to contribute to the all-important task of carrying "the Gospel into all parts of the vast continent." While Benjamin Franklin, in arguing for colonial political and constitutional rights, had insisted that Nova Scotia was an area "of no particular concern or interest"[2] to the colonies, Ebenezer Gay, in talking about the colonial mission to redeem the wilderness, emphasized that Nova Scotia had to be considered as one of the American colonies sharing their common goals. Nova Scotia, in 1768, was "part of our American world."[3]

That Gay's vision of the Protestant settlement of Nova Scotia being the latest stage in the spiritual enlightenment of the "American World" was no esoteric one can be seen by the number of educated ministers who did, at various times throughout this period, undertake to preach in Nova Scotia in spite of "the paths and perils of the sea."[4] Gannett was not an isolated example of New England concern and interest in Nova Scotia's religious affairs. At about the time Gay preached his sermon there were several Congregational ministers, with various qualifications, in Nova Scotia. Chester township had throughout these years the services of the Reverend Mr. John Seccombe of the Harvard class of 1728. In Liverpool the Reverend Mr. Israel Cheever of the Harvard class of 1749 was a permanent fixture in local society. Along with Gannett, these were the outstanding examples of "the sons of Harvard" performing their mission in the remote colony. But these were not the only representatives of New England's missionary spirit. The Congregational Church of Cornwallis was supplied from 1765 to 1777 by Benajah Phelps, a Yale graduate of 1761, and for many years Nehemiah Porter, who "was once an ordained and settled minister over a People" in Massachusetts and "a man of liberal Education," preached at Jebogue in Yarmouth. During the 1760s Samuel Wood, who had been "approbated to preach the Gospel by a Number of Ministers in the Massachusetts Colony," shared his time between Yarmouth and Barrington before returning to New England in the early 1770s. As well as these permanent or semi-permanent New England preachers and ministers there was a considerable number of visiting clerics who stayed only for short periods at a time. For example, in 1770 the

Reverends Mr. Sylvanus Conant and Solomon Reed of the First and Third Congregational Churches in Middleborough, Massachusetts, visited Nova Scotia. Several preachers from Cape Cod made summertime visits to small fishing settlements like Barrington and at least one New England itinerant preacher made the long journey to Maugerville on the St. John River. Considering the remoteness of Nova Scotia there was a surprisingly large number of New Englanders attempting, throughout this pre-revolutionary period, to establish New England religious norms and religious values in the northern colony. While the missionary interest in Nova Scotia was not the result of widespread concern in New England for the spiritual state of the northern Yankees, it is nevertheless clear that the strain of New England thought, represented in Gay's sermon, did influence a discernible number of ministers and preachers to go north in an attempt to transform Nova Scotia into an outpost of New England Protestantism. In the larger colonial context this interest was insignificant, but it had an important impact on this period in Nova Scotia development. This interest from New England may have been desultory but it was far more than was manifested by most New Englanders in the political affairs of Nova Scotia.[5]

The Nova Scotia Yankees themselves, naturally, took much more seriously than New Englanders did the possibility that they were fulfilling an important spiritual mission; they were more ready to accept that their northward movement did have a special religious significance in the North American world. The early arrivals from New England in the opening years of the 1760s were very conscious that they were the first English people to settle in an area formerly under French domination, a colony that had "been wholly a land of heathenish darkness and popish superstition."[6] One of their declared aims was to ensure "that the Everlasting Gospell of the Lord Jesus Christ may flourish in this Remote part, where Antichrist once Reigned."[7] An even more precise statement of their belief in Nova Scotia's providential task was articulated in 1769. The members of the Congregational Church as a Society of Cornwallis accepted as one of their beliefs that "God in his providence . . . after previously Removing our Enemies, planted us in this Infant Colony."[8] When the Nova Scotian farmers and fishermen lifted their eyes from their daily work to ponder the meaning of life and its purpose, it was in these religious terms that they thought. Insofar as they saw a pattern to events that they experienced in the 1760s, they regarded themselves as instruments of God, spreading his word into hitherto "wilderness" and "popish" areas of America.

Because of the special importance attached to this view of themselves there was a persistent concern with the ecclesiastical and moral standing of the Nova Scotia Yankee settlements. One of the most worrying features of this decade, particularly during the early years of settlement, had been the inability of the townships to obtain ministers and preachers. In Cumberland, the people had "from the beginning of their settlement . . . manifested a great sense of their need of such [ministerial] help, and have been unweariedly seeking it."[9] The Baptist elements in the population of Horton township lamented that they had been "several years in these parts without the Dispensation of the Gospell among us" and since some of them had been "members of an imbodied Church in New England" this lack of formal teaching troubled them. But in 1765 the situation in Horton improved with the visit of Ebenezer Moulton, a former Baptist minister in Brimfield, Massachusetts, then resident in Yarmouth, "during which time it pleased the Lord to visit this Land in a very Wonderful and Powerful Manner." By 1770, the Horton Baptists were again without any minister and although they tried "to keep the Worship of God according to the best Gifts bestow'd on us" they insisted on the need to have a minister among them.[10]

Yankees in other areas of Nova Scotia also revealed their concern about religious questions at such a "Critickle Junctur" in their history.[11] The fact that Nova Scotia was as yet still a young, struggling colony did not mean that religious affairs could be neglected or permitted to fall into careless ways. On the contrary, the settlers, mindful of their duties as Christians in a wilderness land, believed they had a special responsibility to ensure that religion flourished. This feeling of special responsibility was spelled out in particular terms by the Reverend Jonathan Scott of Yarmouth. In May 1773, Scott was challenged to explain why he had "publickly reproved" certain Church members for "Frolicking and Dancing" when "these Things are practised by Professors of Christianity in almost all Places without being censured in a publick Manner." Replying to the challenge, Scott emphasized that living in Nova Scotia at this time involved more onerous responsibilities than would be the case where religion was securely established. He explained that "the Church being now in its Infancy" it was, therefore, "a particular and important reason to testify against the Sin of Frolicking and Carnal wanton Company-keeping, not only by the preaching of the Word but also by the Discipline and Censure of the Church." Manifesting the same concern the Cornwallis people had shown in the development of their new settlement, Scott made it clear that "this ruinous Practice" must "be suppressed . . . as an example to the Present Generation and to those that may come after."[12] Some Nova Scotia Yankees, at least in these pre-revolutionary years, took their religious affairs most seriously since upon such conformity to God's laws depended the future of the colony. No matter how many acres they cleared or how many fish they caught, unless their churches were properly organized and disciplined and unless the moral standing of the communities were irreproachable, they could not claim to have been successful in transforming the wilderness colony into a Christian "garden."

This is not to argue that Nova Scotians were interested in their religious affairs to the exclusion of everything else, but merely to point out that religion continued to be a pervasive and demanding factor in their lives. A further indication of this characteristic of Nova Scotian society is contained in the records of the Truro town meetings from February 1770 to November 1773. The records still in existence consist of the notice of one meeting, and its agenda, for March 1770 and the minutes of four meetings held in July 1770, February 1772, January 1773, November 1773.[13] The agenda for the March 1770 meeting included the political question of township autonomy. The Halifax government had renewed its efforts to exercise its control over the outsettlements and had, through the Quarter Sessions, provided Truro with certain town officials. The March meeting was to consider "if it be the mind of the Town that the officers [elected] by them at their Annual Meeting shall serve for the present year or those intruded on them by the Sessions." Unfortunately, no record of the actual meeting exists but it seems clear that the town did, in fact, accept this "intrusion" into their affairs. It was a vital political principle yet Truro did not make it an issue of vigorous public debate. The next four meetings contain no reference whatsoever to political matters. The dominating issue at each meeting was the problem of obtaining and supporting a minister and the allied problem of keeping the meeting house in a good state of repair. In these years the Truro people were attempting to settle "the Rev'd Mr. Cock [as] their Minister" which involved an investigation of the potential public support that could be relied on for his salary. Besides the thorny problem of financial support there was also the more immediate task of "putting the place of Publick Worship in some repair as barns will soon be inconvenient for that purpose." It was these issues that apparently roused and maintained public discussion and absorbed public interest in the early 1770s in Truro and not the political issue of local independence. The "tyrannical" use of royal power made the public issues of the day in the colonies to the south, but in Nova Scotia the overwhelming power of the governor was accepted as one of the unchangeable characteristics of the colony and no organized opposition formed to bring these matters before the people.

The remoteness of most of the townships from Halifax meant that in practice a good deal of local autonomy was retained in spite of the legal changes made in the acts of 1765 and 1767. The appointed Justices of the Peace were often as keen to protect township rights as elected town officials would have been.[14] Nevertheless, the fact remains that an issue that would have raised virulent protest in other colonies did not necessarily produce the same response in the outsettlements of Nova Scotia. If the Halifax authorities had decided to prevent Daniel Cock, a Presbyterian, from preaching in Truro, it might have been a different matter, for this issue was something that deeply exercised their minds and induced them to think of broader issues. Cock was not merely to exercise an "Oversight of our Precious and immortal Souls," which was all that would normally be required of him in a strictly local sense; he had a much grander task than this in Truro, Nova Scotia, for he was to be "a Watch-man upon this Watch Tower of Zion's Wall."[15] Living in Nova Scotia as Christians manning the outposts of the Protestant world, this was the way in which many people of Truro saw themselves. It was the question of finding a minister that excited passions, opened purses and pervaded conversation in Truro in the early 1770s.

With this tendency to emphasize religion rather than politics and bearing in mind the eloquent statements of Ebenezer Gay on the importance of Nova Scotia in God's plan for America, it is not surprising that correspondence from Nova Scotia to New England was about religious affairs and not political issues. As the Truro township records indicate, Nova Scotians in the out-settlements had to face political questions but they did not apparently make any attempt to seek advice from other colonies or identify their local struggles with the larger American strug-gle against British tyranny. They were content to get along at the local level as best they could within the legally established government of the colony. They were, however, not the least reluctant to appeal to other colonies for help and aid in their religious affairs.

In November 1769, the Congregational Church in Cornwallis wrote an appeal to Dr. Andrew Eliot in Boston in the hope that he could obtain some financial assistance for the church which was at this time in danger of losing its minister, Benajah Phelps. The Cornwallis Church people felt that this was a critical period in the progress of their settlement, a testing time when their ability to maintain Christian civilization in the "Infant Colony" would be tried. After "Separation from the Society And Communion of our Christian friends in New-england," when they moved northeast in 1760-61, there had followed five difficult years when no minister could be found. The Cornwallis people felt that Phelps' departure would not merely be unfortunate, but would be somehow a reproach on their community. In these pressing conditions it was to New England that they turned for material assistance and moral sup-port in "the Interest of Religion." Cornwallis, moreover, did not limit itself to this one appeal to Boston. Many of the settlers had come from eastern Connecticut and an approach was also made to the Reverend Mr. Solomon Williams in Lebanon who brought the case to the attention of the Connecticut Council. The Cornwallis people repeated the history of their attempts since 1760 to organize their religious affairs, referring once more to the years of trial before the arrival of Phelps. By the late 1760s, however, "circumstances had become very difficult and distressing, chiefly by means of the fruits of the earth being cut short in 1767 and 1768, and by extraordinary expense in building a meeting house, and especially in repairing their dykes to the amount of near two thousand pounds." Unless they could "obtain relief by the charity of their Christian brethren and friends in Connecticut, the cause of religion will greatly suffer." In response to this appeal, communicated to them by Williams, the Connecticut Council agreed to permit the collection of the contributions made by "the several religious societies in the towns of New London, Norwich, Windham, Lebanon, Colchester, Canterbury and Lynne," from which communities many of the Cornwallis settlers had originated.[16] In 1770, the Nova Scotia Yankees and their former friends, neighbours and contacts in Boston and Connecticut still had in common a belief in "the cause of religion." This was one thing that still provided them with shared goals.

The appeals to New England were not limited to Congregational churches and societies in Nova Scotia. In October 1771, the Horton Baptists wrote to Elder John Davis in Boston to inform him of their circumstances and claim a share of any aid that was to be given to "Disenting Ministers" in Nova Scotia. Although some of them had been members of Baptist churches in New England, they had been, for several years, without benefit of pastoral care. Again, as in the Cornwallis letters, so the Horton Baptists insisted on informing their New England contacts of the trials they had endured and the progress they had made since their first coming to Nova Scotia. They saw themselves in the late 1760s and early 1770s as trying to fulfill the aims they had brought with them in 1760, of setting up properly organized churches in the new colony. Such goals had not suddenly appeared in their minds in 1770 bearing no relation to previous thoughts of what they hoped to accomplish in Nova Scotia. They, therefore, were grateful "for the Kind and Solicitous Care you [Elder Davis in Boston] Manifest towards us" in helping to forward the "well-being of Christ's feeble Flock and Churches in this Infant Colony." To emphasize the concern the Horton people felt for the progress of religion in Nova Scotia as a whole, they included in their letter an account of other Baptist churches in Sackville, Newport and Cape Forchu. What the Horton Baptists were primarily interested in and what they believed would be a similar absorbing concern of their New England correspondents was that "the Everlasting Gospell . . . may flourish in this Remote part where Antichrist once reigned."[17]

The series of letters and appeals from Nova Scotia to New England suggests that some Nova Scotia Yankees were identifying their settlements in the new colony as agents for continuing the 150-year-old colonial task of making a Christian conquest of the wilderness.[18] It appears that through a shared concern of such goals the Nova Scotia and the New England colonists could feel that they were participating in a common cause. It seems clear at any rate that this is how many Nova Scotia Yankees were inclined to think. They believed throughout the 1760s and into the 1770s that the New England colonists understood their aims and aspirations and would support their endeavours in the northern wilderness. But it is very unlikely that New Englanders were prepared to grant these somewhat inflated claims of the British-controlled northern colony. As had happened in the political sphere so also in religious affairs the unique development of Nova Scotia since 1749 changed the circumstances and restricted the capabilities of the settlers in a subtle but fundamental way. While they persisted in looking to New England as the model and the inspiration for their spiritual affairs, they failed to see how much New England had changed since 1760 and how, therefore, their move to Nova Scotia had, by the 1770s, made them different from the New England colonists.

For one thing the Church of England, from 1762 on, was virtually the established church in Nova Scotia. Sometimes the Nova Scotia Yankees succeeded in avoiding the implications of this fact, but it became increasingly difficult for them not to realize that a legal Anglican establishment made Nova Scotia

alien to Massachusetts. The way in which the presence of the
Church of England inserted itself into the thinking processes of
Nova Scotia Yankees was nicely demonstrated in the 1769 letter
of the Congregational church in Cornwallis. The letter was
addressed to "the several Churches in Boston in the Massachusetts Bay in Newengland." There seemed no problem in thus
describing the Congregational churches in Boston for the Congregational Church polity was in practice the established church
in the Bay colony and it was normally never necessary in correspondence between Massachusetts' churches to refer to themselves as "dissenting churches." Yet, having been for almost ten
years in Nova Scotia, the Cornwallis writers thought better of
their first attempt at addressing the letter and inserted the
epithet "Dissenting" to define more accurately the status of the
Congregational churches in Boston. In the long text that followed there were no other words crossed out or insertions made
apart from this one.[19] It is, therefore, a revealing insertion, a
small slip that suggested a fundamental change in the traditional
views and perspectives of the settlers in Nova Scotia at the very
moment when it seemed they were asserting, and acting upon,
the belief that they were merely New Englanders who had
moved to a neighbouring colony. The authorities in Halifax
always referred to the New England elements in Nova Scotia as
"dissenters" and the settlers themselves came to accept this as
their normal status in Nova Scotia. They began to refer to their
pastors as "Disenting [sic] ministers of the Gospel" to distinguish them from the ministers and missionaries of "the Establish'd Church."[20] This proximity to the influence of the Anglican
establishment began to colour the settlers' views of the other
colonies and so by the early 1770s they no longer saw the super-
fluity of talking about the "dissenting churches" in Boston.
Their description was technically correct in the imperial context
as a whole, but precisely because of that it betrayed the fact that
they were beginning to accept English rather than colonial definitions of how society was ordered.

Their experiences in the 1760s tended to blind the Yankees of
Nova Scotia to distinctions which were of paramount importance
in the value systems of the New England colonies. These years
were difficult ones in the new settlements in Nova Scotia. Even

when a minister could be persuaded to settle in a township and material support pledged, it was always likely, as may be seen in the case of Cornwallis, which was one of the more prosperous communities, that such a normal event in a rural community as a bad harvest or extraordinary expense in repairing buildings and equipment might render the settlement incapable of continuing its support of the minister. An observer from Halifax confirmed this characteristic when he pointed out that "as the people are low [in circumstances] it renders them unable to perform their Contracts with their Ministers, for although they are willing and desirous to support the Gospel among them they have it not in their power."[21] This situation presented an excellent opportunity for the Society for the Propagation of the Gospel to make inroads on the position of the "Dissenters" in Nova Scotia. The result was that the S.P.G. devoted considerable attention to Nova Scotia in a declared attempt to change the religious, and hopefully the political, allegiances of the Yankees by reconciling them to the Church of England.[22]

Rather than have no religious services at all, many Nova Scotians were induced to listen to the sermons of the S.P.G. missionaries and have their children catechized by qualified clerics. In 1766 Joseph Bennett, the S.P.G. missionary for the townships of Horton, Cornwallis, Falmouth and Newport, wrote to his superiors that "a spirit of benevolence and harmony was kept up among the people of all persuasions who assemble together for public worship." Even the arrival of Benajah Phelps did not make the Cornwallis people immediately abandon their attention to the Anglican missionaries and for a long period Congregationalists and Anglicans worshipped together.[23] Thus, habits established when no Congregational minister was available began to harden into new patterns of allegiance and respect. The Congregational church was alive to the dangerous possibility of the complete erosion of traditional New England values, attitudes and practices and warned Eliot in 1769 that unless Phelps could be retained the Cornwallis people would in "a Few Years . . . all be Churchmen or Nothing . . . in point of Religion."[24] Phelps, too, saw the danger and after an initial period of cooperation tried to regain the people for the Congregational way. Many of the people who had attended S.P.G.

services did so only because no other preachers were usually available and because it cost them nothing, which "consideration has led many Dissenters to attend on that way of worship who cannot afford to pay towards the subsistance of a Dissenting Minister."[25] But the significance of this trend comes into clearer focus if Nova Scotia is compared to the New England colonies, where the activities of the S.P.G. and the Anglican church were arousing deep-seated fears among colonists that a Church of England establishment was going to be imposed. In New England, the Anglican church was usually regarded as alien to the colonial religious and political atmosphere, a "cold, formal, fashionable religion" of a country "grown old in vice."[26] In Nova Scotia there was not the same pervasive and avowed hostility to the S.P.G. activities. There was no way of avoiding the fact of the Church of England's pre-eminence in the colony and there were many good reasons for gratefully accepting the free ministrations provided by the S.P.G. missionaries. Nova Scotia then was one part of the continent where "a great many of the people in the different towns" were "quite divested of their prejudices against the Church of England."[27] The S.P.G. missionaries, of course, habitually overestimated their influence among the outsettlements and there is no reason to accept their sweeping statements about Anglican success in Nova Scotia. There was no wholesale desertion of the Congregational camp for that of the Anglican. But one thing is certain. The Nova Scotia Yankees were not as prejudiced against, and fearful of, Anglican intentions as were the New England colonists. By the 1770s, the Nova Scotia Yankees had lost one of the major negative reference groups whose alleged aims were crystallizing the traditional beliefs of similar social classes in other colonies into an openly hostile attitude to everything English.

The Nova Scotia Yankees, however, seemed oblivious of the transformation that had pressured traditional New England values into a justification for resistance to the British "plot" against religious liberty. In the New England colonies, religious values and assumptions were beginning to respond to the political and constitutional challenges coming from London. Many congregations now looked for political symbolism in pulpit oratory and were prepared to classify preachers as having Tory tendencies or being good Whigs on the strength of the words they uttered in their sermons. It was still possible to confine preaching "to Spirituals," but pastors were increasingly expected to give either overt or implied advice on the latest developments in the political debate with England. Peter Oliver's Tory version of the seditious influence of the "black Regiment, the dissenting clergy" who on the Sabbath "spun out their Prayers and Sermons to a long Thread of Politics" was a bitter account of the motives and methods of the New England clergy in participating in the resistance movement.[28] But in essentials, Oliver was correct in discerning a growing political orientation among the New England ministers. In a recent study of religion and its influence in moulding the revolutionary mind, Alan Heimert has described how the evangelical elements in the colonies, seemingly the most apolitical part of the social structure, responded to the political issues of the day. According to this analysis, in the pre-revolutionary decade "the very religious life of the colonies came to center on the crisis in public affairs" and indeed "to be defined by it and from it to derive its vitality."[29] Whether all the claims made by Heimert concerning the impact of evangelicalism on the American Revolution are accepted there is overwhelming evidence that these years witnessed most varieties of religion in the New England colonies attempting to relate themselves in some way to the political crises of the time.

This did not happen in Nova Scotia. None of the religious correspondence that went to New England at the end of the 1760s and in the early 1770s contained any references to non-religious affairs. Times were gloomy because of crop failures or too many expenses or divisions within churches, but never because of the political situation in Nova Scotia or anywhere else in the colonies. The Nova Scotia Yankees did not adapt their shared religious traditions to rally support for a challenge to royal authority in Halifax. They did not see the S.P.G. as the insidious arm of a corrupt and vice-ridden Britain embarked on a policy of domination in the colonies. In Nova Scotia, therefore, religion was not forced into being relevant for a political and constitutional debate but continued to derive its meaning and its vitality from local community goals and affairs.

The one theme which did rise above local matters to encompass visions of more grandiose achievements for the Yankees to strive for came to the surface only occasionally as people recalled the special task they believed they had to perform to extend Protestant religion into yet another part of the American continent. But this theme brought no sympathetic response from the New England colonies. Ebenezer Gay, in his 1768 sermon, had articulated a belief in some such role for Nova Scotia but in 1770 Andrew Eliot was merely requested to recommend the representative of the Nova Scotia ministers, and "his cause" to his "friends in England."[30] For Eliot, the problem of Nova Scotia's religious affairs was simply a question of helping dissenters living under the Anglican establishment. It was, therefore, a question that was to be settled in England and not in the colonies for it had no great importance in colonial views of the present and visions of the future. Eliot did not see in the indigency of the Nova Scotia dissenters any reproach to New England or any challenge to the colonists to revitalize their interest in Nova Scotian religious affairs.

The Yankees' concentration on religious affairs to the exclusion of politics and their belief in Nova Scotia's place in the expansion of Protestant Christianity marked them off as out of date compared with many of their more politically orientated New England contemporaries. While New England Christians were coming to identify their special mission with the struggle to maintain American political and constitutional liberty against British tyranny, their co-religionists in Nova Scotia were only dimly aware that such grave issues even existed. They, like Gay, who was seventy-two years old in 1768,[31] tended to stick to old beliefs. In the trying circumstances that faced them in the remote colony of Nova Scotia they looked for strength to the traditional values they had brought with them from pre-1760 New England.

From the first years of settlement in the northern colony, the Nova Scotia Yankees had quite naturally regarded themselves as an integral, if remote, part of the New England religious structure. The presence of qualified Congregational ministers encouraged the persistence of this self-image even though the Massachusetts-Connecticut Congregational way failed to establish a firm base throughout the colony. Only two Congregational ministers, the Reverend Israel Cheever of Liverpool and the Reverend John Seccombe of Chester, were continuously

established in any of the Yankee outsettlements for the entire
period between 1759-60 and the end of the revolutionary war.
There were, however, other townships which had resident Congregational ministers for briefer periods of time ranging from
fifteen years to a few months.

Even when no Congregational ministers were available to
remind the settlers of New England traditions and practices,
there were attempts to follow Congregational patterns of worship. When, for example, the Maugerville settlers in 1763 or
1764 drew up their Church Covenant they ensured that all those
who signed the document had been "orderly dismissed from
the Churches we heretofore belonged,"[32] and they also based the
terms of the covenant on the Cambridge Platform of 1648. In
some Nova Scotia settlements people often retained their mem-
bership in specific New England churches long after they had
moved north. In Yarmouth, such persons were admitted to the
communion service but were denied a vote in church meetings.
In such ways, the Yarmouth church attempted to adhere strictly
to established Congregational norms.[33]

Nova Scotia was, however, it should be reiterated, far from
being a colony with exclusively Congregational tendencies, even
in the Yankees outsettlements. The Reverend Ebenezer Moulton, a native of Windham, Connecticut, and a leading New
England Baptist, moved to Yarmouth in 1761 where he became
a religious leader in the community. Moulton also preached at
Cape Forchu and Chebogue and from 1763 to 1766 he travelled
to Barrington, Cornwallis, and Horton, at which latter place he
participated in organizing a Baptist church. The town of Newport also contained "a Considerable number" of Baptists, and in
Sackville in Cumberland County there had been a Baptist church
organized in the early 1760s. Just as Congregational people in
Nova Scotia looked to New England as the model they were
trying to imitate, so did the Nova Scotia Baptists regard their
New England brethren as sources of inspiration and practical
help.[34]

The Scotch-Irish settlements of Truro, Onslow and London-
derry added another dimension to the religious structure of
Nova Scotia. James Lyon, a Presbyterian minister "from the
Jerseys" officiated at Onslow for several years before moving to

Machias where he became one of the leading figures in the revolutionary cause. During the Revolutionary period the Reverends Mr. David Smith and Mr. Daniel Cock were Presbyterian ministers at Londonderry and Truro. Horton, outside the main area of Scotch-Irish settlement, also possessed by 1767 a Presbyterian minister. The Reverend James Murdoch, ordained by the Presbytery of Newton, Limavady, Ireland, and sent directly to Nova Scotia, based himself at Horton but also preached at other towns in the colony.[35]

It seems obvious that in spite of its small and scattered population there was a great diversity of religious sentiments, attachments and organizations in the Nova Scotia outsettlements. In Barrington, for instance, a group of Nantucket Quakers had been among the first settlers. Throughout the 1760s there was a growing Congregational organization and it also seems likely that the town had some Baptists.[36] In Maugerville a similar diversity existed in the local religious structure. Thomas Wood, an S.P.G. missionary at Annapolis, following a journey up the St. John River, reported that the population consisted of "Dissenters of Various Denominations."[37]

The determination of the S.P.G. to extend Anglican influence in the colony added another element to the religious life of pre-revolutionary Nova Scotia. It is difficult to estimate the precise effect of S.P.G. activities on the religious values of the Yankee settlers, since most of the evidence is literary in nature and is provided by the subjective letters of the missionaries. The Congregational Church in Yarmouth is the only one that has left detailed records over a period of years but no S.P.G. missionaries were active in this area and it is therefore not possible to arrive at any accurate assessment of the number of Yankees who actually became Anglicans or who became openly sympathetic to the Church of England. The S.P.G. missionaries were undermining the New England values of some Yankees at least. A recent study has demonstrated that even in New England Anglicanism was not simply the faith of rich merchants but was, in fact, the religion of a considerable number of poor colonists.[38] In Nova Scotia, where many of the townships had great difficulty in acquiring and maintaining ministers, the S.P.G. missionaries provided a welcome and inexpensive method of obtaining the services of a minister. In most cases the fact that no money was required to pay for the preacher was a sufficient inducement for some Yankees to attend S.P.G. services. And familiarity with Anglicanism led to an increasing acceptance of the normality of that form of religious worship and organization.

One of the best examples of this tendency at work is to be seen in a 1770 letter from settlers in the Annapolis Valley. Written on September 30, the document is remarkable in revealing the changes that had occurred in the values of some Yankees subsequent to their emigration to Nova Scotia. It contains a request by some Congregationalists to Massachusetts but it is a request that the Reverend Mr. Clarke, an S.P.G. missionary at Dedham, Massachusetts, come to Nova Scotia to be their minister. This peculiar action for Massachusetts Congregationalists was explained in this way:

> We the inhabitants of Annapolis and Granville having been educated and brought up (at least the greatest number of us) in the Congregational way of Worship, before we came to Settle in Nova Scotia, and therefore should have Chosen to have a Minister of that form of worship settled among us; but the Reverend Mr. Wood . . . hath removed our former prejudices that we had against . . . the Church of England as by law established and hath won us unto a good opinion thereof in as much as he hath removed all our Scruples.

These ex-Congregationalists now had "the greatest desire to have another minister of the episcopal Forms also settled among us." This confession of new-found attachment to the Church of England was not merely a device to encourage the appointment of a missionary to aid Wood in the area. The inhabitants of Annapolis and Granville promised "most Chearfully and freely" to pay Clarke for one year and assured him of support in the future if their relationship was satisfactory.[39]

Five years after this request was written Thomas Wood confirmed the growing popularity of the Anglican way in the Annapolis Valley. Wood in April 1775 conceded that the increase in attendance was "occasioned partly by several English farmers who came here last summer" but added that "great numbers

. . . [of] Dissenters from New England . . . now flock to my congregations: in so much that our places of public worship will not contain them."[40] Even the presence of a Congregational minister in a community in Nova Scotia did not guarantee immunity from S.P.G. influence. In Liverpool, Israel Cheever, the Congregational minister, was "much disliked by the people in General" and in late 1766 a group of Liverpool people requested aid from the S.P.G. in the form of a missionary and money for a church building.[41]

These then were the main features of religious life in the Nova Scotian outsettlements in 1776 and the pre-revolutionary period. The most prominent characteristics of the structure were instability and a general lack of cohesion. The presence of a variety of religious beliefs in one colony was not unusual in itself, although in the case of Yankee Nova Scotia with its small population, it was perhaps to some extent remarkable. In Massachusetts the same religious spectrum existed from New Lights to Anglicans and the only feature unique to Nova Scotia was the influx of Methodists in 1774-75, particularly into Cumberland County. But an important difference between Nova Scotia and Massachusetts was that in the northern colony no viable Congregational system was organized. The New England settlers attempted to institutionalize their traditional patterns of belief and worship in Nova Scotia but with no great success. Individual communities managed to retain a Congregational minister for varying periods of time but no inter-township organization emerged prior to the revolutionary war. New England Congregationalists were in the same position as the Baptists and other sects in Nova Scotia; they were merely another part of the struggling dissenting elements. Although Congregationalists, whether pro- or anti-revivalist in sentiment, composed the majority of Yankee population, they failed to establish their position in an effective way. Since Congregationalists were struggling along with the other dissenters, the S.P.G. was able to make much more impact on the outsettlements than might otherwise have been the case.

The Nova Scotian Yankees, in spite of the growing influence of the S.P.G., still regarded the New England colonies as a source of spiritual strength and material assistance in their

Christian struggle in the northern wilderness. At times certain elements in New England, usually those living in areas many of the emigrants had left from in the early 1760s, helped out when they were able. But the help was given for old times' sake rather than because of a pressing concern to bring Nova Scotia into the struggle for religious and political liberty. Religion in New England had moved beyond the preoccupations of the 1750s and was, moreover, losing its dominating hold over the colonial mind. As has been recently argued, during these years the leadership in the American colonies gradually became less religious and more political in inspiration and outlook. Ebenezer Gay was not in the vanguard of colonial thought and though he could manage in 1768 to praise Nova Scotia, most colonists must have found it impossible to look favourably on Nova Scotia when they noted its dependent and submissive attitude towards Britain. The religious correspondence that passed between Nova Scotia and New England around 1770 was carried on as if nothing had happened to the American world since 1763. Too much, of course, can be deduced from this correspondence. It was still possible for colonists to write to each other in 1770 without referring to the threats allegedly contained in British policies. But when seen in relation to the Nova Scotian context as a whole and its particular lack of development after 1765, the evidence garnered from church records and religious correspondence becomes far more informative. Religion was one strong bond of sympathy and a complex of shared values and attitudes that could have been used to inform the Nova Scotia Yankees of contemporary trends in New England churches and even in New England society. But the Nova Scotia Yankees made no attempt to educate themselves in this manner. This was one window through which they could have studied recent developments in New England but when they looked, they saw little change from the conditions they had known in the 1750s when only a few of the most informed Americans had begun to imagine a rift between England and the colonies.

For the Nova Scotia Yankees this period was the missing decade. It was during these years that the other American colonies left Nova Scotia behind while they created for themselves a new sense of identity and constructed a new version of their position and purpose in the world. The Yankees in the outsettlements of Nova Scotia could still join in opposing the Stamp Act in small groups but there was no general movement of protest and no sense of solidarity among the settlements.[42] Above all, there was no sense of participation in the "Union" of 1765 that John Adams believed so significant. The Stamp Act did not produce a crisis in Nova Scotia's internal affairs, and it did not serve, therefore, as a critical turning point in the development of the Nova Scotia mind or as a catalyst that enabled traditional ideas to be transformed into the rhetoric of resistance. In the other colonies it was the Stamp Act crisis and subsequent political battles that generated the intense political heat in which "long popular though hitherto inconclucive, controversial and hitherto imperfectly harmonised ideas . . . were fused into a comprehensive view unique in its moral and intellectual appeal."[43] Insofar as the Nova Scotia Yankees protested British policy in the 1760s they did so at a much less intense level than the other colonists, and the protests were never generalized into a popular, colony-wide movement. Such ideas of protest remained submerged and limited in their application; they were not brought into the public consciousness and pressed into service as the basis for a coherent attack on British designs for enslaving the colonies. In Nova Scotia such ideas remained in a stunted form, uncertain of their legitimacy, incapable of raising men's passions and sustaining a revolutionary ideology.

3

Response
to Revolution

Whatever there was of a revolutionary movement in Nova Scotia must be viewed within
the context of the missing decade. For only in the western extremity of Nova Scotia, in Maugerville and in the Chignecto
Isthmus–Cobequid region, was there any significant indigenous
revolutionary activity. The "contagion of disaffection" affected
a fairly large number of inhabitants of these areas but only for a
brief period of time at the beginning of the Revolution. In the
late summer of 1776 a liberating army consisting of twenty-
eight men under the command of Jonathan Eddy, a Chignecto
farmer, left northern Massachusetts. It was Eddy's hope to
galvanize revolutionary support in western Nova Scotia in preparation for a decisive assault on Halifax. After picking up a
few more volunteers on the way to Maugerville and at the
settlement, Eddy's tiny army made its way to the Chignecto
Isthmus. The immediate military target was Fort Cumberland,
the British fort on the Bay of Fundy side of the isthmus. After a
brief, desultory siege, the invaders, in late November, were
driven from the Chignecto by British troops. And Eddy and his
men were compelled to retreat westwards to Maugerville and
then to northern Massachusetts. Largely because of this disaster, the revolutionary movement in Nova Scotia collapsed.[1]

Until 1775 there was no known overt revolutionary activity in the colony. Governor Francis Legge in Halifax may have believed at times that there was an incipient revolutionary movement in Nova Scotia paralleling similar ones in the other colonies, but this belief was more a creation of his imagination than one based on conclusions drawn from actual events. In September 1774, for instance, Legge issued a proclamation condemning various meetings and assemblies that had been held in the outsettlements to promote, what he termed, "illegal confederacies, combinations and public disorders."[2] Yet the extant records of the town meetings for the period contain no reference to political affairs and, moreover, they indicate a distinct lack of interest in such issues. The only exception to this was the Cornwallis meeting held in the spring of 1771 which took steps to "apply for a charter of privileges Both Sivel and Relidgeous."[3] But this was a continuation of the attempt, made most strenuously in the early 1760s, to gain certain rights for the Yankees based on the 1759 proclamation and was not a sign of a locally inspired and organized resistance movement following the example set in the other colonies. Legge must have based his September 1774 proclamation on certain facts he had been given, but the wide scope of the document and general accusations made in it suggest that he had no hard evidence that could describe a coherent protest movement or identify local agitators. Those meetings that did take place were not the beginnings of a rebellion and it seems that, subsequent to them, no steps were taken to link the sporadic meetings into anything approaching the organized protests of the colonies to the south. Legge was unable to name any specific rebellious measures or point to any popular radical orators. In the case of Cumberland County, which was one of the most disaffected areas in Nova Scotia during the early war years, it was not until late 1775 that the people "for the first time" began "hinting" to the Governor their "feeling for the commotions in the British Empire etc."[4] Whatever the governor, moving among the small official circle in Halifax, believed to be the situation, the American sympathizers in one of the most actively "revolutionary" areas in Nova Scotia were certain that prior to 1775 no hint, far less any public movement of protest, had in fact appeared.

That the governor in Halifax was out of touch with the situation in many of the outsettlements was clearly revealed in December 1775. In that month the Council appointed commissioners in the various townships to collect the taxes that were to be raised to support the militia. This was a deliberate step to prepare the colony against American invasion. Among these government appointees in the Maugerville and Cumberland areas were men who were involved in the rebellious movements in those townships during 1776.[5] Since both townships, particularly Maugerville, were remote from Halifax control, the fact that the governor and his Council were unaware that leading men, including two members of the House of Assembly, were prepared to organize resistance to Halifax authority is not surprising. The incident does indicate, however, that the governor's assessment of the general trend of events in Nova Scotia during these years must always be treated with caution. In December 1775 he knew of no revolutionary leaders and there seems no reason to believe that he knew of any in 1774 when he issued his proclamation. Like many British officials in London and the colonies, Legge was convinced that all New England people had too much democracy in their heads.[6] Looking at the large numbers of New Englanders in Nova Scotia he assumed that these people must be plotting in some way against the constituted authorities. Legge was unable to distinguish between the Nova Scotia Yankees and the more politically informed inhabitants of New England.

Those Nova Scotia Yankees who made appeals for American help in 1775 and 1776 did not attempt to convince the revolutionary colonies that the Nova Scotian movement had any origins earlier than 1775. A Maugerville petition, sent in May 1776 to the Massachusetts authorities, specifically explained that their "scituation [sic] being Somewhat Remote from the Seat of these troubles" they had not "been so Immediately Effected as many Parts of the Continent." They had, therefore, "hitherto taken no part in the Present unnatural quarrell." It would undoubtedly have been in the interest of the Maugerville people, endeavouring as they were to encourage Massachusetts' intervention on their behalf, to recall and report any previous examples of their declarations and activities in the "cause of liberty."[7] But they could produce no precedents for their action in May 1776 because there had been none.

This inability to cite precedents for their actions in 1775 and 1776 was not peculiar to Maugerville. The revolutionary elements in Cumberland openly admitted to General George Washington that it was only in 1775 that "publick declarations" were uttered against the British authorities in Halifax and that people were roused against arbitrary government. Until that time such notions of public, concerted action and attempts to organize a protest movement "were not heard" in Cumberland.[8] The revolutionary activities in 1775 and 1776 were clearly a novel experience for the Nova Scotia Yankees. They were only beginning to be aware of, and experiment with, the procedures and politics of local resistance that other American colonists were by then well practised in. While the Thirteen Colonies, after many fruitless attempts to reach an accommodation with Britain, had pushed towards a final break with the mother country and were engaged in open war with her, some Nova Scotia Yankees were just beginning to take the first steps in formulating their case for joining the American cause. In 1775 and 1776 they had only begun the attempt to rationalize an acceptance of the American view that Britain had become a despotic power bent on subjugating the colonies.

Thus while the American colonists formed committees of correspondence, organized periodic gatherings for supporters of the "cause of liberty" and drafted political statements and resolves, the Nova Scotia Yankees had remained quiet. As John Adams realized, all these political and social activities created a feeling of solidarity among the Patriots and enabled them to clarify their position and to keep constantly their goals in public view.[9] In these other American colonies when the final break with Britain came, the Patriots had behind them many years of practice and experience in the aims and methods of resistance.

Because of their failure, especially in the 1760s, to squeeze concessions from the Halifax authorities, by the 1770s the Yankees had apparently reconciled themselves to the reduced extent of liberty in the northern colony and made little effort to use their political voice in the Assembly. Most of them held their land directly from the crown and as one observer in Halifax noted, the "insecurity of real property"[10] in the colony was one of the main reasons for the reluctance of the population to demand political changes. Nearly all the land holdings in Nova Scotia, many of which were never officially confirmed until the late 1760s, depended entirely on the Halifax authorities. The general poverty that prevailed in the outsettlements, in spite of prosperous years in the early 1760s, combined with this factor to prevent any effective political pressure from originating in the outsettlements.

As ex-New Englanders, however, some Yankees were aware that the New England colonies, in contrast to Nova Scotia, possessed certain historical rights that were endangered by designing British ministers intent on reducing the colonies to a weak and dependent status. Thus, when the Yankees openly sympathized with the Revolution they did not do so as Nova Scotians but as New Englanders. This fine distinction is of critical importance. It was not a question of Nova Scotia's liberties being threatened but a question of an attack on the liberties of the New England colonies. Nova Scotia Yankees did not talk about "our" rights but always referred to "their [New England's]" rights. Samuel Doane, for example, on a visit to Boston in 1772, went to the First Baptist Church where he heard "Rev. Mr. Allen preach . . . concerning the excellency of having our liberty." Even with the title of the sermon, using as it did the inclusive term "our," that presumably tempted Doane to identify Nova Scotia, controlled by an all-powerful governor, with the Massachusetts struggle, the Barrington inhabitant quite clearly believed that Nova Scotia was not involved in the struggle for liberty. As Doane put it, the sermon argued that the people in New England were in "a great measure deprived wrongfully of this great blessing by their own nation." He considered the sermon "an outstanding piece of work" that was "very reasonable" in setting out the case against the mother country.[11] Impressed as he was by the logic of colonial resistance, Doane apparently saw no reason to apply similar principles in the case of Nova Scotia.

It might be argued that Doane was not typical of the Barrington people and of Yankee farmers and fishermen generally and that although he failed to link Nova Scotia with the Patriot

movement in New England this was by no means a characteristic of Nova Scotia as a whole. It might further be argued that
in 1772, when Doane visited Boston, it was quite normal for
visitors from other American colonies to talk of the threat to
New England liberties rather than colonial liberties in general
since the main arena of the struggle against British policies had
been in Boston. It was only with the passing of the Intolerable
Acts that many of the people throughout the colonies fully
realized the extent of the British attack of their liberties and
joined together in a general union to defend them.

But there is evidence to indicate that Doane was not an un-
typical Nova Scotia Yankee and that the attitude displayed in
1772 remained unchanged even after hostilities had broken out
between Britain and her American colonies. In October 1776
twenty-seven inhabitants of Barrington put their names on a
petition to the Massachusetts Congress in which they described
their difficult circumstances now that war had broken out. These
petitioners openly admitted to the Congress their sympathy for
the American cause "haveing" as they put it, "Fathers, brothers
and children liveing there [Massachusetts]." Yet even at this
time, when the other American colonies had declared their independence from Britain, these Barrington people made no effort
to include Nova Scotia in the colonial camp. The townspeople
did not identify with the political and military struggle of the
American colonies. They did not refer to the great cause "we"
are engaged in but quite unambivalently talked of "the great
cause you [Massachusetts] are Imbattled in." It is of fundamental importance to understand this persistent nuance in the
expressions of the Nova Scotia Yankees. They used "you" rather
than "we" whenever they talked of the Revolution. As New
Englanders they were, at the outbreak of hostilities, almost in-
tuitively sympathetic to "the great cause" but they did not identify themselves, as Nova Scotians, with the American point of
view.[12]

The American colonists, after the passage of the Intolerable
Acts, regarded these latest moves as final proof of a British conspiracy against all the American colonies. This was not the case,
however, in Nova Scotia. The British army in Boston presented
no new danger to the constitutional and political system in Nova

Scotia, which had since 1749 been securely in British control. The troops under the command of General Thomas Gage were "endeavouring to enslave their friends and relatives"[13] in New England. But the future of Nova Scotia was not at stake; the northern colony was apparently not to be considered in the same context as the other American colonies. Again there was no thought of bringing Nova Scotia into the struggle against Britain. This critical period witnessed in Nova Scotia a concern for "the Distress of New England."[14] In the months of crisis in 1774 and 1775, the Yankees who heard news of events in New England noted "the alarming conditions in America" and they wondered what the outcome of "the disturbances in New England"[15] would be. In spite of their close ties with New England it was with a peculiar detachment that the Nova Scotia Yankees viewed current developments as the colonies moved toward the break with Britain. Some of them sympathized with the colonists' cause but few believed that Nova Scotia was, or could be, part of the American struggle. As in 1765 so ten years later the Nova Scotia Yankees were not part of the colonial "Union."

In these circumstances few Nova Scotian Yankees expected a strong revolutionary movement to emerge in the northern colony. Thus when they talked about revolution they were not dealing with the same concepts that the Patriots in New England believed were contained in that term. In the New England colonies revolution meant organizing local committees and electing representatives to perform the functions of government and to prepare local militia to aid in the military overthrow of royal authority. The term revolution to Nova Scotians had no specific political connotations; quite simply it meant obtaining military help from New England, particularly Massachusetts. On the surface this merely seems to indicate that the Nova Scotia Yankees, because of their weak position, had to look outside the local situation for military strength since their own resources were inadequate.

There was, however, a more profound reason that compelled some Nova Scotia Yankees to place so much emphasis on American military intervention. By 1776, when the Patriots were engaged in war against Britain, there had occurred a radical transformation in attitudes in New England; loyalty to the mother country had been significantly eroded and new loyalties to the new and purified "rebel government" were emerging. This revolution in attitudes had been largely completed before the fighting began. In Nova Scotia there had been no corresponding revolutionary change in attitudes prior to 1776. Thus, whereas military activity for New Englanders was the culmination of a decade of verbal fighting with Britain, the appeals of the Nova Scotia Yankees for military aid had no roots thrusting into previous political protest. The quest for military intervention from Massachusetts became, therefore, an end in itself. This was essentially the meaning of the term revolution in Nova Scotia. There was little attempt to fabricate a political ideology; there were few references to British tyranny or to corrupt ministers of the crown. Instead, there was an obsession with getting American troops into Nova Scotia.

The Nova Scotia Yankees had developed no rationale for resistance. The successive governors in Halifax had made certain that the colony remained firmly under British control. The New England colonies, throughout the 1760s, had regarded Nova Scotia as quite distinct from the other American colonies. Franklin had seen Nova Scotia as a potential British power base from which Britain could intimidate the colonies. Stephen Hopkins had criticized British use of Nova Scotia in the mid-1760s during the attempts to enforce the Navigation and Trade Acts. John Adams had believed Nova Scotia incapable of producing political resistance movements. In the outsettlements of Nova Scotia the Yankees had gradually come to accept this view that the colony was irretrievably under British control. The stereotype image of Nova Scotia as a British military and naval base, held by prominent New Englanders, had affected the Yankees' own view of their colony. They too had come to believe that they were in no position to challenge the British hold on the colony.[16]

One of the Nova Scotia rebels clearly perceived the accuracy of this analysis. Writing in December 1776, Josiah Throop, a resident of Cumberland and an open sympathizer with the American cause, attempted a realistic assessment of the chances of a successful revolution in Nova Scotia. According to Throop, the only way that Nova Scotia could become part of the colonial struggle was for Massachusetts to take under its "protection" the counties of Sunbury and Cumberland, those areas of Nova Scotia that were linked to the continent. Once these areas were controlled by Massachusetts they could be used as a base from which expeditions could be sent into peninsular Nova Scotia until the whole colony "can be subdued."[17] This, then, was how one of the Nova Scotia rebels viewed the situation at the end of 1776. He simply discounted the possibility of the population of Nova Scotia organizing itself politically or militarily into any sort of resistance movement. If a revolution were to occur it would be accomplished by Massachusetts troops who would forcibly subdue the colony.

The same point was also made by the rebellious population in Maugerville in May 1776. The revolutionary committee elected by the townspeople of Maugerville gave no indication that they believed themselves to be part of a general resistance movement in Nova Scotia. Nor did they give any sign that they believed a Nova Scotia-wide Patriot organization might be possible in the future. They made no appeals for solidarity to other groups in the colony sympathetic to the American cause. Indeed they did not even refer to such potential allies. The Maugerville rebels assumed, apparently, that Nova Scotia was incapable of supporting a revolutionary movement similar to that in the other American colonies. In a resolve that inadvertently revealed the colonial mentality of Nova Scotia Yankees, the Maugerville people declared that it "is our Minds and Desire to submit ourselves to the government of the Massachusetts Bay."[18] This resolution is often cited as an unambiguous indication of an open revolutionary movement in Nova Scotia but a closer examination of its context and of its wording reveals the fundamental weakness of the revolutionary cause in Nova Scotia.

The Maugerville rebels did not argue that the political system in Nova Scotia was endangered by new British policies. They agreed that Massachusetts was right in resisting "tyrannical" encroachments by Britain on the colonies. But the only way the Maugerville people could throw themselves into the revolutionary cause was to renounce the fact that they were Nova Scotians and return to the system of politics and society they had lived in prior to their northward movement. There was no question of declaring Nova Scotia to be a Fourteenth Colony.

Revolution meant, to Maugerville, "to Share with you [Massa-chusetts] the Event of the present Struggle for Liberty, however God in his Providence may order it." The American colonists who in July 1776 declared their independence from Britain be-lieved that they were sharing with Massachusetts "the Event of the present Struggle," since it was Massachusetts that had been the focal point of British attacks on American liberty. But many of the residents of these Thirteen Colonies also believed that their social and political systems were threatened by British poli-cies and in joining together they believed they could better resist such attempts. In Nova Scotia, however, it was not a ques-tion of defending Nova Scotia from British power in conjunc-tion with the general American struggle but, rather, simply a question of "submitting" to Massachusetts. It seems clear, there-fore, that the revolutionary elements in Nova Scotia were not so much concerned about fighting against corrupt British power but were primarily intent on becoming, once more, a part of New England.[19]

It is against this background that the Eddy invasion in the autumn of 1776 must be seen. He had been warned in the sum-mer by John Allan, the other leader of the anti-British move-ment in the Cumberland area, against taking any action before a sufficiently large invasion force could be raised and before the people in Nova Scotia could be organized to take full advantage of the intervention.[20] Eddy had refused to listen and arrived at Cumberland in November with his "liberating army." Those people who were sympathetic to the American cause were ap-palled by the size and quality of Eddy's scanty force; they had reckoned on at least five hundred well-trained and well-armed invaders before a serious attempt could be made on the British troops garrisoning Fort Cumberland. The "friends of America" in Cumberland who had been meeting "in a private manner in Order to Determine" what supplies of men and equipment would be needed for the attempt to have any chance of success insisted that there "could be no probability of success and Liable to Every Evil and fatal consequences to the Inhabitants." Since they had learned of the outbreak of the revolutionary war all their hopes had been pinned on the possibility of American in-tervention. Few of them even considered the possibility of

extending local political and military resistance through the
Yankee townships. But now that the American help had arrived
in the form of Eddy's small, poorly equipped and badly disciplined band of freebooters the "friends of America" saw their
hopes crumble.[21]

Eddy increased the uneasiness and hesitancy among his potential allies by adopting a domineering approach. He would
not allow them time to organize nor would he heed their pleas
to wait for promised reinforcements from New England. Eddy
warned the people

> in the name of the United States That they had supplied the
> Enemys of America which had much displeased the States.
> That the Congress doubted their Integrity. That if they
> would not Rouse themselves and oppose the British power . . .
> they would be looked upon as Enemys and Should the country
> be reduced by the States, they would be treated as a con-
> quered people.[22]

Eddy's rough tactics achieved immediate results although in
the long run they did severe damage to the American cause
among the people of Cumberland. Many sympathizers, "chusing
rather to meet any Difficulty than to be thought Enemical [*sic*]
to America" and encouraged by Eddy's assurances that reinforcements were on the way, joined his proposed attack on the
British garrison. The attempt was a dismal failure. Before they
could lay siege, the American forces were dispersed by a sortie
from the fort and were chased to the surrounding forests. Eddy
thereupon decided to retreat to the relative safety of the St. John
River valley and to eventual oblivion. By this time most of the
Cumberland rebels were disillusioned with this commander who
had been sent "from the States." They "began to suspect they
were Imposed on, and that the men who came with Captain
Eddy were Induced to it by an expectation of much plunder."
This suspicion was virtually confirmed when the local people, to
their consternation, saw that "these men were determined to return; many of them declaring they did not come for such business but to seize particular persons with their property." Eddy's
ineptness and alleged duplicity not only brought about the complete failure of the invasion but precipitated the collapse of the

fragile revolutionary movement that had manifested itself in Cumberland. Almost seventy families sympathetic to the American cause preferred to leave rather than attempt to continue in Cumberland in the repressive atmosphere that was bound to follow Eddy's bungling. Of those sympathizers who remained, "many from their Indigent circumstances and Indisposition of their Families," most submitted to the British authorities. As John Allan clearly realized, the result of Eddy's mismanagement was that one of the potential revolutionary areas in Nova Scotia was now an unhappy county in a "Calamatous Situation." Where, before November 1775, hopes of revolution had existed, there was after the disastrous Eddy expedition, only the "utmost distress."[23]

The collapse of the revolutionary movement in Cumberland by the end of 1776 cut out the one great possibility that had been open to the Nova Scotia Yankees at the beginning of the year. The American intervention had come, but far from boosting the morale of the sympathizers and encouraging the establishment of committees and other organs of propaganda, it had forced the Cumberland rebels prematurely into the open and had made them easy targets for suppression by the Halifax authorities. John Allan, for one, saw the changed situation. In February 1777 he began talking to the Massachusetts authorities about helping to evacuate American sympathizers from Nova Scotia, particularly from the Chignecto area. To Allan it was clear that the one trump card in the hands of the Nova Scotia rebels had been played, and played badly, and that there was no longer any chance of a successful revolution in Nova Scotia.[24] He still suggested at times the possibility of an expedition but he only took this seriously when he believed there was the chance of mounting a large, well-organized invasion.

But Allan's main efforts were directed towards obtaining aid from Massachusetts "to Enable them [American sympathizers in Nova Scotia] to Remove their Familys."[25] From this time on the policy of evacuation was the main aim of the Nova Scotian exiles who gathered round Allan in the small frontier settlement of Machias. Allan was also concerned with keeping the Indian tribes between Machias and the Chignecto from joining the British side and he devoted some time to obtaining information about the state of affairs in Nova Scotia in case Congress at some future date became interested in the military conquest of the colony. Thus by early 1777 one of the most prominent leaders of the disaffected elements in Nova Scotia had discarded the hope that an insurrection could be fomented in the colony. The internal Nova Scotian situation, now that the outside help had failed as a catalyst, did not contain in itself the possibility of organized resistance.

Allan's analysis of the situation was common enough among American sympathizers in Nova Scotia. In the summer of 1776 a petition was brought from Onslow in Nova Scotia to Massachusetts. In this petition the inhabitants of the Cobequid township represented "their distressed situation" and prayed "relief either by sending them forces or vessels to bring them away."[26] This request was made prior to Eddy's invasion attempt and indicates the tenuous roots the revolutionary movement had in Nova Scotia. In Onslow the people realized everything depended on intervention or the "sending of forces." Once this failed there was no alternative in their view but to leave the colony. Gradually the people in Onslow, unable to evacuate in large numbers, submitted to the British authorities. By the summer of 1780 American sympathizers in Onslow and neighbouring townships were obliged to comply with the demands of Halifax and sent a "party of militia" to help repair fortifications in the British stronghold.[27] There is little evidence to trace the precise development of events in Onslow but from the available pieces of information it seems plausible that they conformed to Allan's analysis made in early 1777. Hope gave way to disillusionment and distress and eventually compelled even the most open sympathizers with the American cause to comply with the demands of Halifax. In other colonies the strength of revolutionary sentiment and the degree to which the population had been propagandized and organized meant that the Revolution did not require instant military success. In Nova Scotia everything depended on effective intervention. When this failed so did the Revolution.

In both Cumberland and Maugerville the revolutionary movements emerged into public view not as spontaneous mass uprisings of large sections of the population but as sudden outbursts coaxed into existence and inspired by a few politically aware leaders. In these areas the active leaders who urged the people to participate in the movement of resistance had been in close touch with recent events in New England. Whereas the mass of the population had lived "in a Retired Situation" from the "unnatural quarrel" between Britain and her colonies, several key figures were informed of and abreast with latest developments in New England. It was these men who were primarily responsible for explaining the issues to the people and for encouraging them to join the American cause.

In Maugerville the evidence clearly supports this view that certain key figures were the initiators of the local revolutionary movement. As the Maugerville settlers realized, there had been little talk of politics and colonial rights since their arrival in the early 1760s. In their isolated situation they had been out of touch with events in New England. But in 1774 or 1775 a figure who was to assume great importance in the local social structure arrived from Massachusetts. Seth Noble, the first permanent minister to be settled in Maugerville, had not missed the colonial controversy with Britain. He had lived in Massachusetts during the series of disputes from the Stamp Act crisis to the Boston massacre and its aftermath and was well aware of what he believed to be the grave danger which threatened the freedom of the colonies. Noble became one of the leaders of the revolutionary movement in Maugerville. He brought the issues before the people, explained their significance and urged the town to join the American struggle. In May 1776 the Revolutionary Committee elected to organize Maugerville for participation in the American cause consisted of twelve members, ten of whom had been prominent figures in the church of Seth Noble. When the revolutionary movement in Maugerville collapsed, when the hoped for major intervention from Massachusetts failed to appear, nearly all the people who had agreed to the May 1776 declaration returned to their allegiance to Britain. Only Seth Noble along with two ringleaders refused to deny their commitment to the Revolution. These three fled the town and headed for Machias, leaving the settlement once more a community loyal to British authority.[28]

In Cumberland County, John Allan and Jonathan Eddy were the most influential supporters of the Revolution. Allan was well informed of events in the New England colonies and realized what was at stake in 1775 and 1776. He had first arrived in Nova Scotia in 1749 when his father came to Halifax with the founding expedition of Cornwallis. But he had not remained in Nova Scotia. He was educated in Massachusetts and only finally settled in Cumberland in 1767.[29] He had not, therefore, had the same experiences as most of the people in the outsettlements but had remained in contact with developments in the colonies. He subscribed fully to the colonists' version of British intentions and patiently explained to the Micmac Indians how Americans were fighting for their liberties against a powerful, corrupt Britain that was determined to steal colonial property and goods. In reply to the Indians' question, "How comes it that Old England & new should Quarrel & come to blows?" Allan explained the reasons that had impelled the Americans to fight for independence. Allan,

> accordingly gave a short Historical Account of matters from the beginning of the settlement of America, the reasons for the first Emmigrants leaving Europe; the different Charters of the Colonies, the unjust demand of Britain and breach of Faith — usurp'd authority claimed by Britain, the different steps taken by the Americans for redress, and finally the design of Establishing Civil & religious Liberty.[30]

Allan was fully committed to the American cause and his open adherence to it during the critical months of 1776 did much to increase the numbers of American sympathizers. As in Maugerville, one of the major revolutionary figures in Cumberland was not one of the original settlers of the early 1760s but a more recent arrival who had kept up contacts with New England.

Jonathan Eddy, however, unlike Noble and Allan, had come from Norton, Massachusetts, to Nova Scotia in the early 1760s and there seems to be no reason why he should have been better informed of contemporary events or more committed to the Revolution than other Yankees. Eddy had, it should be noted, made a point of involving himself in political affairs. He had been elected in the Assembly for Cumberland township in 1770 and was in close contact with John Allan, the second member for the county.[31]

Further indication that recent arrivals from New England tended to be more disposed to the American side can be extracted from the various petitions sent from the Yarmouth area to the Government of Massachusetts after the outbreak of war. While most of these petitioners requested permits to carry on trade and secure protection from American privateers, several of them asked permission to return with their families and effects to New England. In the collection made by Edmund D. Poole of these petitions there are sixteen requests for permission to return. Since the other petitioners generally showed concern for improving their difficult position in Nova Scotia, in spite of protestations of affection for the American cause, it seems reasonable to deduce that these sixteen petitioners for one reason or another were attached to American values to the extent that they wished to leave Nova Scotia. Ten such requests came from Yarmouth and Cape Forchu and out of these ten there were six families that had definitely arrived in Nova Scotia later than 1767 and two more families were possibly in this group.[32] From this small sample it seems reasonable to suggest, though not in any way conclusively, that the settlers who had arrived in the early 1760s were less likely to support the American cause in a strong and continuing manner in such a way that their living patterns would be disturbed. More recent arrivals, however, were much more likely to make extra efforts to revert to the social and political system of New England.

This kind of evidence, for arguing that a distinction can be made between the goals and values of early and late arrivals in Nova Scotia, is not convincing in itself. Like so much of the evidence relating to the outsettlements it is fragmentary and too limited to yield statistically valid results. It is, therefore, not conclusive. But all these pointers assume more significance when joined to the earlier argument that most of the Nova Scotia Yankees, by moving north in the early 1760s, had missed a decade of political turmoil that had radically altered American loyalties and values. It should not be surprising that most of the leaders and some of the people in Nova Scotia who found it impossible to remain under British control were relatively late arrivals or, for various reasons, were more likely to be better informed about the colonial case against Britain.

In spite of the belated efforts of men like Allan, Eddy and Noble, the Nova Scotia Yankees remained ideologically incapable of organizing sustained movements of political protest. In Cumberland there had been no public committee in existence prior to the Eddy invasion although some meetings had taken place in "a private manner."[33] It was only in the midst of the chaos caused by Eddy's blundering tactics that a committee was finally established to organize rebel strategy. The Committee of Safety in Maugerville was also formed in adverse circumstances. Although Noble had instructed his people in some of the revolutionary ideals, the committee was actually established as the town was threatened by two privateers, who had announced that unless Maugerville joined the American cause an invading army would confiscate property and treat Nova Scotia as a conquered country. For the following twelve months of its existence the Maugerville committee was continually uncertain of its function and hesitant about extending revolutionary rule to the settled area at the mouth of the St. John River.[34]

That the Nova Scotia Yankees were inadequately prepared intellectually and psychologically for revolution may also be deduced from the experience of Alexander McNutt in late 1778. A resident of southeastern Nova Scotia, McNutt for many years had been concerned in one way or another with the colony's affairs. He had been deeply involved in the 1760s in land speculation and had played a key role in the settlement of Onslow and Truro by the Scotch-Irish.[35] After the outbreak of the revolutionary war, the ubiquitous McNutt approached the Continental Congress with a grandiose scheme to transform Nova Scotia into an independent, republican state. In his correspondence with the Congress, McNutt inadvertently suggested that the Nova Scotians were deplorably ignorant of the aims of the revolutionary struggle against Britain and lamentably lacking in the skills required to organize a democratic and republican government. He therefore had found it necessary to have:

> Colected a Variety of Authors upon Government, civil and Religious Liberty, Sermons and Speeches suited to the [Lords of Battle?] Pamphlets, papers, all the Acts of the Assembly of this State; several of the constitutions with remarks upon them, and some material for a new one in order to have it

> printed and laid before the Convention, and a number of
> Copies for the several Townships for their Consideration. . . .

All of these documents were required reading for Nova Scotians, McNutt concluded, because "it is not the errecting of Fortifications, nor Collecting together a multitude of people, that makes a great and flourishing State but a wholesome Constitution, good Laws . . . and a faithful administration."[36] He realized that the Nova Scotia Yankees required a crash reading course in 1778 to bring themselves to the stage reached by the other colonies in 1776 or earlier.

McNutt, however, was ignoring the conditions of 1778. There was a war in progress, an attempted invasion of Nova Scotia had ended in disaster, and communications between Nova Scotia and New England were now subject to constant disruption. The farmers and fishermen of Nova Scotia had no opportunity and little time to examine books on law, government and religion to become enlightened concerning the advantages of independence and republican government. Moreover, after 1775, the gap between a colony still under British control and the new states under republican constitutions dramatically widened and became virtually impossible to bridge. What was required in Nova Scotia before revolutionary ideas could take hold and motivate large sections of the population was, as one American contemporary put it, an "Ecclaircisement."[37] This observer sensed that the Nova Scotia Yankees simply were not aware of the ideas that impelled the colonies to break free from their mother country and could not therefore make an easy and complete identification of their position with the course taken by the other Thirteen Colonies. The whole of Yankee Nova Scotia was essentially in an unenlightened state. What was needed was a massive propaganda effort that could telescope the transformation that had taken place in American values between 1765 and 1775 into one great act of understanding.

4

Neutrality
or Confusion?

It was difficult for the Nova Scotia Yankees in 1776, and increasingly so as the revolutionary war continued, to take an unambivalent moral stand. This is what John Allan apparently did not see when he criticized the Maugerville people for failing to use their "moral agency" after 1776 as so many of the colonists to the south had done.[1] Allan was unable to understand how anyone possessed of moral agency would fail to acknowledge, as he himself had done, the justice of the American cause and identify with it whatever the cost. For him and for many other supporters of the Revolution, the Almighty was assisting them in the struggle against despotic, evil forces.[2] But this kind of simple apocalyptic analysis did not coincide with the Nova Scotia Yankee perception of contemporary events. The Maugerville inhabitants, for example, were not incapable of "moral decision" as Allan implied. On the contrary, the fact that so many of the church members were actively engaged in the events of 1776 and the manner in which they referred to their "transgressions" when re-submitting to British rule in May 1777 indicate how susceptible they were to viewing political issues in terms of the Christian morality they had absorbed since their earliest days in New England.[3] Instead of bestowing approbation on either the British or the Americans, the Yankees appeared simply puzzled by the events of the time.

This general state of confusion was compounded by the nature of Nova Scotian contacts with the emissaries of the Revolution. When Eddy arrived in Cumberland he had resorted to threats against private property in his attempts to compel sympathizers to join the American cause. In Maugerville the American privateers had issued similar threats. In both cases the probability of being conquered by the Americans and then being deprived of property, was put as a likely outcome of the revolutionary war. These types of contacts made it difficult for Nova Scotians to bestow the same moral approbation on the American side that the colonial Patriots naturally and instinctively granted.

Over on the South Shore, the inhabitants of Barrington had similar problems in deciding whether the British or the Americans possessed a monopoly on virtue. The Barrington people were clearly sympathetic to the American cause. Most of them had originated "from the Massachusetts bay for whose welfare we Earnestly pray having Fathers, Brothers and Children liveing there." In such troubled times they had done their best to help in small ways by sheltering escaped American prisoners and shipping them back to the States. They were aware that, by continuing to follow their fishing trade in a British colony, they were doing a "Disservice to the great cause," but unless they fished and traded they could not support themselves. American privateers had "taken severall of our Schooners from us and the fish caught in them to the great Distress of the fishermen which have not done anything but fishing to injure you [Massachusetts] which they could not help being the only way they have to maintain their families." A possible solution to these difficulties, beneficial to both Barrington and Massachusetts, would have been, it was suggested, for the Americans to grant permission to Barringtonians to trade their catches for provisions in the New England states. The Barrington inhabitants still did not identify themselves with the colonial cause — they talked of the struggle "you [Massachusetts] is Imbattled [in];" but they were clearly still attached to their former colony and were anxious not to obstruct the American cause.[4] Of course they were interested in carrying on their trade and this is why they make representations to Massachusetts.

In spite of their attachment to Massachusetts, however, the inhabitants of the southern tip of Nova Scotia were somewhat troubled that no one from New England had kept them informed of the proper course to pursue in Nova Scotia. And they were, therefore, at a loss to know how they could help the Americans. They had "not seen or heard from you any thing who are in Authority." All the information they possessed in October 1776 was provided by "the privateers that have made this a place of Rendezvous." These privateersmen were, naturally enough, very clumsy in explaining the aims of the Revolution to the local people. They made little effort to describe the various ideals behind the revolutionary movement. According to the Yankees of Barrington, the privateersmen assured them that, unless they joined the American cause, "all the Dreadfull Things that can befall any people" would happen to Barrington, "to viz . . . That the Indians are Commissioned to come on the back of us and Kill, burn and Destroy." To the Barringtonians, "Descendents from America," it was hard to accept that they had to be threatened before they could become members of "the free and Generous Sons of America."[5] They were basically well disposed, at first, to the Americans but this type of introduction into revolutionary rhetoric made it difficult for them to accept the fact that the American colonists were battling for the Lord.

It has been suggested that these American privateers were a powerful influence in pushing Nova Scotians from a sympathy for the Americans into a position of neutrality in the war.[6] But things were not as simple as this. In both Maugerville and Barrington the people were able to talk freely with the privateersmen, many of whom may have come from the same New England towns as the settlers. There is no indication that in either town the privateers plundered or otherwise made their presence intolerable; there seemed to be a communicative relationship between townspeople and privateersmen in spite of the threats and warnings doled out by the Americans. In the case of Barrington, resentment of seizures of fishing vessels did not lead to any attempts to bring British assistance or prevent the privateers from using Barrington harbour as a safe refuge.[7] Those Yankees who had emigrated from the coast towns of New England had previously encountered the effects of privateering, most recently in the war between Britain and France. In 1758, a few years before the mass of Yankees had emigrated to Nova Scotia, many New England people had been "much intimidated with the reports of Privateers" operating between Nova Scotia and the New England coast.[8] The French privateers had been alien to New Englanders, crewed by foreigners with a strange language and customs and carrying the frightening possibility of taking their captives to France. But the type of privateering practised during the revolutionary war was quite different in its nature and consequences.

The New England privateers presented a far more subtle problem for the Nova Scotia Yankees. Often the name of the captain, his town of residence and the port of origin of the privateer in New England were well known. The records of the Justice of the Peace in Liverpool, which formally recorded the statements of victims of the privateers in the seas off the township, indicate that from 1779 to 1783 privateers that were complained against were often mentioned by name, captain and home port in Massachusetts.[9]

On the Cape Sable shore in the township of Yarmouth the same paradoxical juxtaposition of familiarity and fear also existed. In November 1775 privateers actually landed men in the township, rounded up leaders of the militia and carried them off as prisoners. The local Congregational minister, Jonathan Scott, criticized the townspeople for openly sympathizing with the actions of the privateer. Fifteen months later, however, this same minister entertained at his home the crew of a privateer which had been forced aground by a British man-of-war.[10] The Nova Scotia Yankees, living in the outsettlements with members of their family still residing in New England, had too many shared values and customs with the privateersmen to regard their activities in a uniformly hostile manner.[11] In such circumstances it is by no means clear that they could use the privateers as a negative reference group to undermine their sympathy for the struggle of the New England colonies.

The privateersmen, for their part, tended not to wage their trade indiscriminately against all elements in Nova Scotia. A distinction must be made between privateering on the high seas when ships and cargoes were seized and taken to New England and privateering expeditions which landed in Nova Scotia townships, and plundered local houses and businesses. In the more conventional privateering, on the open seas, Nova Scotia fishermen and traders generally had no guarantee of receiving special treatment simply because they had close ties with New England. Many Yankees attempted to avoid this problem by applying for special permits from Massachusetts to carry their trade to New England, thus depriving the privateers of any grounds for seizure.[12] It seems that even in difficult wartime conditions a considerable trading network was maintained, especially in the early years of the war, between Nova Scotian ports, particularly those in the Cape Sable shore, and Massachusetts. But any ship in open sea, whatever paper protection it carried, was always in danger of being seized by unscrupulous privateersmen who paid no heed to American laws but pursued their profession for purely personal gain.[13]

The privateering expeditions that landed in Nova Scotia were, however, quite a different matter. These raiding parties selected their victims from among the small number of well-to-do families in the outsettlements whose homes contained valuable booty. Several petitions and letters complaining of the depredations and asking for government protection were sent to Halifax from some of the Minas Basin townships and in those extant petitions the wording reveals who the usual sufferers were. In September 1775 a letter from John Burbidge, a former Halifax resident, then living in Cornwallis, advised the government that "many of the principal people here [Cornwallis] are very apprehensive of more visits from these plunderers." Five days later Burbidge emphasized the state of fear among these people who were "uneasy that the Troops [ffom Halifax] delay their coming."[14] Burbidge was not content to send individual pleas for help to Halifax but joined with other men who feared for their property. The result was a "memorial of Several of the principal Inhabitants of the Township of Cornwallis" to Lieutenant-Governor Arbuthnot, pointing out that Cornwallis was "greatly Exposed to the Ravages and plunder of His Majesty's Enemys from the Adjacent colonies."[15]

In Machias, after 1776, the Nova Scotia exiles, when contemplating the possibility of undertaking whale boat expeditions against the colony, planned on the assumption that they would plunder certain homes known to be wealthy and "call what they took their own in common with the good people of that Province."[16] The ordinary people in Nova Scotia, the settlers who had come from New England at any rate, had apparently little to fear from privateering excursions. Even the German and French-speaking inhabitants of Lunenburg learned to store their valuables in the house of Mrs. Robert Foster in the expectation that her house might be spared because she came from Massachusetts. Also in Lunenburg, as in Cornwallis, it tended to be "the principle [sic] Inhabitants" who were "Plundered of their Interest."[17]

The one communication from the Minas Basin townships that failed specifically to mention that leading citizens were the main objects of privateering attacks came from Horton and styled itself a "memorial of us the Subscriber, Proprietors and Inhabitants of the Township of Horton in Kings County as well as for and in behalf of Ourselves and other Inhabitants of the Said Township as for and in behalf of the other Townships in the said County and about the Basin of Minas." The main motive of the memorialists was not to protect their own property but to "prevent the Destruction of those Settlements by the Enemy."[18] It seems reasonable to conclude that although the raiders attacked selected targets their impact on the countryside was to induce fear throughout the area in general. Nevertheless, in October 1776 the Yankees in the Windsor area were accused of openly sheltering and aiding the raiders. According to one account "the Generality of the people of the Neighbourhood . . . Expeditiously furnished the Privateer Rebells with every Assistance in their Power to forward their getting away." The "country people" appeared to be "fast and firm friends" of the rebel privateersmen.[19]

Once again the fragmentary nature of the evidence prevents a detailed picture emerging of the effect of privateers on Nova Scotia from 1776 to 1783. Much of the evidence for local sympathy towards the privateers comes from the earlier years of the war and it may be that by 1780 there was a great deal more disenchantment with continued American harassment. What can be said from the available evidence is that privateering did not have a one-way, easily identifiable effect of making neutrals of the

Nova Scotia Yankees or of making them ardent British supporters.

The primary influence of the privateers on the great mass of the Nova Scotia Yankees who were not directly threatened by the raids was to make more complex the already complicated predicament in which they found themselves. It was another factor in their lives which made it difficult for them to accept that Americans were fighting a morally justifiable war. Even those people who sympathized with the Revolution found it difficult, because of their comparative political illiteracy, to "regulate their conduct agreeable to the Rules made by the United States."[20] When they did come into contact with New England it was not with any authorities in the independent colonies but with raiders and privateers. The revolutionary ideology which carried so much moral virtue in the new States impinged on the minds of Nova Scotians in a highly equivocal way.

On the other side of the battle lines, the British, by impressing seamen and drafting local militia for work in Halifax, ensured that the Yankees would find no more understanding from one side than from the other. The activities of the press gangs, especially, alienated and intimidated the inhabitants and made them understandably suspicious of the underlying motives of their supposed protectors. The frequent threats of the press gang and the success of the American privateers seemed to provide convincing proof to the Yankees that the British in Halifax were far more interested in impressing Nova Scotians into the navy than in defending them.[21] It was therefore virtually impossible for the Yankees to acknowledge that the British rather than the Americans possessed moral and political virtue. Rather than introducing an element of stability into the colony at the beginning of the Revolution the British military presence added to the existing chaos.

It is an oversimplification therefore to describe the Nova Scotia inhabitants during the Revolution simply as neutral Yankees. This is too unitary a concept to cover such a complicated situation and implies an articulate coherence of outlook among the population. Their predecessors in Nova Scotia, the Acadians, have been specifically used to explain and illustrate the Yankee posture of neutrality.[22] But the Acadians had been, compared

with the post-1760 population structure of Nova Scotia, a homo-
geneous population since the seventeenth century and in the
course of their growth since 1713 had developed traditional and
instinctive attachments to the concept that they were neutral in
the imperial struggle for North America. They referred to
themselves and were referred to by American colonists quite
normally, with no feeling of awkwardness, as "the neutral
French" or "the French neutrals" or simply "the Neutrals."
Such a self-image was an ingrained part of their value system.[23]

It is misleading to identify the Nova Scotia Yankees with this
Acadian neutrality complex. There certainly were some indications that in the revolutionary period they were aware of the
course adopted by their predecessors and made attempts to
appropriate some of the advantages of neutrality. The most
obvious example of this is the petition of 1775 in which the
inhabitants of Yarmouth pleaded with the British Governor to
be permitted to remain "Neuter."[24] Similar hopes of being
allowed to opt out of the war were displayed in a memorial from
Cumberland during this same month in 1775.[25] But in both
these cases it must be noted that no attempt was made to identify
these appeals with any Nova Scotian tradition of neutrality in-
herited from the Acadians. This is understandable in that these
New England settlers would not care to link their behaviour
with their "Papist" predecessors on whose lands they were now
living. Recalling the expulsion of the Acadians in 1755, they
would be further disinclined to draw any parallels. But it does
indicate how awkward it was for the Yankees to adopt the status
of neutrals. The pleas made to Halifax while mentioning the
term "neutral" were, in fact, simply attempts to extricate the
Yankees from the distasteful prospect of having to fight against
New England friends and relations. They were not in any fundamental way, as were the Acadians, claiming to be permanent
neutrals, but were merely endeavouring to utilize the concept
in the face of war between Britain and New England. There had
been in Nova Scotia, prior to 1775, no internal pressure that
induced the population to fear that political relationships between Britain and her colonies had arrived at a critical impasse.
The pressure put on Nova Scotians in 1775 and 1776 came from
one fact — Britain and New England were at war with each

other and it was no longer possible to remain loyal to both. The Nova Scotia Yankees hoped to postpone or avoid committing themselves to either side. There did not exist in Nova Scotia during the revolutionary war a neutrality complex of the same scale and depth as existed in the colony during the Acadian period. This may seem an obtuse distinction to make but it is an important one. The predicament of the Yankees and the Acadians may have been similar but their traditions and beliefs and attachments were quite different and their behaviour in Nova Scotia was not identical.

A better perspective for the Yankee attitude to, and use of, the neutrality concept can be gained by making a comparison with the activities of groups of New England settlers in the territory between Nova Scotia and New Hampshire. In the more northern, remoter areas of this country the people were often cut off from the new government of Massachusetts and were forced to fend for themselves.[26] This area is not usually described as being neutral in the revolutionary war yet at times the people were driven to adopt such a course. In November 1775 some of the inhabitants on Long Island in Penobscot Bay found it difficult to resist the temptation of increasing their income by supplying "the Ministerial forces with Cord wood and other Necessarys."[27] Almost six years later in the area round New Bristol the people began to toy with the prospect of becoming neutrals as the British seemed likely to extend their hold over the country. According to John Allan, who was trying desperately to keep the whole area on the American side, the people had little idea of what neutrality meant in practice but they were nevertheless tempted to use the device if it could be serviceable. As Allan explained, "there is much Confusion now in the Country in respect to Nutrality. Some late Advices from Boston that it would be Compld with if Requested, has sett some Districts much upon the wavering hand, by the influence and persuasion of some, most of the people will fall in with it not knowing the nature and meaning of such a state, nor concerning the consequences should it be permitted."[28] For the settlers in the remote districts northeast of Boston neutrality was one device they could use in the event of a British invasion. They had not thought deeply about what neutral status meant and had

no clear idea of how it would affect their relations with the
United States or with Britain. It was simply a tactic they could
use in a time of confusion or fear.

It can be argued that neutrality was used in much the same way
in Nova Scotia as in these other remote areas, and that it was not
a manifestation of Yankee adaptation to Acadian values but was
simply one way they attempted to cope with the dilemma in
which they found themselves. All of the memorials and petitions normally used to argue the case for neutrality were written
in 1775, just at the time when it was becoming increasingly clear
to the Nova Scotian Yankees that the dispute between Great
Britain and her colonies was not soon going to reach an "Amica-
ble settlement" but rather was going to develop into a protracted
war.[29] All the petitions concentrated on the fact that unless the
Yankees were granted the privilege of not fighting on the British
side they would be forced to fight against their Fathers [and]
Brothers" and "their friends and relations." With a full-scale
war now seemingly inevitable the Nova Scotia Yankees moved
desperately in an attempt to avoid fighting against New
Englanders.

This resort to neutrality was temporary and spasmodic. No
pleas for, or references to, neutrality have been discovered for
the period after 1776. In Maugerville the people definitely
abandoned any leaning towards the neutral status in May 1776.
They joined the American cause and explained to Massachusetts
that it was "impractible for us to Continue as Neautures."[30]
Hoping for speedy military intervention from Massachusetts
the Maugerville people had no need to persist in talking about
neutrality. When they finally re-submitted to British authority
in the summer of 1777 they made no attempt to return to the
position they had held prior to May 1776 when they had believed themselves to be neutrals. From 1776 to 1783 they were
under oath to be loyal to Britain; there were no "neutral Yankees" in Maugerville. The policy of the Maugerville Committee of Safety towards those merchants residing at the mouth of
the St. John River further revealed how little liking they had for
neutrality. They demanded the merchants state their position
but warned them that a declaration indicating the merchants
"are Determined to Stand Neuture [would] not be [a] satisfac-

tory answer." The Maugerville people, from their own experience, well knew that statements of neutrality were only used to
cover up other intentions or retain freedom of action to side with
the stronger forces. Neutrality was something they could not
tolerate or understand. Any men who claimed such status were
"slothful" to use their own epithet, filled with moral animus.[31]
Unlike their Acadian predecessors, the Nova Scotia Yankees had
no deep attachment to the concept of neutrality.

The Maugerville settlers may have toyed with the possibility
of being neutrals in 1775 but had quickly abandoned such
attempts when they submitted to Massachusetts in 1776 and
then to Britain in 1777. The impression gained is one of confusion and indecision rather than of neutrality. While adherents
of the American cause they had been unsure of how they should
proceed and what measures they should take. When they re-
aligned themselves with Britain by "suddenly and Passively"
submitting to an Oath of Allegiance they were still perplexed
and uncertain they had done the right thing. They "appeared
. . . dejected and forlorn and sorry for what is done but how
to Manage the affair they appear at a loss."[32] This sort
of uncertainty and irresolution as to which side they could commit unequivocal, whole-hearted allegiance can be called "neutrality." But it is more precise and accurate to see such actions as
attempts by the Nova Scotia Yankees to disentangle allegiance to
traditional values and sentiments they had absorbed while in
New England from new patterns of behaviour and loyalty they
had adopted since their removal to the British-controlled colony
of Nova Scotia.

A much more helpful way to characterize the Nova Scotia
Yankees during the revolutionary war is that they were a people
in a state of confusion. This characterization has the advantage
of encompassing and explaining the temporary resort to neutrality by some Yankees in 1775. People were confused, and
hoped to avoid the implications of war between Britain and New
England, particularly the possibility they might have to fight
their fellow colonists. Neutrality therefore was a function of the
general feeling of uneasiness, fear and puzzlement about the
shattering upset of the political world they had long known.
The Reverend Jonathan Scott in Yarmouth was, in August

1775, "full of Perplexity about the Distress of New England" and in March 1777 he was still uncertain about the proper attitude to adopt towards the war.[33] In the fall of 1776, when Eddy arrived in Cumberland and insisted on immediate military operations, the "inhabitants of that unhappy County . . . were reduced to the Shocking dilemma of Being Either plundered and butchered by their friends or of incurring the highest displeasure of their own Government."[34] The people in Barrington openly sympathized with the Thirteen Colonies yet were put in the most acute fear of American-inspired Indian attacks on their town.[35] In May 1777 the town of Liverpool observed a day of "fasting and prayer . . . on account of ye sickness and Troubles that have happened here of late." And in September of that year the congregation at Israel Cheever's church was rudely disturbed by gunfire. This was merely one of the British ships in the harbour scaling off her guns but in the tense atmosphere of the time the frayed nerves of some of the pioneer women gave way as they "fainted and went into fitts etc."[36]

On the other side of peninsular Nova Scotia, in Annapolis, the local Justices of the Peace reported that the people were in a state of fear as they heard of the activities of the "Pirates of Machias" on the northern shore of the Bay of Fundy. These local officials were also under orders to "apprehend" any suspicious characters who might be from New England and in the summer of 1775 they arrested Simeon Howard, a "dissenting Teacher" who, as the Justices themselves admitted, had "not been guilty of any Misdemeanours since his Arrival in this Province."[37] In the tense months of 1775 the town of Annapolis was clearly on edge as local officials attempted to carry out Halifax orders and as rumours of privateering depredations spread through the area. In June 1777, two years later, Thomas Wood, the local S.P.G. missionary, reported that "we have been in such confusion here most of the last winter" because of the privateering activities of Americans.[38] The arrival of Loyalists and refugees as the war progressed kept Annapolis a magnet for American raids. The rebel intruders often landed at night and moved through the woods to their selected targets, usually "against the Refugees." As usual most of the long-settled New England populace had little to fear directly from such incursions but their presence caused public unrest as officials attempted to find out who gave aid and sustenance to the nocturnal invaders. According to J. Wingate Weeks, another S.P.G. missionary, writing in September 1783, "the utmost confusion and disorder is prevailing thro' the whole county."[39] The arrival of many refugees was at this time a complicating factor in Annapolis but this was merely another instance of the unsettling effect of the war on the region.

Surveying the general situation in the colony from his base in Lunenburg, the S.P.G. missionary Peter de la Roche confirmed the pervasive mood of uncertainty and alarm. He characterized the period in that part of the world as "these times of war, fears and confusions."[40] The alarming feeling of insecurity that gripped the colony, particularly among the Yankee population, was summed up nicely by William Ellis in Windsor. As an S.P.G. missionary Ellis was prone to exaggeration when discussing the state of the Yankee dissenters, but in this case his exaggeration succeeded in isolating and dramatizing their predicament in Nova Scotia. "The New England people," noticed Ellis, "reckon their situation to be very precarious."[41] Ellis had perceptively captured the mood of the Yankee population during the war years. In September 1777, the shrewd John Allan also observed, from his vantage-point in Machias, that "the whole province is in Confusion, Trouble & Anguish."[42]

The prevailing mood of confusion in the early years of the Revolution contributed significantly to the acute disorientation and anxiety of many inhabitants living in the outsettlements. By missing the critical decade of ideological and political development in New England, the Yankees found themselves locked into the pre-1765 conceptual framework they had left behind. Their world at the beginning of hostilities had suddenly assumed an unfamiliar shape; men with familiar names, from familiar places, were using old words and phrases in a radically new and strange manner. Bitter civil strife pitting New Englander against New Englander and Briton had engulfed their former homeland. American privateers and British press gangs introduced further elements of instability into an already chaotic situation. Until local leaders were able to make some sense out of the confusing contemporary situation, the Nova Scotia Yankees were bound to have remained in a troubled state of mind as they desperately searched for a new sense of identity to replace their disintegrating loyalty to both old and New England. Henry Alline was one Nova Scotian able to perceive answers for the fundamental and perplexing problems facing the Yankees in the midst of the confused revolutionary situation.

Part II

Henry Alline and the Great Awakening in Nova Scotia

5

Some New England Traditions in the Religious Views of Henry Alline

During the war years a powerful moulder of public opinion emerged in the Yankee out-settlements of Nova Scotia. Henry Alline became the popular leader of a major religious revival that, by the end of the war, had spread through most of the colony. The fact that Alline achieved such extensive popularity indicates the strong influence that religious values still exerted on the Nova Scotia Yankees at the height of the American political and military struggle against Britain. The Yankees in Nova Scotia turned to a religious rather than a political figure in their search for guidance on the many distressing problems produced by the war.

Alline's religious ideas were a peculiar mixture. One of the authorities he relied on most was William Law, the famous Anglican spiritual writer, whose *Serious Call to a Devout and Holy Life*, published in 1728, was probably more influential, in popular terms, than any other post-Reformation book except John Bunyan's *Pilgrim's Progress*. John Wesley, the founder of English Methodism, and George Whitefield, his colleague, whose preaching had sparked the Great Awakening in the American colonies in 1740, both had a high opinion of Law's *Serious Call*. The influence of Law can be seen working through all Alline's sermons and tracts still in existence. But Alline had spent all his life among New Englanders and his understanding of Law was distorted by his New England Calvinist upbringing. His religious thought consisted of a tortuous attempt to reconcile a New England Calvinist God with Law's "God of Love," to make compatible the communal religious traditions of the New England way with Law's emphasis on the individuality of the Christian experience. The resultant religious ideas were original but, not surprisingly, somewhat confused and superficial.[1] As a religious thinker Alline was not in the same class as such evangelical preacher-philosophers as Jonathan Edwards or Isaac Backus in New England.

Yet, in Nova Scotia, Alline achieved considerable prestige as a religious teacher. A large part of the Yankee population regarded his ideas as coherent and believable. Many of Alline's basic concepts closely resembled post-1740 evangelical thought in the American colonies but he reformulated these familiar ideas in a way that made them more attractive to the Nova Scotia Yankees. Moreover, by relying extensively on Law, some of whose ideas coincided with Wesleyan Methodist dogma, Alline was able to appeal beyond the Yankees to the Yorkshire Methodists who had emigrated to the Chignecto area in 1774 and 1775. In accepting many of Alline's doctrines the Yankees and the Yorkshire settlers were departing from the religious norms they had held in New England and old England, for Alline was neither an orthodox New England evangelical nor an orthodox Methodist. Thus, in a sense, the religious thought of Alline reflected the changed perspectives that the Yankees and, to a lesser extent, the Yorkshire people had assumed since their respective emigrations to the isolated and sparsely settled northern colony. Religious values that were specifically "Nova Scotian" in character were beginning to emerge. In the wider intellectual world of the eighteenth century Alline's ideas were third-rate and trivial. But to the people in the outsettlements of Nova Scotia, the ideas were fresh, appealing and relevant to their preoccupations and concerns.

Henry Alline was born on June 14, 1748, in Newport, Rhode

Island. His parents, William and Rebecca, had been brought up in Boston before moving south and in 1760, "after long consultation," decided once again to move. This time the Allines convinced themselves that Nova Scotia offered better opportunities than Rhode Island and they moved north with the general migration of New England people. From the time he was eight years old Alline had been concerned and often distressed about religious matters and during his adolescence in Nova Scotia his anguish over the state of his soul and his relationship to God increased in intensity. He continued in this tense, troubled state until March 1775 when at the age of twenty-six he experienced an emotional conversion which convinced him that he had at last found salvation and had entered the earthly ranks of visible saints. After a few more months of uncertainty, Alline was persuaded that he should abandon his vocation as a farmer and go forth and preach his new-found faith to the other townships. From that time until his death in February 1784 his sole occupation was that of an itinerant preacher.[2]

In the course of the revival Alline was subjected to criticism and ridicule from many quarters but his most persistent and knowledgeable opponent was Jonathan Scott. Scott was born in Lunenburg in Worcester County, Massachusetts, in 1744, and in 1758 he was apprenticed to a shoemaker in Roxbury. In 1765 he settled in Yarmouth, Nova Scotia. Scott had been instilled with considerable Biblical knowledge by pious parents and in spite of what he believed to be youthful lapses in his apprenticeship days he retained a serious approach to religious matters. After several years of lay preaching Scott, in 1772, was ordained in Massachusetts and installed as the minister of the Congregational church in Yarmouth.

From his first contacts with Alline, the Yarmouth minister thoroughly disapproved both of his doctrines and his itinerancy. In Cornwallis and later in Yarmouth he attempted to persuade Alline of his errors and urge him to cease promoting the revival which Scott considered to be mere enthusiasm. Scott eventually managed to put his case against Alline down on paper and his long critique of Alline's methods and beliefs is the only extensive detailed contemporary condemnation of the revival that now exists.[3]

The debate between Alline and Scott is of considerable

importance because it illuminates the crucial problem of the effect of New England religious traditions on the Nova Scotia Yankees. Scott was determined that the New England way, based on the Cambridge Platform of 1648 and subsequent re-statements of Congregational doctrine made by such diverse authorities as Jonathan Edwards and Charles Chauncy, should remain the accepted religion of the Yankees during the revolutionary war. Alline challenged the relevance of these New England traditions to the predicament of Nova Scotia and postulated, throughout the war years, his own theory on the nature and purpose of religion. Yet, although Alline insisted that he was an "anti-traditionalist," he was, in fact, utilizing many elements from the New England heritage of the Yankee settlers. Alline simply redefined old values in an attempt to make them functional and relevant to revolutionary Nova Scotia.

When writers first began to analyse Alline's religious thought they usually concluded that the Falmouth farmer had been hopelessly mixed up and had no clear understanding of the terms he used.[4] The notion that Alline's ideas bore no relation to any recognizable theological school persisted until 1948 when Maurice W. Armstrong's interpretation of the Nova Scotia Great Awakening was published. Armstrong argued that "to a far greater extent . . . than has been recognized, Henry Alline was influenced by other writers." Proceeding to trace the reference to religious thinkers in Alline's writings, Armstrong discovered that the Nova Scotia revivalist had taken many of his ideas from "that stream of mystical teaching which had come down through William Law, John Milton and the seventeenth-century English sectaries, from Jacob Boehme." Armstrong believed that Alline could be seen as part of the "revolt against the Calvinistic system [that was] widespread in the eighteenth century." More specifically, Alline turned to pietistic or evangelical anti-Calvinists such as Law rather than to the more humanistic Socinians, Arminians and Free Thinkers. Thus while conceding that Alline had produced a "peculiar mystical theology," Armstrong successfully explained the sources of Alline's postulates and placed the Nova Scotian evangelist in an illuminating perspective.[5]

Alline himself made several references to Law in his writings and his utilization of Law's work is quite certain. The opening arguments of *The Anti-Traditionist*, Alline's most concise and forceful presentation of his theology, follow closely Law's "doctrine that the world was created 'out of nothing' " and the term "Out-Birth," to which Alline attached so much importance, was used by Law in his later writings. For both men the creation of Adam, and subsequently the world of nature, was an emanation from God.[6]

The precise editions of Law's writings used by Alline cannot be definitely ascertained, but in 1766 extracts from a treatise by Law were published in Philadelphia and there are many parallels between this work and the theories propounded by Alline. Alline's notion of the process by which Adam fell away from God into the natural, physical world was similar to Law's description in the 1766 pamphlet. According to Law, "by his fall [man] had broke off from his true center, his proper place in God [and] . . . was fallen into a life of self, into an animal life of self-love, self-esteem and self-seeking in the poor perishing enjoyment of this world." As with Alline's concept of the natural forces operating in this breaking away from God, Law viewed the worldly predicament of man as "the natural state of man by the Fall."

In the material world man was, according to Law, "in a state of contrariety to the order and end of our creation." In each man, however, there existed in the heart "a spark of the Divine nature" as "the eternal word of God." This holy spark was the one remnant left in man from his spiritual existence in paradise and it had "a natural strong and almost infinite tendency, or reaching after that eternal Light and Spirit of God." Since the soul had "come forth from God . . . [and] . . . came out of God," it partook "of the divine nature, and therefore it is always in a state of tendency and return to God." Alline, too, argued his case in these terms. He also maintained that everything about man was alien to God except man's conscience which "held him in possibility of redemption," and he described the conversion experience as a "turning of the inmost soul after God." Alline, following Law, insisted that because the soul "naturally" tended back to God and since every mortal being possessed a soul, the possibility of redemption was freely open to all mankind. The concept of predestined sanctification was rejected by Law and by Alline since it implied God was vengeful and harsh and proceeded in an arbitrary, illogical manner.[7]

Whether or not Alline read this particular version of Law it is apparent that he relied heavily on the Anglican divine for many of his most basic assumptions about the nature of God and of man and of God's relationship to the world. Alline's other major sources were also English religious thinkers, particularly John William Fletcher, "the Shropshire Saint," whose *A Rational Demonstration of Man's Corrupt and Lost Estate* provided Alline with "arguments for the freedom of the will [and] ideas concerning the state of man before the fall," and Edward Young whose sombre and dramatic description of the Day of Judgement was appropriated and embellished by Alline. Although relying extensively on such well-known English theologians it is clear that Alline was not arguing at the same intellectual and philosophical level as these men.[8] Alline's mind was inadequately trained to deal with these intricate, abstract concepts that had been elaborated by generations of English and European scholars and theologians. Alline's basic conviction that his arguments were valid stemmed not from any academic knowledge he may have had, but directly from his conversion experience after which he believed he knew all the "real" solutions to perennial theological problems. He did not fully understand all of the intricacies in the ideas of men like Law but his absolute conviction of his own divinely inspired perspicacity gave his sermons and tracts the appearance of coherence. John Wesley, writing in 1783 to William Black, leader of the Nova Scotia Methodists, clearly perceived the limitations of Alline. Wesley wrote to Black, "I have sent you (with other books) two volumes of Mr. Law's works, which contain all that Mr. Alline would teach if he could: only it is the gold purged from the dross; whereas he [Alline] would give you the gold and dross shuffled together."[9] Alline himself put the case in a more favourable light. He had, he admitted, taken much from other writers but this did not mean that he approved "all their writings or every Part of their Principles."[10]

William Black agreed with Wesley's estimate of Alline's inadequacies and attempted to counteract Alline when the itinerant visited the Methodist areas of Cumberland County. But a large number of the Yorkshire farmers, unacquainted with the world of theological debate, found much that was familiar in Alline's doctrines and responded enthusiastically to his preaching. Alline was elated by his reception in Cumberland and carried with him, to parade before sceptics throughout the colony, a written account of his success in that area. It was Alline's reading of English mystical writers, particularly Law, that enabled him to attract the Nova Scotian Methodists. If Alline had preached Calvinist principles, emphasizing the preordination of Christian history and the limited nature of the offer of salvation, he probably would not have had such an impact on the Yorkshire settlers. But, having read Law and Fletcher, Alline travelled among the Cumberland farmers, telling them of a "God of Love" and reminding them that salvation was open to all. Alline's English sources enabled him to appeal beyond Yankee society to another major social and ethnic group in Nova Scotia.[11]

It is not correct, however, to regard Alline simply as an insignificant spokesman of certain eighteenth-century, pietistic, anti-Calvinist tenets. Alline's almost exclusive attention to English writers obscured the fact that he still accepted many New England Calvinist assumptions. In Yarmouth for example, it was the pro-revivalist Congregationalists, insisting that they were Calvinists, who were Alline's most enthusiastic supporters. Nova Scotia Yankees were convinced that Alline was preaching the same evangelical doctrines that New Light preachers had expounded in New England in the 1740s and 1750s. The superstructure developed by Alline from his reading of Law and others had as its base a complex of New England assumptions. Many of the Methodist settlers believed that he was preaching doctrines long known to them; most of the Yankees were just as certain that Alline was a typical New England evangelist.[12]

At least one man, whose opinion is worthy of some consideration because of his influential position in Yankee religious circles, was convinced that Alline had in fact departed completely from New England evangelical traditions. Jonathan Scott certainly had decided views about Alline. Scott's opinion regarding the contents of Alline's sermons and tracts was unambiguous and to the point. Alline, in Scott's view, uttered "sublime nonsense" and wrote "dreadful jargon." So prolific were Alline's absurd misreadings of theology in Scott's eyes that the Yarmouth minister found it difficult to decide where the major heretical foundation of Alline's thought was located. Scott accused Alline of a whole range of well-known heresies and branded him as both a "Deist" and a "wild enthusiast." The Congregational minister was quite certain that Alline's doctrines and preaching were alien to the religious values of the Yankees. In his critique of Alline's thought, Scott cited various New England authorities to substantiate his charge that Alline was undermining New England traditions.[13]

Scott was correct in noticing that many of Alline's views deviated from normal evangelical tenets current in New England. Alline apparently read nothing produced by Jonathan Edwards, although he may have been acquainted with other New England theoreticians of revivalism. His articulated thoughts, as evidenced in his writings, owe little to New England models. But Alline, it must be emphasized, was not free from all New England traditions. His religious upbringing in Nova Scotia had been formally conducted in the family prayer meetings led by his pious parents who had lived most of their lives in Boston. Alline himself had been in Newport, Rhode Island, until he was twelve years old, and when there had begun to concern himself with religious matters. The preoccupation with religion which Alline retained throughout his years in Nova Scotia had begun in Rhode Island. After Alline experienced his conversion in March 1775 he was soon "convinced that he must preach, but knew not how, where or when." As Alline struggled with the question of his qualification for the work of the ministry, he by October 1775 came to a conclusion as to the best course to follow. He decided he "could not preach until he acquired learning, and therefore must proceed to New England, and endeavour some way or other to get learning there." As far as Alline was concerned the best place to receive education for the ministry was in New England. In spite of the deviousness of his particular views, produced by almost fifteen years of relative isolation in Nova Scotia, he naturally turned to New England, in the belief that his experience would be understood there and in the hope that one of its institutions would accept him as a theological student. He did not consider that his ideas would be regarded as strange by New England evangelicals.[14]

Alline, however, never got to New England. The ship that was supposed to take him "was seized and could not get clear until the Spring." Then a smallpox epidemic broke out which affected Alline's relations, who "advised me by all means to return." Alline reluctantly decided to abandon his attempts to get to New England. This turn of events had a significant effect on him and on subsequent events in Nova Scotia. By failing to reach New England, Alline was forced to rely entirely on his own ingenuity to vindicate his views and to articulate them to the Nova Scotia Yankees.[15]

Jonathan Scott failed to perceive the masked or hidden way in which typical New England assumptions permeated Alline's religious ideology. Scott rightly saw that at times Alline had "driven Things next door to Deism itself" by his apparent reduction of a God, active and interested in the world, to a God who had merely set in motion a natural process.[16] Interestingly, William Law, on whom Alline relied a great deal, was also accused of deistic tendencies, for his denial of the wrath of God.[17] Both men denied such interpretations of their doctrines but their attempts to describe an inevitable fall and a gradual process of redemption through the natural tendency of the soul to return to its spiritual environment did tend to underemphasize the possibility of divine intervention in the affairs of men.

The individualist strain was certainly present in Alline's thought, but individuals who experienced conviction or conversion were quickly channelled into communal activity. While Law devoted a large part of his life to scholarly solitude, Alline spent seven years preaching to groups of farmers and fishermen in Nova Scotia. Alline did not believe that existing churches were helping the redemptive process and he urged the converts in Nova Scotia to set up new churches. The task facing the purified church organization was to promote and encourage a general reformation in the world. Thus, far from basing his message on the concept of a remote deistic Supreme Being, as Scott at times charged, Alline conceived of a God who looked to a special people in the world to be the true supporters of the Christian cause. Logically, Alline should not have been thinking along such lines, for if redemption was to occur outside time as Alline contended and there was to be no earthly millennium, there seemed no good reason to get involved in such urgent missions in this world.[18] Law was a much clearer thinker than Alline on such matters. But Alline's concentration on the things to be accomplished in this world was a manifestation of the New England traditions he believed he had discarded.

In many other respects Alline revealed that he was working with concepts that were familiar to evangelical elements in the New England colonies. The response of the Yankee population of Nova Scotia to Alline becomes more understandable when these underlying similarities are seen. If Alline's doctrines had been entirely novel he would have encountered far more difficulties in persuading the Nova Scotia Yankees to take him seriously. In the Nova Scotia situation it was not necessary for Alline to duplicate accepted evangelical views to sound credible and knowledgeable on the nature and necessity of the new birth. Most of the people in the outsettlements, particularly the young people under thirty, had received little religious teaching since their arrival in the early 1760s. As Scott noticed, the Yankees had experienced a "Want of Instruction . . . of more than Twenty Years Standing." And "for want of proper and needful Instruction" they were "much Exposed" to the influence of a preacher like Alline.[19] To the Yankees in the scattered settlements of Nova Scotia many of Alline's tenets were apparently merely restatements of the evangelical doctrines they believed were held in New England.

Alline's description of a "God of Love" was not as radical a deviation from colonial evangelical thought in this period as it seems, for this God was in the last resort just as implacably vengeful against sinners as the arbitrary Being Alline was attempting to argue out of existence. God, explained Alline, because he was naturally loving, would do all that he could do to save those who perceived and had faith in his plan of redemption. But just as the redemptive process of sanctification was irreversible once conversion had taken place, so the opposite course of final and eternal punishment for sinners was decreed by divine law. All men, as Alline graphically put it, were sus-

pended above the "Jaws of the Yawing Pit" and were in imminent danger of sinking into eternal misery. In his sermons Alline
worked hard to get this point over and, like Jonathan Edwards,
intensely dramatized the precariousness of man's existence in
order to propel sinners towards an awakening. On another occasion Alline repeated his warning of the fragility of human
existence. "Your live [life]," he explained, "is as a bubble on
the Water soon broke and gone" and "should you neglect a few
more hours, your dye is cast, your state fixed and you gone for
ever."[20]

Alline saw no conflict between such apparently pessimistic
imagery and his frequent assertions that God was good and
loving. The matter for Alline was quite simple. God's natural
goodness saved the converted and condemned the sinners. All
that Alline denied was that God was "roiled" or "incensed" or
"vengeful" against sinners.[21] Alline's reasoning on this point
resembled that used by Edwards and other evangelical thinkers.
Edwards had argued the paradoxical proposition that God pun-
ished sinners out of the inherent goodness of his nature. Na-
thaniel Whitaker, the "New Side" Presbyterian, maintained in
his *Antidote against Toryism* that "God's hatred of sin, and the
punishment he inflicts on the wicked, arises from his love of
happiness, from the benevolence of his nature."[22] In Nova
Scotia, Alline impressed upon his hearers that the nature of God
"is all Love and Goodness" and that he "is angry with Sin from
the Consequence of his Nature." In Alline's theological system,
God "is and forever was the opposite of Sin . . . [and] . . . can
no more abide together than Light and Darkness, Heat and
Cold." Turning to a quasi-scientific analogy, Alline argued that,
when "Light scatters Darkness" or "when fire Dissolves the
Ice," it would be absurd to insist that "the Light was possessed
of Malice, Spite or Revenge against the Darkness" or that "the
Fire was incensed by the Ice or mad with the Ice." By analogy
with these experimentally proved truths, Alline concluded that
it was equally absurd to suggest that God was angry or incensed
because he did not prevent sinners from going to hell. Sinners
themselves made "their own Hell" by refusing to accept and
participate in God's redemptive plan. As Alline succinctly contended, God "is as Vengeance to the finally unpenitent because
of sin." When he talked in these terms there appeared little

movement in Alline's thought away from the Calvinist God of
the American evangelicals. Many of Alline's hearers in Nova
Scotia were inclined to make this identification and at least some
of them came away from his sermons determined to spread the
fear of God to sinners.[23]

There was also a fundamental contradiction in Alline's description of the approach of the end of the world. In his sermons
Alline devoted considerable attention to this theme, emphasizing the connection between the urgent necessity of the "new
birth" and the imminent end of the world. To be consistent
Alline should have argued that the world would end naturally,
as it had been created, simply by God's withdrawing his support.
The withdrawal of God's love which acted as the ordering force,
like gravity, and the permitting the remnants of sinful man to
continue their descent to a spiritual existence in hell would, if
Alline accepted his own arguments, lead to the disappearance of
the material world. It would no longer be necessary or have any
function and would vanish in the same way it had appeared with
no attendant cataclysm. Yet Alline often reverted to the more
usual view that the Day of Judgement would be an occasion
when elemental bodies would be "burnt up and dissolved."[24]
This assertion is even more surprising because Alline at times
argued that Christ's kingdom was not of this world, that there
would be no millennium here on earth. If the kingdom of redeemed man was to be entirely spiritual in nature, then there
seemed no necessity to bring the material world to a precipitous
and violent end. On the one hand Alline postulated an "eternal
Judgement" which in effect meant that there would be no final
Judgement in historical time. This proposition arose easily out
of his previous arguments, for it envisaged a steadily increasing
number of redeemed souls returning to a spiritual Kingdom of
God. But Alline also talked of an imminent Day of Judgement
when fire and water would destroy the world. Alline solved the
contradiction in these two versions by ignoring it. He would not
only attest "to a day of judgement but to an eternal judgement."[25] Alline, not for the first time, was going to have it both
ways.

Alline's reasoning on this point cannot be proved logical or
profound, but it may at least be understood. By insisting on a

Day of Judgement Alline was able to impose an urgent pattern on human history. An eternal judgement necessitated no sense of urgency which could mobilize the visible saints to press forward the process of conversion in order to save as many souls as possible before God's offer of salvation was finally withdrawn. If the doors to God's kingdom were to be open forever there was little point in regarding redemption as being all-important in every age; but if the doors were soon to be closed, revivals become all-important, for it was of the utmost consequence to organize for the end of the world. Thus in his sermons Alline emphasized the imminence of a Judgement Day. He issued the gloomy warning that "Midnight Darkness . . . now overspreads the World . . . the Day of Grace Over and the World undone." In such a scheme of things a religious revival was the most significant event of the times.[26] And as the Judgement Day approached all human activities, even war between nations, became irrelevant. The vital task was to awaken as many of the fallen race to their danger and to gather and unite as many visible saints as possible. Only a revival could speedily accomplish these urgently necessary things before the final cataclysm.

Alline, however, took pains to stress that a concentration on the end goal of human history did not mean that normal social activity should be abandoned or its importance underestimated. Alline's ideas, in contrast with those advanced by many enthusiastic sectarians, had little apocalyptic content based on the Book of Revelation and advocated no withdrawal from sinful society by an exclusive group of converts. One of the major reasons for rejoicing by the convert, as Alline took care to explain to his supporters, was "for his life, joy and portion in this life." Alline despised "mercenary Christians" who saw conversion merely as a cause "to rejoice in redemption from eternal misery." Although the sights of converts were "set on things above" this gave them no excuse for neglect of ordinary social duties. On the contrary, they were urged to be useful in society and to attempt to make it conform as closely as possible to the Christian pattern.[27]

While insisting that the converts should continue in their usual social roles, Alline was certain that churches of pure Christians must be gathered out of society to separate from "formal" Christians. The true converts, he insisted, "have an undoubted Right to embody and gather themselves together in Church Order for the Improvement of such gifts and Graces as God has blessed them with." These purified churches were to act together to promote God's cause but they were on no account to have any dealing with "any of those Churches, that hold the form without the Power."[28] Alline denied that in advocating a radical restructuring of existing churches he was "oversetting all religion."[29] He, like many of the Separates, Baptists, New Lights and other evangelical elements in New England, firmly believed that churches composed exclusively of the regenerate were the necessary instruments for effectively promoting the work of redemption.

This position naturally compelled Alline to inveigh against unconverted ministers for the damage they did to the cause of religion, for it was under such lax, as Alline saw it, pastoral care that corrupted churches flourished. Alline could "not believe there are any men on earth who do so much damage to the Redeemers kingdom, as these unconverted ministers." An unconverted man could not, according to Alline's argument, perceive God's great plan of redemption and he could not therefore possibly describe it to the members of his congregation who would thus continue to be unaware of the absolute necessity of conversion. "It is as evident," Alline asserted, "that an unconverted man cannot preach the Gospel as Darkness cannot give Light." Unless "his heart [were] touched with the Spirit of the Word," no man could perform ministerial duties. Alline was careful, however, to emphasize that he had no objection to an educated ministry as such. Providing the pastor had experienced a conversion he was to be allowed credit for his academic accomplishments and oratorical skill. Alline was "not about to reject natural Abilities, nor human Learning when brought in, in their proper Place . . . but their being brought in to supply the Want of Divine Assistance and Authority from Heaven." Proficiency in the various biblical languages, for example, was an undoubted asset to a converted minister but it appeared to Alline "needless for a Man to be at too much Pains in Pursuit of them, merely to attain the Name of a Collegian." In Nova Scotia during the period of the revolutionary war, Alline was repeating the warning that many New England evangelical preachers had delivered against the manifold "dangers of an unconverted ministry."[30]

Other similarities between Alline and evangelical theorists in the New England colonies may also be traced. During the Great Awakening in New England the conversion experience for many had consisted in a perception of the "beauty" of God's ways, a feeling for the "divine excellence" or the "loveliness" of God.[31] Alline defined the experience as a "discovery and felt sense of the love and compassion in Christ" and the perception of the "beauty and amiableness in God and his ways." Alline, during his own conversion, was attracted by the "beauty I saw in his [God's] divine perfections." One of the most impressive consequences of conversion was to see God's plan for man clearly displayed or as Alline put it "the unspeakable wisdom and beauty of the glorious plan of life and salvation."[32]

Too much can, however, be read into these apparent repetitions by Alline of some aspects of American evangelical thought. This is particularly so when drawing parallels between the philosophical speculations of Jonathan Edwards and the emotion-filled theories propounded by Alline. Alline was not another Edwards; he did not approach the New England thinker in intellectual ability. The one thing they had in common was a liking for abstract speculation about the world and God's relationship to man in the world. It is entirely possible that Alline, as Jonathan Scott suggested, did not "understand himself" his own "uncouth and unintelligible Sentences."[33] Whatever the interpretation given to Edwards' thought there is no doubt that he was aware of what he was attempting to understand and the precise location of this attempt within the English and colonial intellectual world. Nevertheless, in spite of these major qualifications, it remains true that Alline's thought resembled in some important aspects the system constructed by Edwards and adopted by many American evangelical preachers.

Since no direct influence can be traced from New England evangelical sources to Alline and yet Alline attempted to deal with similar concepts, it seems clear that Alline independently stumbled upon basic issues facing evangelical thinkers in the colonies in the decades after 1740. However crudely he tackled the issues, he was trying to grapple with the problem of God's method of action in an apparently self-sustaining mechanical world and to decipher the nature and purpose of religious revivals. He persistently made laborious and rather simplistic efforts to underpin all his assertions about God, conversion and revivals by using scientific metaphors in an effort, far beyond his intellectual abilities, to prove the natural or scientific workings of God and his plan for man's redemption. Even his own conversion experience, an intensely emotional moment in his life when, for the first time in twenty-seven years, he became completely and utterly happy, could not be classified as a peculiar and accidental intervention by God in this world. One of the incidents leading up to Alline's conversion had been the appearance of "a large blaze of light in the shape of a circle, with that side next to me open as though it yawned after me . . . ." Alline was convinced that this strangely shaped light was "really designed by God . . . as if it was a miracle" sent to him "in particular." But he did not allow this divine favour to shake his belief in the scientific God. On reflection Alline concluded that the light was probably "one of the common phenomena of nature, such as exhaled vapours of nitre, that had gathered in the air."[34] Alline's explanation of this incident effectively shows his belief in the natural operation of God in the world and indicates that his quasi-scientific theorizing was rooted in a deep conviction that all religion depended on understanding natural laws.

When Scott focused on the strange terms used by Alline, largely drawn from his English sources, he was right to regard these as departures from the religious values of the Yankees. Even less-informed inhabitants of Yarmouth were aware that Alline's ideas were often peculiar. But although they could only "harmonise with some of Mr. Alline's Doctrines" or subscribe only to "a Number of his Doctrines," they did not regard Alline as alien to Yankee evangelical traditions.[35] They did have some reservations about Alline's ideas but they overcame any doubts they may have had because they heard many familiar exhortations from Alline. This is what Scott failed to understand; he did not try to discover why Alline was so popular with the

Yankees in Yarmouth and elsewhere throughout the colony.

The Yankee population in Nova Scotia had little difficulty in identifying Henry Alline's new role. Soon after his conversion "it was . . . published abroad that Henry Alline was turned New Light" and by the spring of 1776 the report that "Henry Alline was turned New Light preacher" caused "many . . . [to] . . . come from other towns even whole boatloads."[36] Neither was this designation of New Light merely a loose use of terminology by Yankees who had been out of New England for twenty years. A recent immigrant to Nova Scotia from Tiverton, Rhode Island, made the same easy identification. "This preacher, Henry Alline," whom people were talking about, "was a 'New Light' and . . . the 'New Lights' were people of God."[37] This Rhode Islander saw nothing alien or incomprehensible in Alline's preaching — it was the same as the New Lights had delivered in New England.

In February 1783 when Alline was preaching in Port Medway he met an old man, fifty years of age, who was moved by Alline's preaching. In an interview with Alline after the sermon he made no effort to seek further clarifications of Alline's theories about the nature of the world or question what Alline meant by "fallen nature interposed." Instead this Yankee settler recalled that when he "was about Fourteen Years of Age [he] was awakened under the preaching of George Whitefield" but this awakening had not proceeded to a conversion and the man was still "a stranger to the New Birth." This elderly man now hoped that Alline would complete the work begun by Whitefield and help him to "experience a saving Grace" that had eluded him at the time of the Great Awakening in New England.[38] In 1783, in this small Nova Scotia fishing settlement, the impact made by Alline was identified with, and compared to, the work of the famous preachers who had participated in the great revivals in the colonies.

The revival inspired by Alline was regarded by the Yankees of Nova Scotia as another manifestation of the same forces that had been operative in New England at the height of the Great Awakening. Simeon Perkins, a leading citizen of Liverpool, Captain of the Militia, Justice of the Peace and prominent member of the Congregational church, kept in his diary an account of

Alline's effect on Liverpool which illustrates this tendency to link the revival with New England precedents. According to Perkins, on Sunday, February 16, 1783,

> Mr. Alline made a long Speech, Very Sensible, Advising all Sorts of People to a Religious Life, and gave many directions for their outward walk. This is a wonderful day and Evening. Never did I behold such an Appearance of the Spirit of God moving upon the people since the time of the Great Religious Stir in New England many years ago.[39]

Nova Scotia was experiencing a similar religious phenomenon as New England had in 1740-41. To Perkins, as Alline preached successfully in Liverpool and many other townships, this seemed the obvious conclusion to draw.

It was of little consequence to many of the Nova Scotia Yankees that Alline's ideas were at variance with some of the tenets of New England evangelical thought. The main outlines of Alline's theories, and above all, the character of Alline's preaching, were accepted by them as typical, effective evangelical exhortation. As Heimert, after making a detailed analysis of evangelical doctrine in the American colonies, has pointed out, "the manner in which a preacher delivered his message was often more revealing of his persuasion than the particular doctrines he happened to espouse."[40] This was even more true in Nova Scotia than it had been in New England. In New England the post-1740 evangelical doctrines were codified, elaborated and debated by many preachers. A protracted public debate persisted throughout the 1740s, 1750s, 1760s, and 1770s between Old Lights, new divinity men, New Lights and Baptists. Thus, although the manner of preaching was considered important, there were also some generally accepted evangelical doctrines that had to be adhered to or acknowledged or taken account of in some way. In Nova Scotia, where there were relatively few ministers and itinerant preachers and where no one church polity was dominant, there was no generally accepted evangelical framework in which the preacher was compelled to work. Moreover, there was no widespread and well-organized opposition to the revival. In these conditions, Alline was able to get away with more looseness of doctrine and individuality of expression than could itinerant preachers, who hoped to be successful, in New England.

As long as Alline remained an effective preacher he could redefine evangelical concepts in his own terms. His success in generating a series of local revivals meant that the content of his theology was considered to be of secondary importance. Amos Hilton, a member of Scott's Congregational church in Yarmouth, summed up this point cogently. Scott had tried to persuade Hilton that Alline was preaching heretical views. The Yarmouth pastor "had given him [Hilton] an exact Copy of Mr. Alline's Doctrines in his [Alline's] own Words which he had published to the World, taken out of his Book entitled, Two Mites etc." These quotations seemed sufficiently incriminating proof to Scott that in Alline's writings "all the Revelation of God's Word is overthrown." Yet to Amos Hilton these criticisms were irrelevant. "It was," Hilton reminded his minister, "no Matter of any great Consequence to him what a Man's Principles were, if he was but earnest in promoting a good Work."[41]

6

The Case of Yarmouth: Scott versus Alline

The remark made by Amos Hilton, that "it was no matter of any great Consequence to him what a Man's Principles were, if he was but earnest in promoting a good Work," explains a great deal about the nature of Nova Scotia's Great Awakening. Alline achieved success because of *how* he preached and because his sermons seemed particularly relevant to the problems arising from the revolutionary crisis. He did not present an accurate exposition of New England evangelical theory; but what he did was to preach with conviction and with results and these, in the final analysis, were the criteria used by the Nova Scotia Yankees in evaluating Alline's work. This response to Alline can be most clearly seen in the case of Yarmouth where most members and adherents of the local church, including Scott, were favourably disposed towards revivalistic religion.[1] Scott tried to publicize the fact that Alline was wandering away from New England religious practices and traditions. But Alline was able to overcome this basic criticism and to persuade people like Amos Hilton that he was a far more genuine revivalist than was Scott. Everything seemed to hinge on Alline's ability, during his preaching, to "awaken" the people. As long as he was successful in this, his doctrinal inconsistencies became irrelevant.

A careful study of Yarmouth also reveals the extent of Alline's success in gaining a following in the remote Nova Scotia communities. Scott, for example, was left with only a few faithful supporters out of a congregation that had, at its founding, consisted of about seventy families. It is also evident that Alline's Yarmouth visits and the subsequent religious controversies which ensued roused the town, as never before in its brief history, to a pitch of public excitement. Whether by friends or opponents of the revival the result was the same — public issues were defined in terms of the revival and its effect on the township.

Alline did not reach Yarmouth until October 1781, but in order to understand his impact on Scott, the church and the people it is essential to know what had been happening in the religious affairs of the community during the previous years. By placing Alline in this context the techniques by which he discredited opponents and gained the sympathy of the people become clearly discernible. It is also possible to demonstrate that Scott, although claiming to be an upholder of New England evangelical traditions, was, in fact, a poor spokesman for revivalist religion, particularly during the revolutionary war period.

From its founding in December 1767, the Congregational church of Yarmouth was clearly revivalistic in character.[2] In its formative years, the church was rocked by dissension but the constant bickering that went on was conducted entirely within an evangelical framework.[3] The congregation was in favour of revivalistic religion but there were varying degrees of "friendliness" towards revivalism. And this led to disagreements as to which preacher would be most effective in initiating local revivals.[4] There is no evidence that the disputes turned on doctrinal issues.[5] The character of the preaching was the issue that decided whether there would be separation and dissent. Scott was well aware of this and noted that John Frost, ordained as the first minister in September 1769, had alienated people more because of his preaching style than because of his lack of evangelical knowledge. Frost, conceded Scott, "had not an entertaining and easy way of delivery in his publick Discourses but the Contrary; which, no doubt, was the Occasion of Disaffection to some that heard him." Within a short time of Frost's ordination, even those who had selected him in face of the opposition of the congregation were somewhat disillusioned by his ministerial abilities. As Scott laconically put it, "the ministerial Performances [of Frost] did not tend to the Edification of the Church so much as they expected."[6]

The disputes turned on the nature rather than on the content of preaching. The forty-two people who separated from the Frost ministry in the summer of 1769 were uneasy at the time of his ordination but they had waited to hear a few sermons before they finally decided they had to separate. Only when they heard a man preach could the Yarmouth people easily judge whether or not he was a genuine evangelical. Ten years later, in October 1781, when Alline first arrived in Yarmouth, the people were long practised, as Hilton reminded Scott, in concentrating on effective preaching rather than right principles.

Late in 1769, in an effort to bring stability to their church affairs, a petition was sent from Yarmouth "to Churches in New England" requesting immediate assistance. The Reverend Mr. Chandler Robbins, of the First Church of Plymouth, presented the petition to his associate ministers who agreed to send assistance "and also chose Two Ministers of their Association for the Purpose, namely Rev. Mr. Solomon Reed and Rev. Mr. Sylvanus Conant." Reed and Conant arrived in Yarmouth in May 1770 but "were very coldly received by the Church at first because . . . they were ready to conclude that the Ministers were not friendly to the Work and Doctrines of Grace." It was not until "the second sabbath after their Arrival," when both "the Church and Society met in one Place for publick Worship and the Revd. Ministers preached to the Acceptance of the People" that the Massachusetts divines were finally accepted by the Nova Scotia fishing community. The inhabitants of Yarmouth did not allow the experience and qualifications of Reed and Conant to overawe them. Like all other preachers who came to the township they had first to demonstrate their preaching ability. Only after the people had listened to sermons by Reed and Conant did the reserve and suspicion give way to guarded approval "respecting their [Reed and Conant] Doctrines and Friendliness to vital Religion."[7]

The preaching of Reed and Conant stimulated signs of "a Revival of Religion in the Place," and having gained public confidence in this way the Massachusetts ministers were able to persuade the Yarmouth people to spurn "the unchristian spirit of Dissension and Disagreement" that had divided the church since 1766. Reed and Conant took advantage of the good impression they had made and succeeded in imposing a solution on the troubled religious affairs of Yarmouth. They recommended that both Frost and Ebenezer Moulton, a Baptist preacher,[8] the leaders of the opposing factions, should "cease their public ministerial Exercise." They could continue to lead in private worship "provided they are cautious not to say or order anything that tends to excite or promote unbecoming Dissension in the Society." Reed and Conant then advised the people to choose a "wise, good and faithful minister of Christ" but urged as an interim measure that "some fit Person" be chosen by a joint Church-Society Committee "to lead in the public worship of God." The Massachusetts ministers "freely" recommended Jonathan Scott, a founding member of the church, as the most suitable person they had met to fill this temporary role. Scott was clearly a compromise preacher who, Reed and Conant felt, would be inoffensive to the conflicting elements in the town.[9]

This temporary arrangement lasted from June 1770 until January 1772 during which time the Church and Society committees haggled over who should be formally installed as minister. The two elements of the community had, following the advice of Reed and Conant, re-united for regular worship but a second separation occurred in the fall of 1770 when Moulton, without informing Scott, came to the meeting-house to preach. Scott thereupon walked out in protest, taking "some of the people both of the Church and Society . . . with him." The more extreme evangelicals were at this stage dissatisfied with Scott and there was even talk of "setting up a baptist Church which Mr. Moulton endeavoured to effect at this Time." Scott, however, possessed greater tact than Frost and by adopting a more prudent attitude to the dissidents the rift was not as deep as it had been three years previously. By the spring of 1771 "the more moderate and sober part" of the disaffected "came off from Mr. Moulton one after another" and most of those who had separated returned to the church fold. Finally in January 1772 the Church and Society committees agreed to offer Scott the ministership on a permanent basis.[10]

By this time Scott was acutely aware of the underlying tensions in the religious community that made the position of any preacher difficult. In view of this fact, he was determined that his position be buttressed by official approval from established Congregational churches to forestall any attempted challenges to his ministerial authority. He "submitted to the will of the people so far as to consent to Submit to examination before a Council of Ministers." On March 21, 1772, Scott, along with representatives of the Church and Society, set out, at his own expense, for Massachusetts. On May 8 he returned, having been officially approved by an Ecclesiastical Council held at Middleborough as a man "likely to make [the Yarmouth Church and Society] a good, useful and faithful Minister of the Gospel of Christ." On May 17 Scott was "unanimously approved" as the minister at Yarmouth by "show of hands."[11] For the first time since its foundation, Yarmouth possessed an ordained Congregational minister.

These years from June 1770, when he was recommended by Reed and Conant as an interim preacher, until April 1772 when he was approved by the Ecclesiastical Council at Middleborough, produced a distinct change in Scott's religious views. Scott had received no formal education as a child but his parents had provided him with "some knowledge of passages of Scripture" and Scott, during his days as an apprentice shoemaker, "often spoke of divine things where [he] could have a hearing." Nothing can be said with certainty about the doctrines he espoused at this stage but by the mid-1760s when he was settled in Yarmouth, he listened "with great delight" to the preaching of Ebenezer Moulton, the Baptist, and on March 14, 1768, he was married to Lucy Ring by Moulton. Scott was, however, not a Baptist.[12] He implied that the marriage ceremony was conducted by Moulton simply because he was available in Yarmouth, not because Scott or his bride were committed Baptists. Scott had been one of the key figures in the setting up of the Congregational church in December 1767 and in the ordination of Frost over the opposition of more scrupulous members who wished to obtain assistance from other Congregational churches. If Scott's doctrinal position is judged from his actions it seems that he was a believer in revivalist religion, but was less extreme than those who were prepared to desert the Congregational church for Moulton's Baptist exhortation.

Scott's appointment as a temporary preacher following the recommendations of Reed and Conant was a great boost to his confidence. Up to that time he had relied for his religious ideas on his own reading of the Bible, and like most Yarmouth people his religious views were determined by his attitude towards "vital Religion" rather than by a conscious identification with any doctrinal writings. His dependence on his interpretation of the Bible lasted up to the late 1760s when he acquired "Will-crites *Guide to Glory*," and the *Westminster Confession of Faith* and *Larger Catechism*. About five months after Reed and Conant had left Yarmouth, Scott received, on November 23, "a Present of two Books on Divinity: The Boston's Four Fold State [sic] from Revd. Sylvanus Conant of Middleborough; the other was President Edwards on the *Affections*." From this time on Scott spent as much time as possible "in Study and Preparation for Publick Service."[13] His religious views were to be determined, after 1770, by what he studied as well as by what he felt. He had moved beyond the stage of merely being an uninformed supporter of revivalistic religion to that of constructing a doctrinal basis for his beliefs. In the process Scott moved closer to the middle of the religious spectrum.

Already at the time of Frost's ordination, in September 1769, Scott had hinted at his attachment to the traditional practices of the Congregational church. Although he had participated in the ordination he had felt uneasy about proceeding with no assistance from other churches. He later made excuses for what he came to consider to have been an illegal, independent action by the church. The approval bestowed on him by Reed and Conant encouraged Scott's drift towards the centre. In the fall of 1770 and during the ensuing winter, Scott refused to listen to the sermons of Moulton as the Baptist preacher led off a group of dissidents from the meeting-house. Scott, certainly, did not

openly attack Moulton but he had moved further away from the
Baptist position than he had been in the late 1760s when he had
listened to Moulton enthusiastically and had not objected to
being married by the man he now, in 1770, considered to be a
stirrer up of opposition.[14] Installed in his position by the advice
of Reed and Conant, Scott was not going to permit unauthorized
preachers to disrupt his public meetings.

Scott's experiences in Massachusetts in April and May 1772,
during his examination by the Ecclesiastical Council, saw the culmination of this trend. He was treated well by all the ministers
he met. Sylvanus Conant, in particular, "manifested a most ten-
der Christian Spirit" toward him as did Solomon Reed, both of
whom, of course, already knew the candidate. But their kind
reception went beyond mere friendship. Conant did everything
in his power to make Scott feel at home and to ensure that the
Council was a success. In addition to kindnesses extended by
ministers and their families, Scott received presents from Peter
Oliver, the Chief Justice of Massachusetts, and his wife—"a
Present of Willard's Body of Divinity" from Oliver and "three
Bands and a large Cambrick Handkerchief as a Present" from
"Madame Oliver."[15]

The impression given by Scott's own account of these events
is that the late April weeks in Middleborough and Plymouth
were an experience in his life which had a marked impact on him.
Scott was still only twenty-eight years old; he had begun his
working life as an apprentice shoemaker before moving to Yarmouth where he had struggled to make a living, first by summer
fishing trips and then by farming. Up to 1770 it seemed his
course through life would continue to be indistinguishable from
those of the other farmers and fishermen of Yarmouth. Even
when travelling to Massachusetts in 1772 to meet the Council,
Scott had done so as an ordinary ship hand. He "worked his passage because there were not Seaman enough to work the Vessel"
and one night "stood at the helm till I blistered my hands
through my mittens which were thick."[16] In Middleborough
Scott, for a time, had moved out of this rough world into a genteel atmosphere where ministers discussed difficult doctrinal
points and wives of important men gave him presents for Mrs.
Scott.

This is not to argue that Scott suddenly changed his values.

The ministers with whom he got on well in Massachusetts were those who favoured revivalistic religion or at any rate were new divinity men. Solomon Reed, Sylvanus Conant and Chandler Robbins, all well-disposed towards properly controlled revivalism, seem to have been Scott's most solid supporters at the Council. But to have convinced the other ministers on the Council, like John Shaw, of Bridgewater, who was anti-revivalistic, that he was acceptable as a Congregational minister, Scott must have shown a decided attachment to the Congregational church structure.[17] On the one hand he had to confirm his position as a revivalist but he also had to persuade the Council that he was not an incipient Separate. Thus Scott had to prove his grasp of both "Doctrinal and Experimental Religion."[18] Presumably he had in the months after 1770 informed himself of the new divinity tenets and had repeated Edwards' warnings about the dangers of separation from the Congregational order.

Thus, although in 1772 Scott returned to Yarmouth still professing a belief in revivalist religion, his views had changed considerably after his two years of studying and his experience in Middleborough. He, as a legally ordained minister, was now deeply committed to the Congregational way. Scott, who had assisted in Frost's dubious ordination in 1769, was to argue in 1783 that Frost had been a poor choice for he "appeared not to have so much Regard to the regular Ministers of the Gospel, as I think would have been becoming, and for the Honour of Religion." Now that Scott had become a "regular Minister of the Gospel" he adopted a much more impatient and superior attitude to unqualified preachers who showed no respect to legally ordained pastors like himself. Much of Scott's criticism of Alline originated from the complete loyalty he devoted to the Congregational church after his transformation of 1770-72. Scott quoted the Cambridge Platform of 1648, Cotton Mather's *History of Witchcraft* and various Conventions of Massachusetts ministers in an effort to demonstrate Alline's deviant views. While primarily depending on Edwards, Scott also brought Charles Chauncy into the struggle against Alline. This suggests that although he was a revivalist, Scott's allegiance was to the Congregational establishment rather than to a particular doctrinal strain within the Congregationalist tradition. As Scott put it in one of his tirades against Alline, the enthusiastic rantings of the Falmouth preacher endangered the "best regulated, and most strongly united Churches of Christ that there now is, or ever was on earth."[19] Scott was still a friend to "vital Religion" but this, after 1772, necessarily took second place behind his loyalty to the New England Congregational system. His advice to the Yankees at the height of the Great Awakening, in November 1782, was "to keep to the Old Paths."[20]

The people of Yarmouth expected Scott to join the revival inspired by Alline. They knew their minister was friendly to revivalist religion and regretted that he made no effort to help Alline. Some of his congregation insisted that if Scott had lived up to his avowed ideals that he favoured "the Doctrines of Grace" the revival would have been even more successful than it was. John Crawley, a leading Yarmouth inhabitant, put this point directly to Scott. If Scott "had agreed with Mr. Alline, he [Crawley] thought there would have been as great a Revival of Religion in Yarmouth as ever has been since the Apostles Days."[21] Thus when Scott cited all the specific deviations Alline had made from New England traditions, much of it seemed irrelevant to most of the people who were still, as they had done in the 1760s, judging a preacher by his effectiveness, not by his principles.

The change in Scott from a public preacher into a Congregational minister had cut him off from the people. Moreover, after his ordination, Scott had been constantly bickering with his church on the amount and nature of his salary. And frequently he had been involved in bitter personal conflict with influential members of his congregation. Four months before Alline first preached in Yarmouth, Scott was experiencing serious problems in retaining the respect of his church. As Scott himself recognized, during the trying revolutionary years it was difficult to expect his people to look to him for effective leadership. In November 1780 he noted in the church records that his actions had "given Occasion for you to be suspicious and fearful of even following me any more."[22]

The most frequent accusation made by Yarmouth people against Scott, during and after Alline's three visits to the town, was that Scott was a poor revivalist preacher and that, more seriously, he was trying to sabotage the success achieved by

Alline in his evangelistic preaching. Already during his stay at
Middleborough, Scott had revealed some weakness in his manner of preaching. Some of the pro-revivalistic congregation of
Conant in Middleborough had been quick to point out that Scott,
at times, dangerously approached Arminian tenets in his exhortation from the pulpit. They reminded the candidate for the
ministry that he must always remember that the necessity of the
new birth was the essential doctrine for evangelical pastors to
stress above all else. According to these critics, Scott had suggested that good works could be the starting point for the
Christian life. From the pulpit of a leading New England
revivalist church, Scott had seemingly relegated the primacy of
conversion to a position of secondary importance.[23]

Until Alline appeared in 1781, Scott had been able to avoid
any direct criticism from his people of his preaching but the
Yarmouth minister was aware, at times, of his deficiencies in this
respect and the various disputes that frequently troubled his
congregation revealed the undercurrents of dissatisfaction. Once
the people of Yarmouth had a successful evangelical preacher
in their midst Scott's shortcomings were finally fully exposed in
public. John Crawley, Justice of the Peace and member for
Yarmouth of the Legislative Assembly from 1772 to 1774, put
the issue quite tersely. Crawley informed the pastor that "his
[Scott's] Doctrine was killing to him." Another church member,
Amos Hilton, reiterated this condemnation of Scott. Hilton, like
Crawley, was certain of Scott's failing. Quite simply, "Mr.
Scott's Preaching did no Good" whereas "Mr. Alline's Preaching was blessed, and every Family where he was received had
partook of the Blessing."[24]

Scott made his position even more vulnerable by actively
striving to prevent Alline from preaching in Yarmouth. This
was a difficult decision for Scott to justify to the people as the
church, since its foundation in 1767, had been openly revivalist
in sentiment. Out of the nine male members of the church in
1782 only one, Moses Scott, brother of the minister, did not
"attend Mr. Alline's meetings." With varying degrees of enthusiasm all the others went to hear Alline preach and were impressed by his effectiveness in inducing religious concern and
awareness among the people. These eight members, apart from

one, did not, however, formally separate from Scott's church but attended separate weekday meetings instead of those organized by the minister. Yet, although, as Scott himself admitted, "a great Part of the Church had agreed with Mr. Alline and had approved of the Proceedings and Work that he had promoted," the church remained formally intact. Since it was a revivalist church those who tended to support or sympathize with Alline had no reason to separate and form another revivalist organization. But although most of the members remained within the Congregational church they became bitter against Scott for opposing Alline when the minister should have, in their opinion, co-operated in promoting the revival. Alline's preaching had "good Effects" on the people and Scott, as a revivalist pastor, was obligated to support this effective evangelist — this was the argument urged again and again to Scott. Scott's crime, in short, was that "he opposed the good Work that was begun in the Place." The Yarmouth minister seemed to be acting as an Old Light minister utterly opposed to revivals. In Scott's own words, he was regarded "as the Chiefest Obstacle in the Way of their real Good and spiritual Welfare" and "treated as the great Obstacle in the Way of their spiritual Good and Advantage." This was the constant refrain of the dissidents within the church, that Scott was completely unjustified "in not receiving Mr. Alline and [not] countenancing the good Work, the Work of God (as they constantly termed it) which he had promoted among the People in this Place, and elsewhere."[25] Scott, in other words, appeared to have abandoned the revivalist principles he had once supposedly espoused.

Naturally, Scott went to great lengths to prove that he was not betraying his earlier beliefs. He argued that Alline was a false prophet inducing a false revival by playing on the emotions of the people. To discredit Alline he attempted to shift the ground of attack from Alline's manner of preaching to his doctrinal lapses. Scott used his reading in theology to draw attention to Alline's deviation from New England evangelicalism. He based his criticism on a detailed examination of Alline's major theological work.[26] In fact, well before Alline ever appeared in Yarmouth Scott had publicized his case against the Falmouth preacher. Scott had drawn attention to what he considered to be Alline's heretical beliefs to "a Number of the

People of his Charge" and "those to whom Mr. Scott opened these Opinions [of Alline], looked upon them [as] very erroneous and horrible and expressed a low Esteem of the Author of Them."[27]

Scott discovered so many peculiarities in Alline's doctrines that he was able to fill over three hundred closely worded pages in a point-by-point critique of Alline's ideas. In his rebuttal he went to great lengths to discover the absurdities adopted by Alline, pointing out that Alline had grossly misused biblical passages, confusing the "common language" used in the English translation with his interpretation of the "types." Alline, in Scott's sober estimation, was "an ignorant, self-conceited novice"[28] who knew nothing of the learned and complicated discipline of biblical interpretation. Beyond this, Scott charged that Alline had completely misunderstood evangelical concepts and had produced a theological scheme that was quite alien to traditional Calvinist beliefs. Scott believed that Alline had deliberately, in both his preaching and writings, set out to "overthrow and destroy the Doctrines of Calvinism, Root and Branch."[29] Scott made extensive use of Edwards to press home his assertion that Alline was oversetting Calvinist doctrine and thereby ruining true revivalist churches like the one in Yarmouth. He concentrated on Edwards' disapproval of extreme enthusiasts who had itinerated without official sanction during the Great Awakening in New England, and placed great emphasis on Edwards' insistence on the necessity of external order.

In view of his detailed denunciation of Alline, Scott found it difficult to understand why his people did not spurn the Falmouth preacher. He was puzzled because the people had, through him, been fully informed of Alline's departures from "orthodox" evangelicalism. As Scott put the puzzle to himself

it was not through mere Want of Information that they now countenanced and caressed this Man upon the Ruins of their own professed System of Religion and Doctrines; but they in a sort carried a Light in their Hand while they were engaged in this tragical Work; and therefore their Rapid Proceeding in the Face of their own professed System of religious Principles cannot be ascribed to the Want of Timely Notice and Warning, but to some other Cause.

Scott failed to appreciate, however, the gap that had occurred between him and the people once he had begun to use book learning to explain the evangelical case. He was perfectly correct in asserting that Alline made novel interpretations of the Bible and directly contradicted such authorities as Edwards on matters of church organization. But these points were irrelevant to the people who had no scholarly knowledge of the inner logic of evangelical thought.[30]

Alline, unlike Scott, had not returned to New England since emigrating to Nova Scotia and had not read Edwards, and his formulation of revivalist doctrine was not consciously based on New England precedents. This enabled Scott to attack his doctrines but it also permitted Alline to speak in terms most of the Yarmouth church understood, where Scott was operating in an unfamiliar evangelical world based on scholarly study.[31] Scott, to his surprise, found that it was the people "who have appeared to have a serious disposition, and a great Veneration for the Doctrines of Grace, or Calvinistic Principles and Doctrines, as they are called" who sided with Alline against him and were "some of his greatest Abettors."[32] These people believed Alline to be a better spokesman than Scott for the evangelical cause or "the Doctrines of Grace."

Scott found it impossible to bring his knowledge of Edwards to bear on the situation in Yarmouth because Alline and those who were affected by his preaching refused to be drawn into what they considered to be an irrelevant doctrinal debate. Alline played a masterly game of avoiding such a debate with Scott and thereby deprived the Yarmouth minister of the opportunity of showing his superior knowledge of evangelical thought. On Monday, October 22, 1781, two days after Alline had arrived in the area, Scott attempted to confront Alline and force the Falmouth preacher to answer his criticisms. Scott had laid the trap very carefully. He had invited Alline to his home and on the Monday morning he took Alline "aside with him from the Family, in Order to lay before him Things . . . for which he invited him to come to his House." Scott was careful to ensure that a witness, Mr. Joseph Robinson, was present to testify to his expected exposure of Alline's inconsistencies. Before Scott could begin, Alline immediately attempted to avoid a detailed theological discussion by presenting Scott with "the Account of his [Alline's] wonderful Success . . . at Cumberland." But Scott was not to be deflected from his purpose. He returned the document without comment and embarked on a long account of the heresies he had found in Alline's work. This barrage of criticism must have lasted for at least an hour. Throughout it all Alline remained silent. When Scott had finished, Alline made no effort to disprove the criticism but, according to Scott, replied with "an Air of Contempt and Disdain, 'I have Nothing to say; you have settled the Point, and have termed me an Imposter, and have censured me very high'." Whether Scott did in fact adopt such a superior, censorious attitude cannot be known from the evidence although it is certain he spoke for a long time and had nothing to say in favour of Alline or his preaching. But what is clear is that Alline, by remaining silent and giving the appearance of being on the receiving end of a bitter denunciation, created the impression that Scott had indulged in a display of temper. Alline thereby side-stepped the specific doctrinal condemnations made by Scott. That same afternoon Alline "held his first Meeting in Yarmouth, about a Mile from Mr. Scott's, at the house of Mr. Joseph Robinson."[33] Robinson had been the carefully chosen witness who was to have testified to Scott's superior evangelical logic in the morning interview. Alline's tactics, and not Scott's, had worked.

The following day Alline was at the house of James Robbins, a deacon of the church, where he gained more support. At Robbins' house "a Number of Persons were gathered, before whom he [Alline] complained of the ill Treatment he met with from Mr. Scott the Day before." This method of discrediting Scott seemed to have been effective, for the image that Alline propagated of an angry minister opposed to a sincere and successful evangelical itinerant "gained him Pity, and forwarded his Design to get Footing in this Place." Such proceedings, understandably, annoyed Scott since he believed he had tried to keep the Monday morning discussion on an academic level and by Thursday he had lost patience. That same day Scott met Alline at the house of Daniel Crocker, another deacon of the church, where the minister again attacked Alline. Whatever his mood on Monday had been, by this time Scott was openly upset and made little attempt to argue rationally. Scott "rebuked him [Alline] sharply for his Conduct in this Place, where he had no Right to appoint Meetings, nor spread his Opinions."[34] All this accomplished was to vindicate Alline's assertion that Scott was an intemperate opponent of revivalistic preaching. During these four days Scott had been successfully manoeuvred away from his strong doctrinal position to a much weaker one where he appeared to oppose Alline simply because he did not like him.

Scott mistakenly believed at this stage that his methods had been successful, for Alline left Yarmouth on the Friday of that week, after having preached in the town only twice. Scott rationalized that Alline "being thus detected so soon after his Arrival on the Place, by having his Principles and practices exposed to his Face"[35] had fled the town in disgrace. But the battle had only begun, as Scott was soon to discover.

Whether Alline deliberately or consciously adopted certain tactics in his attempts to "get Footing" in Yarmouth cannot be deduced from existing evidence, but either by intuition or design he completely outmanoeuvred Scott. By leaving immediately after what Scott himself realized was a peremptory rebuke, Alline gave the impression that he had been driven out of the town by the intolerant minister. He proceeded to Argyle where there was no settled pastor and achieved immediate success among the settlers there. He then moved on to Liverpool and other towns along the coast, in all of which places the people responded favourably to his preaching.[36]

News and rumours of Alline's success soon spread back to Yarmouth and the people regretted having missed out on the "great Reformation" Alline was accomplishing. Scott himself saw the process at work as he gloomily noted that

> the Sound of Mr. Alline's wonderful Reformation at Liverpool and Argyle, and other Places, quickly reached Yarmouth, and excited warm Attention among Mr. Scott's People, and fully determined their Minds not to neglect a second Opportunity for having the Benefit of Mr. Alline's Preaching among them.

The people indicated their feelings to Scott in no uncertain manner and at this time no more "than Two Persons among them . . .

ever consulted their Pastor what was best for them to do in this Matter." Alline had turned the situation in Yarmouth to his advantage. Instead of persisting in a verbal tussle with Scott he had left town as the injured party and preached successfully in other settlements. When he returned to Yarmouth on February 6, 1782, there was nothing Scott could do to prevent the people from flocking to hear the successful preacher. During a thirteen day stay in Yarmouth, Alline preached eighteen or nineteen times and

> such was the Rapidity of the Proceedings, that Mr. Scott did
> not know of his being in the Town, until he observed the
> People hasting by his House to attend the second Meeting
> which was appointed after this, his [Alline's] second Arrival
> in Yarmouth.[37]

Once he had been a public success in neighbouring settlements Alline was assured of an enthusiastic reception in Yarmouth.

When he had gained a hearing in Yarmouth, Alline was able to undermine further Scott's position. Scott argued that Alline was not an ordained minister and that he had no right to itinerate and break into the churches of other pastors. But before he had embarked on his lengthy preaching itineraries Alline had been officially ordained by the churches that had been formed by his followers in the Minas Basin area. Between 1776 and April 1779 his travelling had been restricted to the Minas Basin and Annapolis Valley townships, all of which were within a few days walking or riding from each other. On April 5, 1779, " a general council" of the churches of Horton, Cornwallis and Newport met and after "a day of fasting and prayer . . . concluded to proceed the next day." On April 6, Alline "received the imposition of hands by nine delegates" and was thereby ordained to the work of the ministry. The ordination was not to one particular church but as "an ITINERANT PREACHER" since Alline had insisted that he could not be tied to one locality.[38] Only after he had received this sanction did Alline feel free to visit more distant townships. All his preaching on the St. John River, the Chignecto area, in the Cobequid townships and in the fishing settlements from Yarmouth to Liverpool occurred in the years following this ordination. When he arrived in Yarmouth the first thing he gave Scott, along with the account of his Cumberland success, was "the Certificate of his Ordination."[39] Alline considered this certificate to be his credentials to preach throughout the colony and on this basis he rejected Scott's allegation that his itineracy was illegal.

Scott maintained that the ordination as "a preacher at large" was worthless since it had been granted by "separate men of his own Party."[40] But Scott failed to take account of the lengths to which the New Light churches had gone to ensure that the ordination was as legal as local circumstances would permit. They had even written to Scott himself in August 1777 to enlist his aid in the proposed ordination in an effort to make the operation as official as possible. In spite of criticism from opponents of the revival, Alline gave the appearance of being legally ordained.

When Scott objected to Alline's qualifications at the time Alline was preaching in Yarmouth, Alline countered by reminding the people of the ordination of John Frost over the Yarmouth church in September 1767. This immediately put Scott on the defensive for he had been one of the full church members who, in 1767, had proceeded with Frost's ordination over the protests of the Society. During Alline's stay in Yarmouth, Frost's ordination was used "to justify the Ordination of Mr. Alline." Scott, once more put on the defensive, was reduced to explaining why he had been wrong in 1767. At the time of the Frost affair, Scott, along with others of the church brethren, had been uneasy about the legality of the ordination but nevertheless, being much influenced by Frost, he had overcome his scruples. Indeed as late as April 1770, just before Reed and Conant came to Yarmouth, Scott had reaffirmed his approval of Frost.[41]

By 1781 the people of Yarmouth were hearing a different story from Scott. The Yarmouth Congregational minister now described Frost as a preacher who had too little respect for "regular Ministers of the Gospel" and who evinced dangerous separatist tendencies. Scott had no evidence that Frost had "ever separated from any Church while he lived in New England." Yet in 1782, Scott maintained that Frost "appeared to me to favour the Separations from Churches that have in Years past taken Place in that Land."[42] It must have seemed strange to hear these charges made by Scott who had been one of Frost's closest supporters up to the spring of 1770.

Alline could not have known the history of this episode before he came to Yarmouth but once there he drew a parallel between his and Frost's ordination. He bestowed his approval of the right of churches to ordain without assistance and "excited others" to adopt this line of argument. In an attempt to retrieve the situation, Scott repeated the justifications made by the church brethren at the time of Frost's ordination and pointed out that they had never considered it in their power to ordain him an itinerant minister. He also went at considerable length into biblical and New England precedents to prove the complete illegality of the ordination of itinerant preachers.[43] Scott easily found scholarly references to support his case but he could not cope with the local situation in this manner. Alline had discovered another weakness in Scott's position in Yarmouth and the Yarmouth minister, argue as he might from books, could not get round the fact that he appeared to be condemning what he had once practised.

Another effective way that Alline was able to undermine Scott was to suggest that during his visit to Cornwallis in the winter of 1778-79 Scott had acted in a similarly intolerant manner towards the revival in that locality. Such references were particularly harmful to Scott since that visit to Cornwallis had been linked with the unpleasant episodes, in the summer of 1779, when it appeared that Scott and the Cornwallis church were perhaps scheming to deprive Yarmouth of its minister. At least some people in Yarmouth were prepared to believe that Scott had not been doing the good work he claimed he had been accomplishing in Cornwallis. Even before 1781 there had been some reservations within Yarmouth about the aggressive attitude taken by the Cornwallis church towards Alline and his followers. In March 1780 the Yarmouth church members had mildly reprimanded their Cornwallis counterparts for manifesting "a bitter and censorious Spirit on account of the Separations that have taken Place among you." When he came to Yarmouth, Alline made the most of Scott's suspected complicity in the anti-revivalist campaign in Cornwallis.[44]

In all these direct and indirect attacks on Scott the most telling criticism levelled was that he was an "opposer of the Work of God" whereas Alline was "promoting a Work of God." Once the issue was put in these terms the success of Alline in awakening the people became of crucial importance and as long as Alline continued to be an effective preacher Scott was unable to convince people that Alline was an impostor. Alline seemed to realize that this was his strength. On his first meeting with Scott he had given him an account of his success at Cumberland and he had returned to Yarmouth in February 1782 only after a successful two-month campaign in fishing towns along the coast. In Yarmouth the followers of Alline made little effort to ponder Scott's doctrinal warnings but usually simply pointed out to Scott that "Mr. Alline's preaching was blessed" where "Mr. Scott's Preaching did no Good."[45] Alline was a successful revivalist, Scott was not. The issue was as simple as that.

Such a process of thinking was not peculiar to Nova Scotia Yankees but was deeply rooted in New England evangelical thought in the post-1740 period. The dogma from which all such thinking stemmed was that a revival, while proceeding among men and precipitated by great preachers, was in fact, a "Work of God." No man by his own efforts could produce a true revival in religion. During a revival in Connecticut in the mid-1760s, Jacob Johnson, in describing "the Rule" by which a "Work of Grace" could be recognized, put the case cogently and clearly. A basic principle was that a work of grace was not a common thing nor was it "obtained by a mere common use of means, as reading, hearing etc." A revival was "a supernatural work, as really above the Power of means to effect, as opening the eyes of the blind, or raising the dead was." In short, concluded Johnson, the "Spirit of God must necessarily effect this great work for the will of man cannot."[46] A genuine revival could be ascertained by determining

> whether our professed experiences agree with the rule, and whether our lives and conversations agree with our profession. If so, then we have indeed experienced a work of grace. And in this way we shall become epistles, known and read by all men: And so a work of God will be made manifest, when, and where ever it is.[47]

These rules, as explained by Johnson, resulted in a precise definition of revivalism, the genuineness of which could be tested in each community by "Experience and Observation." This was the experimental approach to religion that constituted one of the basic tones in American religious life after 1740.[48]

While no-one in Yarmouth could articulate their view of revivals in the manner of Johnson, it is certain that they made similar assumptions and drew similar conclusions. Johnson himself had conceded that the work could be known "either by intuition or reflection"[49] and in Yarmouth people were not unwilling to give full reign to their intuition on these matters. With no references to outside sources, either to Johnson or anyone else, people in Yarmouth repeatedly demonstrated that their conception of the revival phenomenon was similar to that propounded by more articulate evangelicals. They referred without hesitation to "the good Work, the Work of God (as they constantly termed it) which he [Alline] had promoted among the People in this place and elsewhere." And "with much Zeal and Confidence they asserted That he [Alline] was sent of God." The argument advanced to support these assertions was that Alline's "Works were a full Proof and Evidence of it etc."[50] The reasoning, if attenuated, followed that of Johnson. A revival was a work of God; Alline could accomplish nothing on his own and thus must be an instrument of God.

In his sermon Johnson had pointed to the recent conversion of two obscure country people in New England as evidence that the millennium was fast approaching. Likewise in Yarmouth in 1782, the specificity of conversion in a particular locality permitted generalization about the genuineness and wider significance of the revival. A turning point for Alline in Yarmouth occurred in October 1782 when the wife and daughter of Cornelius Rogers were converted. Up to that time Alline had achieved a considerable following but these conversions finally offered convincing proof that Alline was promoting a work of God. From "this day forward . . . the Separation greatly increased,"[51] as Scott became even more isolated.

In this context Scott's lapses into displays of temper seriously weakened his claim to be a friend to revivalist religion. Scott had not experienced a conversion. During the 1760s when he had

been most concerned about his own spiritual state and had listened to Moulton's Baptist exhortations, he had been disap-
pointed that, although his "ear was very attentive his heart was
not renewed."[52] From that time on, Scott had relied on his
intellectual understanding of the revivalist case to support his
pastoral responsibilities. But when he fell into many disputes
with church members after 1776, when he attempted to get
more money out of the church in 1779 and when he lost his
temper with Alline in 1781, more and more people suspected
that he was not a converted believer. After all, a work of grace
could be seen from the effects as they appeared "in the temper of
our hearts or the tenor, and course of our lives" and, in his
struggle to defend his ministerial status during the revival,
Scott, neither in his temper nor his behaviour, showed much
evidence of his acquaintance with important evangelical truths.
In contrast, Alline could not only attest to his experience but he
was effective in "communicating of it to others." As Alline
related his success at Cumberland and many other places and
showed his powers in Liverpool and Argyle, it became increasingly clear to people in Yarmouth that a work of God was being
made manifest. They had witnessed "real" conversion in their
own town and knew that other places were experiencing the
same phenomenon. Alline may have been able to fool a few
people for a short period but the extent and duration of his
success had only one meaning to evangelical minds. They were
witnessing a divinely inspired revival.

In his writings Alline developed the same theme as Johnson
had, that revivalists could be distinguished by certain signs or
rules. One of these signs was that the converted sinner would
give outward evidence of his change and involve himself
actively in the general revival. Alline reminded the people that

> when Christ speaks of true faith He declares that if a Man had
> a spark as a grain of mustard seed, it would remove the moun-
> tains and raise the dead. So that it is an infallible Truth that
> whosoever has but one spark of that true faith in exercise; he
> would feel the effects of it in the removing of sin . . . and in the
> raising of his dead mind from the state of death to a real
> knowledge and activity in a divine life.

He went on to emphasize that those who claimed to be revivalists yet criticized a revival when one occurred were false
evangelicals. "Such professors of Christianity," asserted Alline,
"knew no more of the New Birth, and that true faith, which is
the operation of the Spirit of God, than Simon the Sorcerer."
They possessed only "the shadow or representation" of the
revivalist case but not "the substance."[53]

Scott was impotent in the face of such an argument. The Yarmouth minister, it bears repeating, did consider himself to be a
revivalist. He believed that revivals were the "means whereby
He [God] performs his whole gracious and great work of
Mercy in awakening, convincing, humbling, regenerating and
externally saving miserable and spiritually dead Sinners of Mankind." Neither Alline nor his supporters in Yarmouth would
have disputed this view. The difference arose when Scott refused
to agree that the general awakening caused by Alline was a
genuine work of Grace.[54] To the ordinary, uneducated people in
the Yarmouth church the revival was obvious by its effects in
their community and was so general throughout the colony that
it was inconceivable that it could be false. If one false prophet
could accomplish such things then it became difficult to place
faith in any revivals at all. Their fundamental faith in the
necessity of revivals encouraged them to accept Alline, who was
promoting one, and to reject Scott, who had some of the rhetoric
but could produce no such happy effects among the people. As
Cornelius Rogers, another Church member, put it, Scott had
"the Form of Godliness but denied the Power."[55]

It is important to understand the detailed mechanics of the
struggle between Alline and Scott in Yarmouth. Scott's writings
contain so many references to Jonathan Edwards that it appears,
in rejecting him, the Yarmouth Yankees were rejecting their
New England background and were subscribing to an entirely
new evangelical theology. But Scott was rejected not because he
quoted Edwards but because he actively opposed the revival and
because he was a poor revivalist preacher during the period of
Alline's itineracy. There is no evidence whatsoever that the
people felt they were repudiating the religion they had known
in New England. The major dissidents within the church who
were active in opposing Scott were all men with families who

had reached maturity before leaving New England to come to Yarmouth. They never criticized Scott for his references to Edwards but always specified their dislike of his manner of preaching or his attitude towards the revival.[56]

This close study of events in Yarmouth has not been made because Yarmouth was typical of Yankee Nova Scotia but simply because it is the only case about which detailed records exist. It may be that Yarmouth was typical, but not enough evidence from other places affected by the revival has been found to prove that this was the case. Indeed the extant evidence suggests the uniqueness of Yarmouth. Other towns, such as Liverpool, possessed a Congregational minister but Scott was a revivalist pastor where Israel Cheever was an Old Light and this made the debate between Alline and Scott a more paradoxical affair than it was elsewhere. And in contrast to the Minas Basin, Cobequid and Cumberland areas where the Yankee population lived near Scotch-Irish or English settlers, the Yarmouth population was entirely New England in origin and isolated from contact with other large ethnic groups. Nevertheless, the Yarmouth case study possesses more than local significance. It shows clearly some of the tactics adopted by Alline and his followers to undermine opponents of the revival and it dramatizes how so much of Alline's success depended on effective preaching rather than doctrinal expertise.

Moreover, Jonathan Scott, by 1783, had become the focal point round which colony-wide opposition to Alline gathered. Beginning in June 1778, Scott received letters from opponents of the revival in Cornwallis, Maugerville and Liverpool pleading for his help and advice in coming to grips with the effects of the religious turmoil.[57] Both in response to these pleas from other towns and to the local crisis in Yarmouth, Scott on behalf of the opponents of the revival embarked on a full-scale denunciation of Alline and his works. Thus the developments in Yarmouth, although not necessarily typical, do provide clues to the nature and methods of Alline's success and present detailed pictures of the two major religious protagonists in Nova Scotia during the revolutionary war.

7

The Anatomy of Revival

One of the most difficult problems in dealing with revivals as social phenomena is the question of how many people were influenced at a particular time by such an event. Even in social systems like that of New England in the mid-eighteenth century, where most communities had churches which kept records, it is not always possible to make an accurate assessment of the number of people whose values were altered by a general religious revival. In the case of New England, however, the evidence from literary as well as record sources indicates the extensive influence of the evangelical thought and revivalist activity in the decades after 1740. Few historians question the extent of the revival phenomena in New England although there is disagreement as to the nature of the phenomena and their effect on the social and political structure and on the values of New England. Unless it can be shown that a revival impinged on large numbers of people it is not legitimate to suggest that it exerted an impact on the values of the society within which it occurred.

Although Nova Scotia's population in the 1770s was far smaller than that of any of the New England colonies, there are serious difficulties in estimating the numbers involved in the revival. Yarmouth is the only town for which detailed church records exist and there are, therefore, virtually no statistical sources to provide numerical information. An assessment of the nature and size of the Nova Scotia revival as a social movement has to rely primarily on literary evidence. This is unsatisfactory and leaves many detailed questions unanswered. Nevertheless, a careful use of such evidence may provide an approximate estimation of the size of the revival. Moreover, when all such evidence shows a unanimity in its description of the movement and contains no contradictory accounts, then there is reason to believe it reflects with some accuracy the actual situation at that time.

Before examining this evidence it is worth making a point that is often overlooked, or left unmentioned, in various studies of revivalism. It is a simple point but an important one if the social impact of a revival is to be considered. Those people who experienced conversion did not constitute the total number of those affected by the revival, and it is likely that they often formed only a minority among the total numbers influenced by the revival. The term "awakening" which is used to describe the revivals in New England in 1740-41 and Nova Scotia from 1776 to 1783 is not synonymous with "conversion." The awakening was only the first stage in what could be a prolonged road to conversion and it meant only that an individual or a group were made newly aware of the norms they ought to adhere to and the goals they ought to strive for as avowed evangelical Christians. A time of awakening then did not necessarily mean a period of mass conversions but rather a time of unusually acute concern for the religious affairs and religious character of a community. The case of Yarmouth clearly demonstrates this point. It was only on Alline's third visit, in October 1782, that the first conversions took place yet, since October 1781, when Alline had first arrived, the town had been in a state of religious excitement when separate meetings were set up, rumours of Alline's progress talked over and the attitude of the local minister criticized.[1]

In other towns the same behaviour pattern was repeated. In Maugerville when "Mr. Henry Allen [sic], a New-Light travelling minister, came to preach" the immediate result was a revived concern for religious affairs. After Alline's sermon was over, Mary Bradley, a young girl at the time, "was astonished to see people talking and shaking hands, as I never before had witnessed. Some looked of a cheerful, loving, and happy countenance; others were in tears and cast down."

Even when Alline left, conversion became a "common subject of conversation" in the town.[2] In Maugerville, as in Yarmouth, the effect of Alline's preaching was to make religion a prime topic of public interest. There did not need to be actual conversions, although these did occur in increasing numbers, but people talked about such matters with a new interest and intensity. In Liverpool, Simeon Perkins, commenting on the impact of Alline on that town, summed up these occurrences in an apt phrase. Drawing a parallel with the Great Awakening in New England, Perkins described the effects of Alline's preaching. It created, noted Perkins, a "Great Religious Stir."[3]

In these circumstances of public interest and excitement there was no uniformity among supporters of the revival. At least four distinct groups, each representing varying degrees of attachment to the revival, can be distinguished. The first group was composed of the committed followers of Alline, usually those who had experienced conversion and had formed new churches under Alline's influence. The churches of Horton, Cornwallis, Falmouth and Newport, which ordained Alline in 1779, provide the most obvious examples of this complete attachment to the revival.[4] Such people constituted the core support group. Outside this core group were those who actively sympathized with the revival, although they were not prepared to form new or separate churches. The four male members of the Yarmouth church, Daniel Crocker, John Crawley, Amos Hilton and Cornelius Rogers, are good examples of this type. They remained within the Congregational church, although Rogers eventually refused to attend Scott's sermons, yet they were "prevailed upon to justify the Proceedings of Mr. Alline in his entering in among the People, and the good Effects that followed his Preaching upon the Minds and Morals of a Number of the People." As Scott discovered in Yarmouth, these active sympathizers could be just as persistent in support of the revival as the core group which actually formed "a strong Party." The active sympathizers "within the Church, who are not drawn off" were "a more difficult and dangerous Opposition."[5]

A third group, more difficult to define, can be described as passive sympathizers. These people were not so adamantly or publicly attached to the religious revival as the active sympathizers but, nevertheless, they were prepared to go out of their way to look benevolently on the revival and aid it if they could. Simeon Perkins in Liverpool represents this trend. A prominent member of the Congregational Society, he went to Alline's meetings when the preacher was in Liverpool, entertained Alline at his home and generally bestowed, in public, recognition and approval on the revival. Unlike Stephen Smith, a fellow merchant, Perkins did not immediately join the New Light party that separated from the Congregational church, although, in keeping with his basic revivalist sympathies, he eventually became a Methodist.[6] The commander of the British garrison at Fort Cumberland when Alline was preaching in the area in the summer of 1781 is another example of this group. He listened to a sermon by Alline, invited the preacher to dine with him and treated the Falmouth itinerant "with great civility." According to Alline, this valuable ally "acknowledged the truths of the gospel, and promised me whatever assistance I wanted, while travelling in that county, as he was the chief commander." Alline was not misled as to the intensity of the soldier's commitment to the revivalist cause. The commander at Cumberland "had no real religion, yet he could not oppose, but encourage the gospel."[7] This was the outstanding characteristic of this third group of passive sympathizers. Whether they were serious about the details of the evangelical case, as Perkins was, or whether they showed no deep concern about conversion, they had one thing in common in that they would rather encourage than oppose the revival. These people were not as active in the cause as were the four leading dissidents in Scott's church but their sympathy allowed them to give either tacit or overt support to Alline.

The fourth group, probably the largest of all, was composed of those people who left their homes to go and listen to sermons by Alline or, later, by his close followers. Not everyone who went to hear Alline was favourably disposed. On one occasion in Liverpool when Alline was preaching, a man who had obtained a good position "near under the pulpit," looked up as Alline was "delivering the truths of the gospel of the Lord Jesus Christ and cried out, that is damned foolishness." Alline encountered several incidents of this type but apparently usually managed to overawe the taunters. Compared with the number of meetings Alline held, such encounters were rare and on the whole he was eagerly listened to whenever or wherever he preached. The only place where Alline really felt the weight of public disinterest was in Halifax which he visited in connection with the publication of his book and sermons. The reaction to Alline in Yarmouth seems typical of his reception in other towns in the colony. The people in Yarmouth "would hear Mr. Alline; and they had a desire to hear him." In July 1782 Alline, while in Cumberland, "was often obliged to preach in the fields on account of the great concourse of the people." In the fall of 1781, in Annapolis County, he "preached often to great crowds of people."[8] These people who gathered to listen to Alline were not all core supporters, passive or active sympathizers, or debunkers of the revival. There is no evidence to support any analysis of these crowds of hearers but it seems reasonable to suggest that the majority consisted merely of people who were interested in the revival, while the three support groups and the debunkers were a minority. These people in the four groups of pro-revivalists were the ones most directly, and beneficially in their own estimation, affected by the revival. It is these people who are referred to when discussing the followers or supporters or sympathizers of the revival.

One important dimension of the Great Awakening in Nova Scotia can be easily established. The geographical extent of the movement may be deduced conclusively from the evidence and it can be shown that every settlement, apart from Halifax, Chester and Lunenburg, was touched in some way by the religious movement. Most of the specific references to places are contained in Alline's own account of his itinerancies. Although every statement made by Alline cannot be cross-checked certain key ones can and it is clear that, in spite of at least one discrepancy over dates, his account is accurate as to the places he gained a hearing. Indeed, in the case of Yarmouth, about which there is a great deal of local information, it seems that Alline underestimated his effect rather than exaggerated it.[9]

Between April 1776 when he first preached in public and

April 1779 when he was ordained as an itinerant preacher, Alline concentrated on travelling among the settlements in the Minas Basin and Annapolis Valley. Every township in these areas was visited by Alline at least once. Annapolis, the most distant point from Alline's base in Falmouth, received visits from him on ten separate occasions, on each of which he spent at least a few days and often several weeks in the town. In the area of Cornwallis, the largest and most central community, Alline conducted twenty-five preaching campaigns. Newport and Horton both received frequent visits. And on his expeditions to Annapolis, Alline usually made his presence known and sermonized in the settlements of the valley, including Wilmot and Granville.

After his ordination, Alline extended his activities to other areas of the colony. He visited Maugerville on the St. John River four times, stopping in at many of the small settlements along the river. In 1781 he journeyed to Cumberland County, holding meetings at points along the way before reaching Fort Lawrence from where he proceeded to ascend forty miles up the Petitcodiac River. Sackville, an important Chignecto settlement, was included in this campaign.

In the winter of 1781-82 all of the major and many smaller settlements between Yarmouth and Liverpool were reached by Alline. Later in 1782, he returned to Cumberland County from where he sailed for present-day Prince Edward Island and eventually reached the town of Pictou back on peninsular Nova Scotia. From here Alline crossed the uplands and worked his way through Truro, Onslow and Londonderry. All these itinerancies to the furthest parts of Nova Scotia were interspersed among his continued travels in the Minas Basin and Annapolis Valley regions.

In every settlement he visited, no matter how small, Alline preached at least one sermon. Even if he remained for only a day he was able to deliver at least two public exhortations. According to Alline's daily account of these campaigns he received a hearing everywhere he stayed. In such cases as Cornwallis, Maugerville, Yarmouth, Argyle, Annapolis and Liverpool, other more objective evidence indicates that Alline's reports were substantially accurate. Jonathan Scott was fully aware of the colony-wide extent of Alline's influence and likened it to "the rising of the Cloud which has covered our Heavens and darkened our Air." While disapproving of Alline's activities Scott confirmed the wide geographical extent of the revival. The whole province

> is overspread with religious Contentions, Divisions and Separations; so that there is scarce a Church or religious community that I can hear of in this Province but what our Author [Alline] has broke in upon, and drawn off a Party from it by some Means or other.

The extent of Alline's influence was impressive. As Scott sadly noted, for seven years, from 1776 to 1783, Alline had "been industrious in spreading his Tenets; by travelling from town to town; and making it his business to inculcate his Religion from Place to Place through all Parts of this Land." He had, in short, been "industrious in filling this Land with his Preaching and Books from one End to the other."[10]

The question of the popularity of the revival is more difficult to determine but several pieces of evidence indicate that it was the largest social movement that had ever occurred in the colony. According to Scott, who had contacts in Cornwallis, Annapolis, Maugerville and Liverpool, Alline had "got a Party to adhere to him in most Towns; and such as support him in his Proceedings."[11] Scott believed that in most towns Alline had succeeded in establishing a core group which formed a party and groups of sympathizers who supported the revival in a less committed fashion. He was of the opinion that the geographical extent of the revival was paralleled by its widespread popularity among the people. Other evidence supports this assessment.

In Liverpool during Alline's visit of December 1781 and January 1782, his first sermon was, according to Simeon Perkins, attended by "a Great Number" who "in General Approved of his preaching." In the opening week of January, outside Liverpool, Alline "preached twice every day . . . and the houses were crowded." On January 5, Alline preached in the evening at the house of Stephen Smith and Simeon Perkins noted that "many People attend and are generally pleased with him." After Alline left Liverpool on January 7, the religious interest and public excitement continued as Israel Cheever, the Old Light Congregational minister, became the focus of public debate when he preached against the revival. On February 2 at the house of Simeon Perkins

> A large Concourse of People . . . near 150, attended, which is till of Late a Very Strange thing in this Place, Such a meeting having Scarcely been Known in the Place Since the Settlement of it, till Since Mr. Alline was here.

This was no temporary phase in Liverpool social life, and when Alline returned to the town ten months later the revival had reached such a scale of intensity that Perkins could only compare its effects with the Great Awakening in New England "many years ago."[12]

When Alline returned to Liverpool in November 1782, a number of supporters were waiting for him on the wharf and they informed him that "the glorious work of God, that had appeared since [Alline had] left them . . . was still going on in the place." Alline remained until December 2 preaching "every day and sometimes twice a day; and the houses . . . were crowded almost all the time." At one meeting Alline claimed that "almost all the Town assembled together."[13]

This evidence from Liverpool is important not only for the indication it gives of the duration, size and intensity of the revival in that town, but also because it provides cross-references for Alline's own account of events and enables Alline's accuracy to be confirmed. For instance, when Alline first came to Liverpool in December 1781 he felt that at his first preaching he "had but little encouragement" from the people, yet at this time Perkins was certain that Alline was "generally liked by the People."[14] And Alline's belief, evident from his diary, that his second visit in November 1782 saw a large upswing in attendance and religious excitement is substantiated by Perkins' version of the increased public interest.[15] Alline, indeed, provides more information than does Perkins on the opposition he encountered there. In Liverpool, then, Alline did succeed in establishing a New Light group and in inspiring in the town a public debate on such a scale that no-one could recall anything like it since the town had first been settled.

In 1779, after his ordination as an itinerant preacher, Alline travelled up the St. John River to Maugerville for the first time. According to Scott, during this campaign Alline "gained many Followers upon that whole River" including "a Separate Party from the Church of Maugerville."[16] When Alline reached Maugerville the people, hearing he was there, were so anxious for the preacher to begin his work that they "came on board to fetch [Alline] ashore." His sermons "took much hold of the people" and for days at a time he was busily "engaged in preaching and discoursing with the people." Since the departure of Seth Noble, the Maugerville church had been without a pastor and had fallen into a "broken state." Alline maintained that on this visit he managed to persuade "the greatest part of the old church" along with some new members to renew the covenant and reorganize the church.[17] The account of Mary Bradley testifies to the unique effect of Alline among many of the Maugerville people. As in Liverpool religious matters raised by Alline became "a common subject of conversation."[18]

For the Minas Basin townships of Falmouth, Newport, Horton and Cornwallis, where the first New Light churches were formed, there are numerous references by Alline to the large size of his following. Early in his preaching career, word of Alline's new role was spread from Falmouth and "many would come from other towns, even whole boat-loads." Again Alline distinguished those who came to hear the word of God from those who came to scoff, but it seems obvious, at any rate, that he was a major public spectacle. In November 1776, Alline's preaching seemed to make an impression on the people in Horton and he "gained the attention of the people." After three days "the people seemed to have hearing ears" and on his last evening in town, "there was such a throng of hearers that the house could not contain them." In January 1777, the inhabitants of Newport were anxious to hear Alline, and they being "much scattered," Alline moved about the township preaching every day. During the summer of the same year, in Cornwallis, "a great number met almost every evening and continued to eleven and twelve o'clock at night." No precise figures can be extracted from such references and the size of the New Light churches in the area at this time are not known, although they were firmly established by the time of Alline's ordination in 1779. But Scott, who had spent the winter of 1778-79 in Cornwallis, believed he was well acquainted with the progress of Alline in the neighbouring townships and his comments confirm Alline's statements. Scott knew, for example, that "the Separate Party [that] had been drawn off" from the Cornwallis church by Alline "boasted that they were the greatest part of the Church and was not, therefore, to be charged with Separation." And in Wilmot, Horton, Falmouth and Windsor, Scott was aware that Alline "had his separate Followers who warmly adhered to him at this time."[19] The Reverend Mr. William Ellis, an S.P.G. missionary based in Windsor, confirmed the pervasive influence of the revival in public affairs. Writing in September 1776, Ellis informed his superiors that "Fanaticism has taken a strong hold"[20] of the people in his area.

Scott, while receiving information on Alline's effects elsewhere in the colony, was also trying to cope with local problems occasioned by the revival. As in most of his writings on the extent of the revival, Scott in the church records always took care to point out that the core support group of Alline was only the tip of the iceberg and that many more people were influenced in some manner by religious excitement. In the fall of 1782 "the Separation" from the church in Yarmouth, "greatly increased . . . even to near twenty Heads of Families." Besides these avowed separatists, a majority of those who remained within the church favoured the revival. As Scott put it, "his own People [were] equally involved with the Rest" and would not "be reasoned with or . . . receive Conviction or Instruction from his publick Preaching or private Discourse." During this third visit to Yarmouth, Alline succeeded in inducing his first conversions in the town. "This," in Scott's words, "was the Occasion of such Joy and Triumph, that after the Meeting . . . a considerable Number of Men, Women and Children [went] with Mr. Alline . . . in the Evening, singing aloud as they passed along the Highway." When in the summer and fall of 1783 Scott tried to raise subscriptions in Yarmouth to support the cost of printing his long rebuttal of Alline's views only ten people were prepared to advance anything and

some of the Members of the Church smartly objected, and
manifested warm Disgust against the Pastor on Account of
this Book before it went to the Press, and before they knew
what it contained; and were averse to give the Book a reading
after it was printed.

By this time Scott was convinced that the twenty people who had
begun the separation were only a small part of the pro-revivalist
party. After the book incident the disaffection towards Scott, by
separates and non-separating sympathizers of Alline, continued
and increased.[21]

At the other end of the colony in Cumberland County, Alline
was also extremely successful. At Fort Lawrence, in July 1781,
such a crowd attended Alline's preaching that he "was obliged to
preach in the open field." In August, this time at Cumberland,
"the hearers were so numerous" that Alline, once again, was
obliged to preach in the fields. In Annapolis County, south of
the Minas Basin Townships, Alline, during his travels, "visited
and preached to all of the societies . . . through the whole
county." According to Scott, Alline gained a considerable number of followers in this county, partly from the Congregational
church of Reverend Mr. Asarelah Morse. At Wilmot, "great
numbers attended" Alline's meetings. Alline believed he was
extremely successful in stirring up interest in settlements of the
area. In Annapolis County Alline maintained he "preached
often and to great crowds."[22]

The credibility of Alline's own account of his itinerancies is
increased by the frankness with which he described unresponsive
towns. When he arrived among the Cobequid townships of
Truro, Onslow and Londonderry where there were two Presbyterian ministers, Daniel Cock and David Smith, among a predominantly Scotch-Irish population, Alline received a cold
reception. As he travelled through the country he met with
open hostility. The reason for this, according to Alline, was that
the two

poor dark ministers there . . . informed the people that there
was a strange imposter from the country up the bay . . . who
was neither college learned, nor authorised by the presbytery

... [that] He was a New Light, he was a separatist, and one that broke up their churches.

The result of these advanced public warnings was that

the poor dark people [most of them] conceived such an opinion of me [Alline], that they would gaze at me, as I passed their doors, with as much strangeness as if I was one [of] the antediluvians; and when I came down to the public house I was even refused a bed or a room for any money.

Alline eventually found lodging in a private home. As he was led by the reluctant owner to his room, the people looked at Alline as if he "had some distemper that was catching." The curiosity of the people about this man against whom dire warnings had been given soon, however, got the better of them and "some of them hearing me sing," asked to speak with Alline and "began to be free." Soon the "man of the house called . . . [Alline] . . . and desired . . . [him] . . . to pray in his Family, and numbers of people came in." Alline took advantage of this initial breakthrough to announce that he would preach in the afternoon at four, thus allowing time for news to spread and anticipation to excite the people. In spite of the efforts made by the local minister to stop him from preaching, Alline went ahead as planned and such "a great number attended . . . the house could not contain them." The following day, after a morning of public debate with the local minister, Alline found he "had more houses [open to his preaching] than I could supply." In both Truro and Onslow, he "not only preached often, but discoursed also with the people, who often filled my room and stayed till twelve at night."[23] Even in such hostile areas, Alline's persistence eventually gained a public hearing. Once this had been achieved he could use all his oratorical skill and begin to establish support groups.

In many of the smaller settlements of Nova Scotia the whole population often turned out to hear Alline. In July 1781 while in passage from Windsor to Amherst Point, Alline "got to Partridge Island, and preached there about seven in the morning to . . . about 20 in number."[24] Almost two years later, in July

1783, at Port Medway, a small settlement near Liverpool, Alline preached a sermon at which "almost every Person in the place" was present.[25] During the last months of 1782, Scott and the people of Yarmouth heard that

> in Barrington, Liverpool and other Places . . . down the Shore
> . . . the religious influence that accompanied his Preaching in
> different places was said to be very great, and by some was
> called [a] great Reformation.

At the nearby settlement of Argyle which had no minister, Alline met with little or no resistance. "The Body of the People embraced him and his Preaching; and great was the religious Commotions among them."[26]

The revival not only affected a large geographical area of Nova Scotia but it also had considerable support throughout the colony. No precise proportion of the population who were pro-revivalist can be deduced from the evidence but there is no reason to disbelieve Alline's rough estimation that his support consisted of "some thousands in the province."[27] If the term supporters is used to include all four groups — the committed core, the active sympathizers, the passive sympathizers and the interested listeners — Alline's approximate total is a reasonable one. In the Nova Scotia outsettlements, with a population of a little more than ten thousand, such a degree of support for the revival clearly made it a social movement of great consequence. This is not to suggest or imply that a majority of the population outside Halifax, Chester and Lunenburg was under the direct influence of the revival. The evidence does not support such an assertion and merely piling up references to large audiences does not permit any specific totals to be estimated. The points to be made are simply that the revival extended to most of the out-settlements, that nearly every outsettlement possessed some type of pro-revivalist party, that such a widespread public stir in the colony was unprecedented. The Great Awakening in Nova Scotia was, therefore, the first large-scale social movement to affect the outsettlements as a whole.

The next important question to be examined is whether the revival attracted people from particular social groups, whether, in other words, it was a class-based social phenomenon. Again, the evidence is very fragmentary but it does permit some conclusions to be drawn. There was certainly nothing in Alline's preaching to indicate that he was directing his message towards specific groups or classes who felt disenchanted with the existing social system. Indeed, all the references towards society in his sermons and writings reveal an unquestioning belief in the existing stratification of society. There is no hint that he wished to change the social system or that he urged his followers to do so. This did not mean that Alline or his supporters manifested deference towards those above them in the social structure. Alline insisted that "earthly dignity" or a "conspicuous Station in the world will not make a man of God" and in the evangelical scheme a person who was not a man of God was not worthy of respect. But this distaste for the unregenerate was confined to a moral or spiritual animus. As far as normal social activity was concerned Alline advised people that he "would only observe the Command of God and encourage them in the Place and Station for which God hath designed them."[28]

In a sermon preached at Liverpool in November 1782 Alline elaborated on the changes he felt that the revival ought to effect in society. At the outset, he informed his audience that he intended to make "an application" of his chosen text and to ensure that everyone understood how the sermon applied to them, he would "singularise my hearers as in their degrees and several stations of life." As he proceeded with his discourse Alline emphasized the important role to be played in forwarding the revival by the principal men of the town. The "leading men of the Town in Civil affairs" were the "Counsellors" of the people and it was their duty to "be as pillars in his [God's] House and as nursing Fathers to his people." Alline considered such men, being in controlling positions in the social structure, as key figures to be enlisted in his support if the revival was to have general success in the community. Again, Alline was not deferential. He informed the leading men that because their influence was great they could easily undermine the moral values of the town when "your ways are perverse and your examples ungodly." It was "a shocking sight," continued Alline, "to see the capital men of the Earth who ought to be a Terror to evil doers

. . . sitting in the seats of the scornful and joining with the ungodly, wallowing in vice and debauchery and walking in luxurious paths." Alline hastened to add that the leaders of the community at Liverpool displayed no such scorn for godly ways but reiterated that it was his duty to impress upon them that they must walk in godly ways and "be the happy instruments of such benefit to immortal souls." Even if it created difficulties in their public life these men must promote the religious welfare of the people.[29]

Alline was quite blunt in insisting that he must condemn and criticize ungodly men, no matter how important their positions in society. But it was also no less clear that absolute moral condemnation did not necessarily imply criticism of the social system controlled by such men. Alline felt under an obligation to condemn what he conceived to be sinful practices, but he would still "treat you [capital men] with all that respect that is due your station and would be far from giving any wilful offence."[30] In his sermons there are no signs that Alline believed himself to be, or was looked upon by his hearers as being, a social leveller.

For Liverpool and Yarmouth there is some evidence to confirm the view that the revival was not based on particular economic groups within the outsettlements. In Liverpool one of the known supporters of the revival was Simeon Perkins who was the leading inhabitant of the town. He was elected as county representative to the Legislative Assembly in 1765, 1770 and 1785. In 1764 he was appointed Justice of the Peace and Justice of the Inferior Court of Common Pleas and from 1772 on was Lieutenant-Colonel of the Militia of Queen's County. During the 1770s the Halifax authorities always regarded Perkins as the most influential figure in Liverpool and invariably turned to him for assistance in the local administration of policies.[31] Perkins' prominent social and political position was based on his entrepreneurial activities, which extended to the West Indies and made him one of the most prosperous members of the community. When Alline, during his November visit, publicly acknowledged the part played by "the capital men" of Liverpool in forwarding the revival he was not bestowing empty praise. In other towns, such as Windsor, prominent public figures had actively campaigned against Alline, who was not reluctant to reprimand them for opposing the work of God.[32] But in Liverpool it was obvious to Alline and the people that leading citizens such as Perkins were favourably disposed towards the revival.

In Yarmouth John Crawley was a key figure in encouraging the popularity of Alline. "Esquire Crawley," as he was called, had moved to Yarmouth from Marblehead in 1762.[33] During the 1760s his farm stock consisted of fourteen cattle and three hogs which, along with six cleared acres, made his property one of the most substantial in the town. The only other inhabitant to outstrip Crawley in stock ownership was James Robbins who possessed twenty-one cattle, twenty-two sheep and five hogs and who later became a deacon in the Congregational church.[34] As early as September 1761 Crawley had been appointed a Justice of the Peace and a member of the committee for dividing town lands by the Council of Nova Scotia. In 1772 he was elected as member of the Legislative Assembly for Yarmouth township.[35] Like Perkins in Liverpool, Crawley in Yarmouth was regarded by the Halifax authorities as a mainstay of local government.

When Alline came to Yarmouth these two prominent men, John Crawley and James Robbins, became supporters of the revival. Both remained in Scott's church but Robbins "frequently attended Mr. Alline's Preaching" in February 1782 and, although he never became a member of the core group or an active sympathizer of the revival, he was regarded by others as favourably disposed toward Alline. Although he did not actively encourage the revival he refused to criticize its effects and thus

> the Party who favoured Mr. Alline, both those of the Church, and those who were not of the Church, interpreted the Conduct of Deacon Robbins as favouring their Cause and they did not fail confidently and repeatedly to proclaim it abroad.

John Crawley's work on behalf of the revival was more positive as he took a leading part in the attack on Scott, condemning the minister in no uncertain terms for not assisting Alline in promoting "a Revival of Religion."[36]

The adherence of Perkins, Crawley and Robbins to the revival suggests that at least in Yarmouth and Liverpool the religious commotion was not an overt manifestation of lower-group resentment of the prevailing social system. Some social distaste for Alline and the revival was voiced but usually by ministers who resented the success achieved by an uneducated and unordained preacher amongst their own people. Scott, for example, described Alline disparagingly as a man of "no liberal Education and but ordinary school Learning" and on one occasion asserted that Alline has never been acquainted with "the Restraints of Decency and Good Manners." But Scott found it impossible to continue with this line of argument, for he himself could lay no claim to a liberal education or a genteel upbringing. Even when he was searching desperately for ammunition against Alline he saw no point in trying to make social distinction an issue. He could accuse Alline of bad manners but he made no effort to bring in Alline's social origins. Like most of the inhabitants of the outsettlements, Alline was a small farmer and in most of the Yankee townships the question of the class basis of the revival support was irrelevant. As Scott realized, all his people, both those who sympathized with the revival and those who opposed were "of small Ability as to temporal substance" and "a considerable part of them are poor People."[37]

There was, however, one area in Nova Scotia where the revival did seem to contain certain social implications. William Ellis, the S.P.G. missionary at Windsor, was convinced that the revival in the Minas Basin townships was "a piece of that levelling principle which pervades the whole continent."[38] Ellis made this remark in September 1776 just as the revival was gaining popularity in the townships west of Windsor. That there was a persistent tendency by some to regard the revival as socially subversive was revealed in April 1781 when Alline first entered Windsor to preach. In contrast to Liverpool, Alline discovered "the great men of the place [Windsor] very much opposing."[39] So acute was the fear that the revival was a manifestation of social revolution that the authorities in Windsor were prepared to take active steps to ship Alline out of the colony. According to Alline, he "was threatened by some of the leading men of the government to be silenced, and put on board a man of war."[40] The authorities, apparently, were prepared to use the press gang to rid themselves of a leader they considered to be dangerous.

There was a certain pattern to the socio-economic response to

Alline. The closer the revival was to Halifax the more possibility there was of "principal" people regarding it as socially subversive and the more likelihood that such men would prefer to identify with more socially respectable churches where these were available. The greater the distance from Halifax, the less possibility there was of the revival working itself out along these social lines. Neither was this pattern confined, as at first sight appears to be the case, to the predominantly Yankee settlements out of the Halifax orbit. The English Methodist farmers in Cumberland, including some of their prominent citizens came out in support of the revival.[41] Thus, as a general rule, the fringe towns of the colony, from the Cobequid townships through Cumberland to Maugerville over to Yarmouth and down the coast to Liverpool exhibited few signs of social cleavage following the pro- and anti-revivalist lines of division. The heartland townships round the Minas Basin, on the other hand, contained a few people who were prepared to view the revival in the terms posed by William Ellis and by those who had adopted the values and perceptions of official Halifax. Yankee religious fanaticism in the outsettlements was something the anglophile "sober and conscientious"[42] elite, whether in Halifax or in the tiny satellite of Windsor, was determined to attack and to destroy.

The revival itself, under Alline's leadership, did not generate social conflicts in most of the outsettlements.[43] Only in Halifax did some of the social tensions triggered by the revival actually manifest themselves in what may be regarded as class friction. But in the colony's capital the inarticulate members of the lower rungs of society were the ones who vociferously opposed the revival and openly persecuted its few supporters.[44] If the fundamental thrust of the revival had been one based upon a class appeal, one might have expected that in Halifax, which during the war years had experienced considerable class conflict, the urban mobs would have embraced the revivalists and not attacked them.

After 1783, as the religious enthusiasm in the outsettlements began to be channelled into institutional forms and Baptists, Methodists and New Light churches spread throughout the colony to compete with Presbyterian and Anglican churches for allegiance, religious affiliation probably became an important factor in group distinction within Nova Scotia society. But this process was only beginning in 1783. The Great Awakening may therefore be viewed as the "activating and unifying force in hitherto politically passive and segregated groups" and the "important precursor of political awakening and a forerunner of political organization."[45] In common with other such movements in previously unintegrated societies, the revival in Nova Scotia led to a new sense of unity or at least a new intensity of interaction.

8

A Charismatic
Leader

By 1783 Alline had achieved an unprecedented popularity in nearly all of the outsettlements and was the undisputed leader of a major religious revival. He established himself as a charismatic leader and as such he became an agent for initiating a change in some of the cultural values of Nova Scotia society. As has been pointed out in a recent study, charisma is an elusive concept and the model of social change induced by a charismatic leader very much open to shallow and slip-shod application.[1] It is, therefore, essential to lay out in careful detail the reasons for describing Alline as a charismatic leader and to indicate precisely his impact on the value system of the Nova Scotia Yankees, to show why his ideas were accepted as being relevant to the predicament in which they found themselves during the revolutionary crisis.

The importance of charismatic leadership was first defined by Max Weber, who formulated a theory to explain the nature and consequences of such a phenomenon.[2] Weber's model has since been effectively criticized and is no longer accepted as the best description of the role of charismatic leaders in producing social and cultural change. Nevertheless, the Weber model does present a useful starting point and, as has recently been pointed out, some of the more modern applications of the concept of charismatic leadership often ignore the rigour of Weber's definition. In particular some scholars have failed to accept a central element in Weber's model, namely, that the charismatic leader must be recognized by his followers as possessing divine or supernatural sanction. It is not sufficient to describe as charismatic a leader with unusual organizational ability to attract and maintain a large following among a people.[3] A leader may possess extraordinary power but unless he is specifically regarded as an instrument of some supernatural agency he cannot easily be referred to as a charismatic leader.

Weber defined charisma as the term applied "to a certain quality of an individual personality by virtue of which he is set apart from ordinary men and treated as endowed with supernatural, superhuman or at least specifically exceptional powers of qualities . . . which . . . are regarded as of divine origin or as exemplary, and on the basis of these the individual concerned is treated as a leader." In this formulation the vital addition was introduced that such a leader's "charismatic mission breaks down if his mission is not recognized by those to whom he feels he has been sent."[4] As Claude Ake has emphasized, in criticizing some loose applications of charisma to modern political leaders in Africa, "what alone gives validity to charisma is that followers perceive their leader as possessing it."[5] If Alline is to be defined as a charismatic leader it must be shown, not only that he regarded himself as divinely sanctioned, but that his followers also accepted that his powers were of divine origin and on this basis treated him as a leader.

Alline himself assiduously cultivated the notion that he had been sent by God and he was utterly convinced that he was merely God's instrument. Such beliefs stemmed from his conversion experience which Alline believed had been produced directly by God Himself. Shortly after the conversion, "the Lord discovered to me my labour in the ministry and call to preach the gospel." From April 1775 until his death in February 1784, Alline was committed to a belief that God had chosen him specially to convey God's "glad tidings of salvation and messages of peace to my fellow men."[6] So certain was Alline of this divinely appointed mission that in his sermons he often identified himself with God or Christ, emphasizing the immediacy of his contacts with the Supreme Being who controlled the universe. Alline believed that he, like Christ, was acting as an intermediary between God and man. "The Lord," Alline frequently informed his hearers "is come with a stammering tongue, to seek you."[7]

The easy manner in which Alline transferred the attributes of Christ onto himself was shown clearly in one of his sermons, *A Gospel Call to Sinners.* Alline opened the sermon by reminding the people what Christ had accomplished in his efforts to forward the redemption of man, yet within one sentence Alline managed to slide into the identification of himself with the Messiah:

> How hath he Christ stooped from his realms of immortal glory, waded thro' the disorders of your miserable world in the agonies of death and the miseries of hell, with his vesture dipped in blood, travelling from kingdom to kingdom, from town to town, from village to village, for to seek his bretheren; knocking from heart to heart with bleeding hands, and an aching heart, till his head is filled with the dew, and his locks with the drops of the night! yea, and this night (tho' with a stammering tongue) is come to your doors . . .[8]

From the "realms of immortal glory" Alline, at the very beginning of his discourse, had quickly shifted attention to the important role he was fulfilling, on God's behalf, in the villages of Nova Scotia. Many of Alline's sermons were preached during his travels or immediately after he had arrived at a settlement, whether early in the morning or late at night, and the technique adopted in this sermon was obviously designed to make full propaganda use of the physical fatigue he must have often shown. Alline probably took care not to wipe the drops of the night from his locks when he preached such sermons.[9]

The credibility of Alline's self-proclaimed role as God's messenger was strengthened by the complete transformation that had taken place in his outward character. During his adolescent years in Falmouth he had been regarded as "one of the most careless, merry and light-hearted youths in the whole town." The change from youthful profligacy to devout piety and missionary zeal therefore appeared all the more dramatic to the neighbouring townspeople, particularly those in the same age group as Alline. On his first visit to Horton in November 1776, Alline sensed the impact of this complete transformation on the minds of the people. For the inhabitants of Horton, "it was a strange thing to see a young man, who had often been there a-frolicking now preaching the everlasting gospel. The People seemed to have hearing ears and it left a solemn sense on some youths." Initially, as Alline first began to preach in Falmouth people came out of curiosity but as he grew more confident in his ability to exhort in public or, as he put it, as "God gave me great boldness and freedom of speech in declaring the wonders of redeeming love," of these people who had come "to watch for my halting" many "seemed to be struck with awe."[10]

During the next seven years Alline devoted all of his interest and energies to his preaching, forsaking his parents, neighbours and friends in his determination to proselytize throughout Nova Scotia. In this manner Alline was able to pose as a paragon of the virtuous and excellent revivalist minister. A contrast with the predicament in which Scott, an avowed revivalist, found himself reveals how such exclusive devotion to preaching enabled Alline to be much nearer "a type of the Messiah" than his most persistent critic. Alline refused on several occasions to be pressured by followers in various parts of the colony to settle as a permanent minister in any one locality. Unlike Scott, therefore, Alline never had to cope with the multitude of disputes that frequently occurred between minister and people over salary, housing, land and the other secular aspects of the pastoral relationship. By avoiding being established in any particular church Alline also succeeded in stepping aside from doctrinal disputes about such issues as infant baptism or conflicts over the organization and the source of authority within the church. On several occasions Alline arrived during his itinerancies at places where such arguments were taking place among followers of the revival and was in a position to point out how trivial or "nonessential" such matters were when compared with the great task of advancing the redemptive process.[11]

Alline's extensive travels, in themselves, heightened the

image of the uniqueness of the Falmouth preacher. Travelling between the townships was an unusual practice yet Alline, for seven years, did nothing else. In nearly every township or settlement he visited, his first arrival was greeted with public surprise and subsequent visits with eager expectation. In areas such as the Minas Basin townships where the revival was well established Alline often sent word ahead to give notice of his expected time of arrival and his audience would be ready waiting to hear the word of God. Even if no formal notice was sent ahead rumours often reached a town about Alline's proximity or his successful preaching in neighbouring settlements. On several occasions Alline's followers sent out messengers to the evangelist to escort him to their area and when he left settlements he was often accompanied by a knot of followers who sometimes travelled with him till his next preaching halt. Apart from his visits to the fishing settlements between Yarmouth and Liverpool and to the St. John River Valley, Alline moved about the colony on horseback, which was another factor to add to his conspicuousness. As the revival persisted in Nova Scotia after 1783 travelling preachers became common but Alline's itinerancies were at the time a source of admiration because of their novelty. In March 1782 on his return from Liverpool, Alline was received by his followers in Horton, Falmouth and Windsor "as almost one from the dead: for the report that I died on Cape Sable shore was so believed, that two of my Christian brothers went through to see how it was and get my writings."[12] In both the localities in which he was travelling and in those areas he had left behind his extraordinary activities were a source of widespread interest and concern.

Alline also possessed considerable skill in public debates, particularly with ministers, and this provided another reason for his growing prestige. When his opponent was a pronounced anti-revivalist, Alline had little difficulty in defending his theological position. In February 1779 on one of his many visits to Annapolis, he was "sent for by one Mr. F [isher] a minister of the Church of England." In the open discussion that ensued Alline "was enabled (when he . . . discovered his [Fisher's] Arian principles) before all the society to hold out the truth of the gospel . . . and charged him with destroying souls."[13] In debates with Anglican and Presbyterian ministers Alline was well able to detect and isolate anti-evangelical doctrines, label them with ease and expose the "emptiness" of such a form of Christianity.[14]

It is apparent from various confrontations that Alline did not outmanoeuvre his opponents because he possessed any extensive knowledge of theology.[15] His success did not depend so much on the content of his arguments as on the manner in which he presented them. He gave the appearance of familiarity with these perennial theological puzzles because he was supremely confident that God had revealed all the "real" solutions to him. Argue as they might, ministers could not shake Alline's faith in his own infallibility and the Falmouth preacher happily proceeded to chop logic with men who knew much more about the issues than he had garnered from his limited eclectic reading. Moreover, Alline's lack of sophistication enabled him to put the issues in a simple manner which the ordinary people could more readily understand. This supreme confidence in his own logic and understanding infuriated many of Alline's ministerial opponents and in the final analysis his most effective tactic was to goad his better informed opponents into losing their tempers. In this way the pastors lost much of their public credibility as men of God.

Some of Alline's success in dealing with ministers was clearly accidental — he did not plan every move. But there are some indications that he was aware of the importance of the image a religious leader had to create in public and that he possessed considerable skill in building his up to the detriment of others. In May 1777, for example, when in Cornwallis, he was confronted by "a number of men, enemies to the work, with the minister with them." In face of this interruption to his meeting Alline deliberately restrained himself: "I was obliged to keep my tongue as with a bridle, lest I should speak unadvisedly with my lips." While he held back his own words the commotion continued as "the contest rose so high" and the disputes raged with "much warmth." Eventually Alline struck upon a solution that shifted the initiative back to him. In his words, he took

> out my watch, and held it on my knee, telling them, that I did not come here to wrangle with them, but to defend the truth, which I could not do for want of an opportunity, therefore, I

> intended to allow each one five minutes to discourse, and I
> would have my five minutes, and if any man exceeded five
> minutes I would leave the room immediately.

According to Alline this ultimatum surprised his opponents. But
the stratagem worked. Alline was at his best when he could range
freely without having to reply to detailed theological points
and thus the five-minute system enabled him to deliver an effective public exhortation. Having brought the situation under his
control, Alline "was enabled to the conviction of the spectators
to hold up light and support the truth."[16]

In his dealings with ministerial critics, Alline tended not to
overstate his effectiveness as a public debater or to inflate the
importance of such successes. Indeed, it was his insistence that
such debates were a waste of time that strengthened the impression of his altruism and buttressed the image he was trying to
sustain of a preacher concerned entirely with promoting the
work of God. By constantly under-emphasizing such verbal victories, Alline distinguished his position even more decisively
from that of the clerics who attacked him.[17] He was able to pose
as a persecuted servant of God who had little time or inclination
to indulge in petty theological squabbles.

An important characteristic of charismatic leaders is that their
prestige is increased if the established authorities attempt to
persecute them. If the persecution is not too effective and the
leader remains at large then he is able to pose as a martyr for the
cause of the common people. His authority, therefore, as an
exceptional leader is consolidated.[18] In Nova Scotia in the 1770s
and early 1780s there was no political movement organized to
overthrow the British authorities and the revival led by Alline
was not a cloak for a political uprising. But it was a phenomenon
largely confined to the outsettlements with their "dissenting"
population, and was successful because it fulfilled certain functions in a period of crisis. Thus when the Anglican authorities in
Halifax, or their agents, appeared to threaten Alline, this increased his prestige as a leader of the people.

Alline mentions several incidents in which he was threatened
by the authorities and these usually occurred the closer he came
to Halifax. Windsor, with its military garrison and contacts with

the capital, was a dangerous place for the evangelical preacher and it was in this town that he was threatened with impressment into the British navy.[19] Such quasi-official threats, however, were rarely used against Alline and too much cannot be argued from such desultory occurrences. Nevertheless such threats, no matter how rare, did serve the purpose of highlighting Alline's conspicuousness. Indeed if they had been more frequently issued and carried out they would have destroyed Alline, since once removed from the colony he would have been in no position to undermine opponents and consolidate his leadership.

The very act of travelling in the colony during these years appeared highly dangerous. This was particularly the case in all the coastal areas as American privateers scoured the coasts. Scott, for example, had great difficulty in making the voyage from Yarmouth to Halifax.[20] On at least two occasions Alline was actually taken by privateers although he was subsequently freed. Moreover, Alline travelled throughout the year and on many occasions he had to struggle through severe snowstorms and bitter cold when no-one else was voluntarily out of doors. The fact that Alline was in poor physical condition probably served to increase admiration for his persistence and reverence for his mission.[21]

Whenever Alline was directly abused by drunkards or ruffians he usually attempted to turn the situation to his own advantage. In July 1781, for instance, while in Windsor, "an officer of emigrants" accosted Alline "with his reproaches in the public street, saying, he wanted that I should convert him." This officer then began to denounce Alline "in a most shocking manner, and threatened my life." Alline proceeded to the house where he was going to preach and as he was sermonizing two more "ruffians went by the house . . . with drawn swords," swearing they would kill him. Later that afternoon, at about five o'clock, another "officer" came to the house and after being "turned . . . out of doors" began to curse and "laboured to break open the door with a stick of wood." Soon a crowd of about twenty people had gathered round the door, "many of them swearing they would be the death of me."[22] Some of Alline's friends in the house advised him at this stage to take flight by the back door.

He refused to leave, reminding his followers that he "was

called there by God." He then "told the people of the house that I would go out among them and see if I could not pacify them" and in spite of warnings of his friends not to go out since he would almost certainly be killed, Alline stepped outside to confront the mob. According to Alline,

> They came around me, and one of them, lifting up his hand, swore he would be revenged on me. I caught him by the fore-part of his coat with meekness, and begged him to consider what he was about and to act like a rational man. He cursed and swore for a while but did not strike me. By this time the officer and others in the company became so calm as to talk with me. I was then told by the officer that he would advise me as a friend to desist from preaching, or leave the place. I told him I should obey God before man. He then told me my life would be taken away in a few days if I continued preach-ing. I told him I would preach when I was called; neither was I about to leave the place, until duty called me from it: and after some more conversation with him and others of the com-pany, I bid him good night, and went in the house.[23]

This incident explains a great deal about Alline. It indicated how he utilized every situation to sustain the image that he was called by God, that he possessed the courage and meekness shown by Christ and the disciples when they had been confronted by enemies. It also demonstrated that Alline had remarkable pow-ers of persuasion. He was in a potentially explosive situation with a mob that had no interest in his avowed mission yet he was able to calm them and eventually talk to them. Alline possessed a powerful personality and a gift for dealing with people, even those overtly hostile. These Windsor ruffians had not the slight-est concern for Alline's views yet he managed to transform them into a docile audience.

This Windsor affair also may reveal that Alline's success was not entirely accidental. He studied the situation and decided to take a calculated risk. As the hostile crowd first began to gather round the house Alline noted that they "did not come in the house although there was not one that resisted them." He reas-oned from this that in spite of "all their rage, there was an awe upon them." Alline's decision then to go into the midst of the mob was partly dictated by his cool assessment of the discrepancy between the mob's avowed intentions and its actual desire to carry out these intentions. While his followers panicked he, quite calmly, deduced that if the mob were intent on doing him actual bodily harm they would not have hesitated to force an entry. Relying on his interpretation of the situation Alline was able to amaze his frightened followers by posing as the meek and courageous servant of God. He gave himself no credit — it was simply that "God was stronger than a strong man armed."[24] By skilful exploitation of such incidents Alline established himself as an extraordinary religious leader who was under God's special protection.

In his sermons Alline adopted a number of devices that added to the effectiveness of his preaching and created an impression of his uniqueness. One of his most striking methods of gaining and holding the attention of his hearers was to burst into verse or song, either in private houses or in fields or on the open highway.[25] In the Cobequid townships Alline received a cold reception until a group of people hearing him raise his voice in song "knocked at the door and asked me if they might come in and hear me sing." In August 1781, while in Cumberland County, Alline toured the area, often preaching three times in one day. In the evening, after one of these hectic days, he "set out with about twenty people on horseback" and, noted Alline, "We sung as we were riding, then prayed and sung again." Several days later, in Sackville, Alline led his followers as they sang and prayed in the street.[26] Such public singing was, according to Scott, a new feature of religious life in Nova Scotia and Alline used this innovative technique extensively and with apparent success.

In Yarmouth, after Alline had induced his first conversions among the local populace, an "Occasion of such Joy and Triumph," the revival supporters made a public demonstration of solidarity. When the meeting was over

> a considerable Number of Men, Women and children, with Mr. Alline, went from the Major's to Mr. Roger's, in the Evening, singing aloud as they passed along the Highway; and were singing when they arrived at Mr. Roger's House where

Mr. Alline had another Meeting, attended with a Throng of
People who were, many of them, greatly affected.[27]

The dramatic effect of this singing procession was heightened
since the three-mile journey was undertaken just as evening
was falling and the latter part of the trip was completed in darkness as they passed through the most thickly settled part of the
town. On their way these supporters of Alline, "as they passed
the Houses, which stand so near together in this Way as in any
Part of the Society, . . . exercised themselves by singing aloud as
they went along in the Night, in the Highway." According to
Scott "this was the first Time that ever divine Worship was
performed in such a Manner in the Streets of Yarmouth." Scott
was extremely critical at Alline's introduction of "new Customes
or Modes of divine Worship" but such tactics were effective in
publicizing the revival and extending its influence beyond the
core group of supporters. As Scott realized, Alline was attempting to display to as many people as possible that "he had gained
the Victory . . . and therefore he would shout the Triumph along
our streets."[28]

In spite of the fact that Alline wrote several pieces for the
press, including a long and involved treatise, in the typical
evangelical hope that after his death they might be useful, he
delivered his sermons extemporaneously. He preached without
any notes and wrote few sermons. So convinced was he that he
understood "almost every essential truth of the gospel" that the
lack of notes did not prevent his speaking on any topic demanded
by the people. In January 1781, for instance, near Annapolis, an
"enemy to the cause . . . desired Alline to preach from a particular text he would give me." Alline informed him that he "would
not preach to satisfy curiosity, because I must labour for the
good of society; but I would as willingly preach from one text
as from another, if the Lord gave it to me." The questioner
agreed that this was a reasonable condition and mentioned the
text. As the man recited the passage the words of the text, in
Alline's words, "seemed immediately to be given to me, and
took hold of my mind. I told him I would preach from it for it
was a blessed text."[29] Speaking without notes enabled Alline to
represent his preaching as inspired by God. If "the Lord gave it
to me," he could preach well. In contrast to Alline, Scott had,

since his ordination, written many of his sermons and during the
height of the revival in Yarmouth had even announced in advance the detailed contents of a particular sermon he wished to
preach on external order. Such formal Christianity seemed to
some Yarmouth people to be the essence of anti-revivalism.[30]
Alline on the other hand, by preaching incessantly, with no formal aids, seemed an outstanding example of an evangelist whose
preaching was the result of direct divine inspiration.

There are some indications that Alline was successful throughout the war years in sustaining this image of a supernaturally
endowed charismatic leader. Certainly in the extant sermons, a
small proportion of the hundreds he preached, it seems clear that
wherever he went in the colony he invariably identified himself
as an extraordinary revival preacher undertaking a special task
for God. His preaching was powerful and successful and by
using several impressive innovative tactics he was able to rouse
people's interest throughout the colony. There seems no doubt
that he was an exceptionally able public debater and that he was
adept at undermining the public credit of those ministers who
were determined to halt his "triumphal" progress.

In response, those people who were supporters of or sympathizers with the revival accepted that Alline was the instrument
of a supernatural power. In January 1778 Alline was surrounded
by the "strong bulls of Bashan" as he experienced a profound
feeling of doubt as to the validity of his conversion and as to the
certainty that God had called him to preach the gospel. But as
Alline typically put it, "my God remembered me" and convinced
him that he had been specially chosen "for the work I had before
me which God knew, though I did not." When he returned to
Falmouth in February his friends, on hearing Alline's account
of "how God had appeared" for him, "rejoiced that God had
brought" him through it. His supporters had no doubt of God's
purpose in all this — God, they believed, was preparing Alline
"to fit . . . [him] . . . for a great work."[31]

In Yarmouth Daniel Crocker, John Crawley, Amos Hilton
and Cornelius Rogers, the four prominent pro-revivalists in
Scott's church, were certain that Alline had been entrusted with
his preaching mission by God. With "much Zeal and Confidence," they asserted, "that he [Alline] was sent of God." Both
the core supporters and the active sympathizers in the Cape

Sable fishing settlement believed that Alline's preaching had been sanctioned by God. These people in Yarmouth,

> throng his [Alline's] Meetings Night and Day — vindicate his Authority as one sent of God, and evidently approved of by God — they are attentive to his Counsels, and punctual in executing them without Delay — they become warm Advocates for a Number of his Doctrines, and quietly put up with them all — they rely upon his Judgement in pronouncing his Adherents converted — they approve of his examples, Walk and Behaviour, as coming nearer to that of the Apostles than any they had seen before.[32]

It is difficult to be precise about the number of people in Nova Scotia who believed Alline had been sent to them by God. When dealing with religious movements it is easy to deduce from mere weight of internal references to divine intervention that a particular leader believed he was divinely inspired and was regarded as such by his followers. Such assertions about a revival and its leader may appear to be truisms of a trivial nature. However, certain features of the situation in Nova Scotia from 1776 to 1783 make this particular case of a charismatic religious leader more than a trivial epi-phenomenon within the social system as a whole. Prior to Alline's emergence into public view no leader had ever appeared who gained public attention throughout most of the outsettlements. The movement he led, by 1783, had no parallels whatsoever since the Yankees had moved into the colony in the early 1760s. Alline believed himself to be a messenger and instrument of God and he cultivated this image at every opportune moment. His extensive popularity is certain and it seems reasonable to conclude that he achieved this because people accepted his message and the role he cast for himself. In the case of Yarmouth, at any rate, it was not even necessary to believe all of Alline's theories in order to accept his divinely appointed mission. Even those who agreed with only "a Number of his Doctrines" or "harmonised with some of Mr. Alline's Doctrines" were convinced that he had been sent of God.[33] Alline adhered to no one particular church and had had little education and he could not, therefore, be identified as a leader who derived his authority from traditional institutions or traditional ideas. He and his followers insisted his authority was derived from his direct communication with the Almighty. His ascendancy in the outsettlements of Nova Scotia was unprecedented and was not soon emulated. After 1783 a whole host of evangelical preachers traversed the colony but none attained the unique exclusiveness in leadership established by Alline. He was not merely the leader of a small religious sect submerged within a larger social system, but rather, the charismatic leader of the most significant social movement that had even taken place, up to that time, in Nova Scotia.

9

The Message

During the revolutionary war most people in the outsettlements, particularly those of New England origin, were confused by events and uncertain regarding where their loyalties should be directed. For years they had been dependent on New England, looking to their former colonies for ministers to staff their churches, for financial aid in time of need and for advice on how to organize their religious affairs. Alline enabled the Nova Scotia Yankees to overcome their culturally dependent status. In his sermons he propagated the view that the New England colonies were wrong to indulge in war and urged the Yankees to see that they had performed a salutary act by staying out of such illegal and sinful undertakings. He made such views all the more acceptable by inveighing equally against the corruptness and sinfulness of Britain. By adopting such a posture Alline was able to resolve much of the confusion that had gripped the Yankee mind since the outbreak of the Revolution, for it now appeared that these people in Nova Scotia had a unique identity and a special role to fulfill in a troubled world.

Alline's message appeared relevant to the people of the outsettlements of Nova Scotia because he claimed, among other things, to understand the confused times. This factor is of critical importance in explaining Alline's charismatic appeal. As one scholar has recently emphasized, "it is only when the message

conveyed by a charismatic to social groups is relevant and meaningful within the social context that authority emerges."[1] Alline
accepted the reality of the pressures brought to bear on the
people by the war and explained the significance of the colony's
predicament. Where other people, such as Scott, could only discover gloomy uncertainty in the contemporary world, Alline was
sure that he could decipher a pattern to events — a pattern
which, if accepted, placed the people of the outsettlements in the
forefront of human history. The character of Alline's message
was confident, assertive, optimistic and in their critical situation
the people turned to him for reassurance, explanations and
solutions.

Alline's view of the world in which he lived was determined
in its overall structure by his belief that the world was in its
latter ages and heading rapidly towards the Judgement Day.
Such a belief was common enough among American evangelicals
in the middle of the eighteenth century.[2] But Alline imbued it
with a special urgency and derived from it various conclusions
about the contemporary state of man that distinguished his
interpretation of the course of history from evangelicals in, for
instance, New England. The basic premise from which Alline
worked was that this was a "dying world" which had not long to
survive before God would demand a final reckoning as he wound
up the redemptive process.[3] Various signs convinced Alline of
the imminence of the end of the world. In marked contrast to
the spiritual harmony that had, according to Alline, existed in
paradise, he emphasized that "now there is Separations, Wars
and disorders."[4] The war and its attendant disorders were de-
picted as dire signs of the impending day of doom. "This
world," he reiterated on another occasion, is "under so many
disorders, darkness and sin."[5] Alline accepted that wars and
disorder in human affairs were not unique to this period, for
these evils had existed since the first appearance of man on earth,
but he believed that these convulsions in the world had reached
an unprecedented, and, therefore, significant, intensity. In his
long treatise written sometime before 1782 Alline made no
effort to conceal his fear of an imminent judgement. "O the
Midnight Darkness," he exclaimed, "that now overspreads the
World . . . the Day of Grace is over and the World undone."[6]

Alline did not construct an eschatological theory to fill out and elaborate his bare assertions about the declining stage of world history. He made no attempt to utilize the passages in Revelation that specifically dealt with these issues and which formed the basis of most sectarian and evangelical speculations about the proximity and nature of the final judgement. Indeed his references to this famous book are meagre both in his sermons and other writings. At first sight such omissions appear odd for an emotional evangelical thinker but Alline's position becomes more understandable when it is realized that he had no formal training or guidance in biblical interpretation. He felt much more at home in "opening" and "applying" the "types" in the Old and New Testament narratives of the prophets and disciples than he did in elucidating the complicated passages in the key chapters of Revelation. For the most part Alline ignored the Book of Revelation, usually the most essential and fertile source of apocalyptic theory.

In spite of this peculiar gap in Alline's thinking he was saying essentially the same thing as other contemporary evangelical theorists — that the latter days were coming to an end and that the signs of the times must be studied to discern hints of the approaching millennium.[7] But a belief which Alline held with unique intensity, and which distinguished his position from most New England evangelicals, particularly during the revolutionary war, was that all wars without exception were symptoms of man's sinfulness. The source of this belief is not certain although it seems possible that, as in the definitions of the nature and necessity of the new birth, he used some of William Law's ideas. Law was a convinced pacifist. In the treatise published in Philadelphia in 1766 Law and Anthony Benezet stated the case for the uselessness of all human battles. "War is repugnant," insisted the authors, "in its cause, in itself, and in its consequences; it can be but comparatively irrepugnant, with respect to the degrees of its own evil." To these religious philosophers war was fundamentally anti-Christian since it seemed the ultimate in earthly sinfulness. Since the Fall, man had existed with an animal body and animal passions and sin occurred when the soul or heart of man failed to control these human or animal desires. To commit acts of war was simply to give completely free reign to passions quite alien to God; "war like all other evils . . . is . . . the gratification of those very appetites and passions from which it derives its birth." War was "a sad consequence of the Fall of man and his subsequent apostasy, when he was abandoned to the fury of his own lusts and passions as the natural effect of breaking loose from the Divine Government, the fundamental law of which is LOVE." All wars were, in short, the result of sin and only compounded the unregeneracy of those who indulged in them. War was part of the "disorders of nature and of life" and, most important, distracted man's attention from the only goal of existence, his own redemption.[8]

Whether Alline developed his abhorrence of war from a reading of this Philadelphia publication of Law and Benezet cannot be known for certain but what is beyond question is that his reasoning, in the sermons and tracts he wrote for Nova Scotians, followed precisely the same logic as did Law and Benezet. According to Alline, man was sinful and living in a disordered world; when he indulged in wars he was letting loose even more sin and this in turn produced even greater disorders in the world.[9] In the years after 1776 such reasoning had a particular relevance. Where most evangelical preachers in New England came to regard the war as justified and necessary to protect the Christian cause in the New World, the most influential evangelist in Nova Scotia insisted that no good could possibly come out of the war and that both Britain and New England were wrong to indulge in such massive displays of sinfulness. The war, asserted Alline, had produced a more chaotic world and this "lamentable disorder" was simply the result of sin.[10]

It was not unusual to regard the times as sinful but Alline's conclusion that New England was partly responsible for such alarming signs among men became the basis upon which the Nova Scotia Yankees discerned a radically different pattern in current events than that perceived by their former friends and relatives in New England. To the American Patriots it was axiomatic that "an unjust war had been commenced against" the colonies. The view that the war had begun as an unprovoked attack by Britain on the colonists enabled the Americans to justify their resort to arms.[11] Sylvanus Conant, of the First Church in Middleborough, took pains, in 1777, to explain that "as for the bloody contest between Great Britain and these United States, it is our opinion, upon careful enquiry, that we are not aggressors in the quarrel."[12] Such reasoning permitted Americans to overcome any feelings of guilt they may have had about going to war against another Protestant power. The British administration appeared "to have many of the features and most of the temper and character of the image of the beast which the apostle represents."[13] As the war with Britain commenced a whole body of evangelical literature emerged to persuade the American people that they were fighting in a just and noble cause.[14]

Like many New England preachers, Alline was certain that the war between Britain and America, two Protestant nations, was a sign that Christian history had reached a critical juncture. The apparent increase of sinfulness, particularly in the new states, duly lamented in American jeremiads, was also taken by Alline as an important sign that matters were coming to a head as wickedness and disorder, long familiar in Europe, had now established a footing in the New World.[15]

Alline's sense of world crisis was even deeper and starker than that suggested by Conant and other Americans who speculated on such matters for, unlike them, Alline had no belief in the continuing validity of New England's or America's salutary role. As he surveyed the situation from Nova Scotia, among a people subjected indiscriminately to both British and American pressure, Alline became convinced that New England, as well as Britain, had been led into evil ways. While New England jeremiads used public lack of virtue to urge the people to reform and redouble their efforts in the cause of Protestant progress and American liberty, Alline accepted the apparent increased wickedness in New England at its face value and concluded that New England had in fact lost all public virtue. New England, insisted Alline, must share responsibility for the present extensive sinfulness and disorder in the world, because of her sins.[16] Alline held similar basic beliefs about the nature of the world and the course of Protestant history as did the religious spokesmen of American mission but while they argued that Britain had sunk into corruption, Alline extended evangelical logic to its limit and concluded that New England too had degenerated. It was on such a reading of the times that Alline based his gloomy warning that "the Midnight Darkness . . . now overspreads the World."[17]

In an effort to persuade Nova Scotians of the great crisis facing the Christian world as a result of the war and other disorders of the period, Alline urged the people to take note of the omens. With a tremendous explosion of feeling, and yet with characteristically tight control of his delivery, Alline recited the signs of the times:

> The Great Men and Kings of the Earth grown proud and lofty; all Manner of Debauchery spreading like a Flood; Stage Plays, Balls and Masquerades received as an Indulgence from Heaven; . . . while the Heralds of the Gospel, if any hold forth the Truth, are accounted as mad men and Enthusiasts; Libraries glutted with Tragedies, Comedies, Romances, Novels and other profane histories . . .; cursing, swearing and blaspheming, not only the language of Troops and Mariners but also of Towns and Countries and received as expressions of Politeness; Drunkenness a Common Amusement accounted neither Sin or Disgrace; the Rich exalted, the Poor trampled in the Dust; Signs and Wonders seen in the Earth, Air and Water; Wars and Rumours of War, yea, the most inhuman Wars spreading Desolation thro' the world like a Flood; and these most alarming Prodigies . . . as little regarded as the Shadows of Evening.[18]

The people in the outsettlements of Nova Scotia were, according to Alline, surrounded by a world crisis of unparalleled severity.

One of the most striking aspects of this passage is the manner in which Alline blended local manifestations of the crisis into external or general dire signs. In the outsettlements there were no "Stage Plays, Balls and Masquerades" nor any "Libraries glutted with Tragedies, Comedies, Romances, Novels and other profane histories." But there were "Troops and Mariners," present as a result of the war, who did "curse" and "blaspheme."[19] Rumours of American and French attacks on the colony were also common from 1776 onwards.[20] According to

Jonathan Scott, who had been forced to spend some time in Liverpool in March and April 1776, there was in the town "little else but profaneness and carnal discourse."[21] These local signs were boldly linked by Alline to the wickedness of "Great Men and Kings" and thus the plausibility of the general crisis was increased by the undisputable indicators in the townships themselves.

The passage makes a clear and unambivalent condemnation of the revolutionary war and its effects. To the Americans, even those who, like Sam Adams, found the increasing profaneness alarming, the war was an ennobling struggle for political and religious liberty. In marked contrast to this American attitude, Alline urged the people of the outsettlements of Nova Scotia to view the struggle as a "most inhuman war" that was "spreading Desolation through the world." In the beginning of the war, as the Maugerville and Barrington incidents had demonstrated, the New England settlers in Nova Scotia had taken ambivalent attitudes towards American privateersmen, fearing for their property yet at the same time remaining on speaking terms with their former countrymen. With his definition of the war as inhuman Alline insisted on an unequivocal rejection of any friendship with the emissaries of a wicked nation. He himself was only captured twice by privateers, once simply because he possessed a horse and the Americans feared he might ride to a British garrison and reveal their presence, and on both occasions was treated extremely well. Yet Alline would not condone any friendship whatsoever towards those American ships for, he asserted, "those that wish well to their souls must flee from privateers as they would from the jaws of hell."[22] Nova Scotia must remain uncontaminated by the contagion of sin and war. The description of the world crisis, of which the war was one of the most alarming symptoms, was not, therefore, a mere rhetorical flourish on the part of Alline. From it he was able to guide the people on how to respond to the crisis as it affected them.

Alline, in this passage and at various other times, was attempting to explain to the Nova Scotia Yankees the source of their feelings of insecurity, uncertainty and confusion. Once the situation was understood then appropriate responses could be made. As Alline put it to the people of Liverpool in November 1782, what he was trying to accomplish was to "lend you an omnicient eye or discover to your view a map of the disordered world."[23] The catalogue of the alarming signs of the times was not, therefore, designed to induce pessimism or deepen the feelings of hopelessness among the people but was intended to explain the world. Alline became a prophet who understood the times when most other local, influential leaders found little coherence. He produced "a map of the world" on which he would indicate Nova Scotia's predicament and define her role amidst general disorder.

Singling out New England as well as Britain as being responsible for the war enabled Alline to undermine the dominant cultural influence exercised by New England over the Nova Scotia Yankees prior to 1776, especially in the area of religious affairs. It was a particularly delicate operation to condemn the various New England churches from which many of the Yankees had moved and to which they had often turned for help. Alline was careful to keep his criticisms as general as possible, making an oblique rather than a direct attack on traditional Yankee practices. He argued that the disorders of the world proved that the "love of man for God waxes cold." Not only was a "great part of the world overspread with heathenish darkness" but even "the Christian corners had sunk into formality, glutted with Anti-Christian errors." Formal, empty religion had taken over and there was an ever increasing tendency for people and churches to become "negligent of the cause of Christ." A typical example of these desertions from God's cause was the acceptance by many churches of the controversial "Half-Way Covenant." In Alline's view, such practices in which "some Churches will receive part of the Way, baptise them and their children . . . and make them promise to do so and so; then set them to own a Covenant called by some a half-way Covenant" put the Christian cause into reverse gear for, like the Roman Catholic church, it was a reliance on the mere "foresaking of vices and Practice of Externals." Alline simply could not accept that these churches that used the Half-Way covenant were genuine in Christ's cause. It was partly a result of such lukewarm adherence to divine law that meant, in these days, that the "Power of Godliness was scarcely to be found on earth."

Alline denied that New England, where the Half-Way covenant was in common use, was displaying the "Power of Godliness."[24]

In sinking into these indifferent ways New England was
merely reflecting a general characteristic of lukewarmness to the
cause that was spreading through Christian nations. All these
people who joined churches "and signed Paper Covenants without one spark of saving Grace . . . [were] . . . feeding only on the
Morals and Externals of Religion." Confined to Papists this
practice was ominous enough but it had, according to Alline, now
become common "among those that are called Protestants." A
church polity employing such devices was "spreading the Bor-
ders of Anti-Christ . . . and altho' they may call themselves the
Churches of Christ, yet they are Enemies to his cause."[25]

That New England could lay claim to a long history of
unique service to God's cause in no way excused a lack of zeal in
the mid-eighteenth century. Where Sylvanus Conant had encouraged the people of New England "in this day of trouble
and affliction . . . to retrospect the behaviour of our pious ances-
tors," Alline warned of the dangers of relying too much on the
former pre-eminence of the Puritan founders. It was a sad fact,
Alline reminded Yankees in Nova Scotia, that many people too
often neglect to "increase much in spiritual Wealth" because
"they imagine that their good old Fathers have dug deep
enough."[26] In such troubled times, the present generations had a
duty to do some digging on their own account.

These adverse references to the lack of zeal and purity
among churches in Christian countries served to explain and
justify the separate churches and meetings that were set up by
the revivalist party in Nova Scotia. In Jonathan Scott's view, the
Congregational church polity of Massachusetts was the best
regulated system of churches that "there now is, or ever was on
Earth."[27] In face of Alline's encouragement to separatist tendencies, Scott counselled loyalty to the Congregational way and
advised adherence to the old ways.[28] But Alline was clever
enough to avoid direct attacks on particular Congregational
churches in Nova Scotia and Scott found it difficult to stigmatize
the Falmouth preacher as being anti-Congregationalist. In
January 1779, for example, Alline had "met the Congregational

Church [of Cornwallis] to consult about methods for my ordination that I might be more useful."[29] And later that year some of Alline's supporters in Cornwallis had written to Scott requesting his assistance, as a Congregational minister, in the ordination of Alline. Alline had succeeded in drawing off over half the Cornwallis church into a separate party. It may have been these people who Alline referred to as the "Congregational Church." At any rate it is clear that at a local level Alline made no attacks on Congregational churches as such. He kept his criticism on a general level which enabled him to concentrate on the apparent degeneracy of Congregationalism in New England and avoid antagonizing local adherents in Nova Scotia. Alline explained to his followers that they might be accused of "forsaking the good old Way, turning away from their ministers, separating from Churches, encouraging separate meetings and the like." But he assured his supporters they were actually striving to realize the pristine ideals of the Congregational way by attempting to set up pure churches of visible saints. It was the opponents of the revival who had "left the good old way by sinking into the Form of Godliness without the power." The followers of Alline were, in contrast, "now returning back to the Liberty of the Gospel, and separating from the Seats of Anti-Christ." As for the proposition that the revivalists, "altho' . . . among legal ministers and Churches . . . ought not to leave them; but remain with them in Hopes to reform them, and do them some good," Alline could find no validity in it. The historical progress of God's cause had always been achieved by a vanguard of purified churches separating from the formalism of established churches. For his part, Alline could not find "either Scripture or Reason for Zion's staying in Babylon,"[30] Separation was justifiable if it was designed to forward God's cause. In times of general indifference to the cause such purifying separations were essential to restore momentum to the redemptive process in which mankind was engaged.

From such reasoning Alline was able to explain to the people the significance of the revival that was taking place throughout their townships. In a world sinking into general disorder their colony was to fulfill an exemplary role. The revival was producing visible saints who were forming purified churches and in the midst of world chaos these people were maintaining a firm centre of order. They would be in the vanguard of God's cause and ensure continued Christian progress. In order to convince followers of the validity of attaching such significance to the revival, Alline had to demonstrate that converts were appearing in large numbers in Nova Scotia and that they were a dramatic example to the outside world that God's cause was being led by his chosen people.

The starting point for such an explanation of the importance of the revival was that an experienced conversion was certain evidence that a sinner had been transformed and had entered the earthly ranks of visible saints. Without this certainty the Nova Scotia converts could not be sure of their suitability or worth to perform an exemplary role in the world. Alline had a stock paragraph which he used to drive home to the people who felt conversion must be accepted as irrefutable evidence of the change from sinner to visible saint. It was impossible, Alline lectured, to be converted yet remain unsure of being in a state of grace,

> For it strikes at the very Nature, design and consequences of the Kingdom of Christ among men; for if there is no knowledge but only a guesswork and all a matter of uncertainty who are the sons of Belial, or whether a man is converted or not, then the Pharisees, the Anti-nomians, Hypocrites and the true Christians are all lumped in one promiscuous crowd.[31]

Those who participated in the revival could be assured that they were the "Children of God." They were withdrawing from the promiscuous crowd in order to preserve the essence of true Christianity.

The change in character produced by conversion was "so great, and so obvious," Alline continued, that the convert could easily distinguish his new status from that of the sinful part of mankind. In reply to the arguments, made by such "revivalists" as Scott, that new birth was necessary but that "a Man may be in a safe State, viz be born again and not know it," Alline asserted that this was merely "a tiresome Road to Hell."[32] To Alline it seemed that these arguments denied the possibility of Christian progress, for if converts were unaware of their new state they could not embark on an active campaign to alert the rest of the world to their danger and arouse sinners from their insensibility.[33] Such arguments for the necessity of pure churches were common in separatist and Baptist circles in New England after 1740. In Nova Scotia, as Alline co-ordinated such reasoning with his general assumption of world degeneracy, the concept of revivified and purified churches emerging to lead the Christian cause took on much more than local significance. Those who did not believe in the necessity of a new order of true Christians in these dark times were advocates "for the Powers of Darkness" and supporters of the Anti-Christ. They had "made God a Liar."[34]

It was constantly impressed upon the "Children of God" in Nova Scotia that they must not retreat from the world of sin. Withdrawal from the "promiscuous crowd" did not entail exclusive attention to the internal well-being of the society of the regenerate. Alline emphasized in his sermons that "example is far more successful than bare precept." It was the duty of the converts to be concerned for the welfare of their fellow men. The revival, in other words, was not to be used as an excuse for avoiding the troubles caused by the war but rather every opportunity was to be utilized to spread the good effects of "the work of Grace."[35] The task facing the followers of the revival was to extend his kingdom. Those "who have known and eaten of the heavenly food from the blessed Redeemer, can neither rest on their external performances, on their past experiences, nor on their expectations of future happiness."[36] Alline defined as mercenary Christians those who regarded their conversions as reason for neglecting the state of the world. The converts who exhibited a "false confidence are confident of heaven and happiness hereafter; but those that have a true confidence are thirsting after heaven and the enjoyment of God while here. . . ."[37] In order to create a "heaven begun on earth" the true Christian must publicize his presence and be active in bringing other sinners into the vanguard of progress.

The followers of the revival were, therefore, to be examples "to those poor blinded Souls, that are incapable of judging between Christ and Anti-Christ." They were, as Alline reminded them in 1782, the "salt of the earth, the light of the world and as CITIES ON HILLS." This was the message that Alline delivered to the revival supporters as he extended his travels throughout Nova Scotia. In the midst of a cruel war the revival was creating in the northern colony a solid basis upon which the Christian cause could once again gain strength and resume its progress. As the visible saints of Nova Scotia fulfilled this special role the world, their charismatic leader assured them, "will take notice."[38] For the revivalist party in Nova Scotia these were years when the world was taking notice of these remarkable events in the northern colony.

This part of Alline's message, that the revival supporters in Nova Scotia had, in the chaotic times of war and disorder, a key role to play in forming the new vanguard of visible saints in this world to take over from a degenerate New England, was primarily directed to the core group of followers. Those who had experienced conversion, or who were under such strong convictions that they expected shortly to enter the ranks of the converted, could regard themselves as leaders of the Protestant cause throughout the world. These "true Followers of Christ," as Alline confidently described them, "were travelling in the Unity of the Spirit and Bonds of Peace" and whenever and wherever they met together, in any of the towns or settlements in Nova Scotia, they formed "Christ's visible Kingdom."[39] Within these groups of core supporters a tremendous sense of unity and purpose was generated. They believed that their souls were "cemented together" with "that spirit that binds on Earth and . . . in Heaven." They "enjoyed much happiness" as they "engaged in the Redeemer's cause."[40] In the one place in the world, as they believed, which was producing true converts the visible saint of Nova Scotia expected to "invite his fellow Men" and "spread Redeeming Love from Pole to Pole."[41] Accepting this description of the state of the world and of their unique role in maintaining the Christian cause, the core followers of the revival were able to discern a pattern to contemporary events that had previously appeared confusing or meaningless to them. They "rejoiced, as it were, in a new world."[42] Alline had given them a new frame of reference within which they could locate themselves and find meaning and direction.

Alline's message was, however, not designed merely to increase the happiness and solidarity of the core supporters of the revival. His belief that he understood the times led him into a more general explanation of the role that the people of Nova Scotia were to fulfill. Alline pointed out that while the other Protestant nations were indulging in sinful war, Nova Scotia was experiencing a great religious revival. In evangelical terms since revivals were works of God such phenomena were "worthy of . . . serious and careful attention,"[43] to decipher the meaning of a divine intervention at a particular point in time. In the case of Nova Scotia the significance of the revival was clear. God was bestowing a mark of favour on the people of the colony and indicating to them, and to the world, that these were his chosen people who had become the central rock of purity in generally sinful times. Nova Scotia had been chosen to take up the leadership of the Protestant cause.

Alline reviewed the history of the Yankee settlers in Nova Scotia and concluded that their emigration to the northern colony in the early 1760s had been the initial step in a divine plan to create a new base in the world for God's people. As he went from town to town in the colony, Alline urged the people to think of the "miseries you have been extricated from, what dangers you have escaped, what kindness received, what favours enjoyed, and beyond what thousands could have expected, and beyond what thousands have enjoyed." God, in other words, had been good "to you in particular." The clearest proof of this, announced Alline, casting minds back to the northward emigration, was

> Your being called away from the approaching storm that was hanging over your native land, and sheltered here from the calamities of the sweeping deluge.

While those left behind in New England presently suffered "under the disolations [sic]," the Nova Scotia Yankees had "been hedged about with the kind providence of God and screened from the impending storm in this peaceable corner of the earth."[44] The movement to Nova Scotia in the early 1760s, had not, according to this view, been an accidental occurrence. Alline was bringing a new coherence into the Yankee view of their past.

As New Englanders up to the 1760s the Yankee population
of Nova Scotia might have expected to share the fate of their
former colonies for, if the war was a punishment for the sins of
New England, they, who had once shared in these sins, ought to
have received appropriate punishment. The point was put by
Alline in this way:

> how are we screened from the trials of our (once happy)
> Nation in the convulsions of the present day? How have we
> sat in peace while this inhuman war hath spread devastation
> through our neighbouring Towns, and Colonies like a Flood!
> not my dear hearers because of the cleaness of our hands or
> past righteousness: for surely we have not only had our hands
> equally engaged in the sins that have incurred the lamentable
> disorder, but have likewise perpetuated the same crimes.

The crimes Alline referred to were those of sinfulness and
lukewarmness to God's cause. It was these characteristics of
society, believed Alline, that had brought the scourge of war to
New England. As they looked back over the 1760s the Nova
Scotia Yankees could not discover anything radically better in
their colony, for there had been no general reformation prior to
1776. Yet the fact remained that the punishment of war had not
been inflicted directly on the people of the northern colony
although they had "remained unfruitful and incorrigible." Yet,
in time of war, the people were living under "distinguishing
advantages" compared with their former colonies. The reason
for this distinction was quite clear, Alline assured his hearers, for
as the people

> daily expected the impending cloud and to share the bitter cup,
> heaven's indulgent hand . . . interposed and averted the
> blow.[45]

Not only had God called the people out of New England but
he was now shielding his people from blows that were being
delivered against New England.

In interpreting contemporary events in such a way Alline
revealed that he instinctively accepted the same basic beliefs

about the nature of the world that many New England evangelical preachers had shown in their writings on the war.[46] The
thinking of Alline and these men was characterized by the
belief that human history was moulded or directed by an all-
encompassing Providence. All major events, such as wars, were
therefore related in some way to God's overall purpose in the
world. One New England minister argued that "God in his
providence" had been the hidden power that had made the Thirteen Colonies "his glorious instruments, to fulfill scripture
prophecies"; another was convinced that "the merciful influence
of Providence" had breathed "a general spirit of union into, and
through the Thirteen Colonies"; and Alline believed that
"heaven's indulgent hand" had intervened to protect Nova Scotia. Alline and the other evangelicals agreed if the intentions of
God, working through Providence, could be deciphered then the
events of the time could be understood and their significance
explained.

    Although many American evangelicals had no doubt that God
favoured the American cause, they were no less certain that the
war was partly a punishment for past sins and a reminder that a
reformation had to take place before the independent state could
emerge victorious. As Sylvanus Conant explained, "our Heavenly Father, provoked with our numerous and aggravated offences
hath visited us with the sore and terrible judgement of war."[47]

    This feeling, that God was angry with an increasingly wicked
people, was quite common in New England during and after
the war. Further evidence of the extent of such feelings can be
seen in the case of Windham County, Connecticut, a region that
had been deeply influenced by the religious movements that had
swept New England since 1740 and from where some of the
Nova Scotian Yankees had emigrated.[48] In 1780 the ministers of
the county issued a statement in which they confessed that they
were

> deeply affected with a sense of the awful and abounding sins
> that prevail in our land [?] the lamentable declension of re-
> ligion that we behold: the amazing insensibility of the inhabi-
> tants of the land under the most signal displays of the holy
> indignation of God ... for all our iniquities ....

The Windham pastors concluded that, in these days, New Englanders had departed "far . . . from the right ways of the Lord
God." The people had "greatly offended" God.[49]

Three years later, just after the war had ended, the Warren
Baptist Association in Windham County, in a pastoral letter,
offered its view of the times. The letter rejoiced that the long
and very distressing war had finally drawn to a close but noted
that "many are sorrowful and complaining . . . at these times."
Elaborating on the reasons for this sorrow the letter continued:

> the burden of taxes, the great scarcity of cash, with the pressing
> calls for money from every quarter have drawn a terrible
> gloom over many minds; which is greatly increased by a view
> of the untried scene of political existence into which we have
> entered, where none can tell what is before us; and we have
> no such arm of flesh to trust to as formerly. Added to which
> are a great variety of disappointments and losses, with the use
> of corrupt schemes to repair them, and to get more power and
> gain, among all orders of men in the land, which make a
> number think our cause almost desperate.[50]

The war, with the subsequent economic and political dislocation
as the new states attempted to organize their political systems on
a radically new basis, had caused many of the Warren Baptists
to believe that society, as they had known it prior to 1776, was
disintegrating and getting out of control. To many, it was difficult to adjust easily and quickly to the effects of the war and the
Revolution.

But to New Englanders, and Americans in general, such
doubts and fears about the changes that were taking place in the
economic and political life of the new nation were only one part
of the picture. Although, at the beginning of the war, many
had felt "oppressed and distressed on every side" they did not
despair, for as Americans they believed that "the providence of
God is favourable to our cause and our country." A belief in the
rightness of their cause, the struggle of the colonies for their
political liberty, was what gave coherence and meaning to the
war. The continuing progress of Protestantism was bound up
with the cause of American liberty.[51] In September 1783 the
Baptists of the Warren Association, after noting the almost des-

perate state of their cause, returned to the accomplishments achieved by the new states. "The American Revolution," according to the pastoral letter, "is wholly built upon the doctrine that all men are born with an equal right to what Providence gives them, and that all righteous government is founded on compact or covenant, which is equally binding upon the officers and members of each community."[52] Even the Baptist elements in New England, concerned as they were over the apparent increase in disorder, gave unequivocal loyalty to the new nation. They had been affected by the transformation that had taken place in the American colonies in the decade or so before 1776 and had come to identify independence from Britain as a further step forward in Protestant history. However despondent American jeremiads sounded, their fundamental faith in the necessity and righteousness of the war of independence remained.

If Alline had remained in New England he would probably have viewed the revolutionary war in these terms. But, along with several thousand other New Englanders, he had moved to Nova Scotia in the early 1760s. In the northern colony the traditional values of these Yankees were not pressured by political debate into a revolutionary ideology. The colony was relatively isolated from such change since the Yankees missed that decade of intense public debate. Thus when Alline analysed the effects of the war he came to many of the same conclusions that New England spokesmen such as Conant had arrived at — that the war was a judgement by God, that New England displayed increasing evidences of "backsliding," "lukewarmness" and "degeneracy," and that God had a reason for visiting this war on the American part of the world. But Alline had little knowledge of, and no commitment to, the cause of American liberty which, for New Englanders, gave direction and meaning to the war. Viewed from the outsettlements of Nova Scotia, the signs of the times seemed even more alarming since the war had, apparently, no meaning other than a clear indication of increasing disorder in the world. Alline, like Conant and others in New England, concluded that God's purpose must be operating somewhere in these momentous times of change but his conclusion was quite different from theirs. God was not looking to New England but to Nova Scotia. While utilizing many traditional

New England beliefs Alline began to turn the Yankee mind of Nova Scotia on to a unique track of its own. They were special members of the New England community who had been "called" to Nova Scotia to serve as a saving remnant while New England abrogated her mission to lead the Protestant cause.

These unique favours that had been extended to the Yankees of Nova Scotia since the early 1760s were signs that God had singled them out for a special purpose. The most incontrovertible proof of God's special interest in the colony was the revival that was spreading throughout the land. In evangelical definitions a revival was a supernatural work, granted by God to encourage his people. Such an extraordinary dispensation of God towards these people of Nova Scotia was a convincing sign that he had marked them out for a special task. In normal times a revival was a cause for communal joy and expectancy but when such occurrences were apparently disappearing from the warring Protestant world they became even more significant. Alline drove this point home by emphasizing that

> above all, when they are thus wading thro' the terrible storm, and we have been expecting soon to share the bitter cup, we have been blest with the greatest of all blessings . . . . O the goodness, the unspeakable goodness of God to such a people.[53]

The revival was clear evidence, open to public view in nearly every settlement, of God's goodness to the people of the colony. "What great things," Alline noted in January 1778, "has God done for this desert land."[54]

Such manifestations of divine favour were, however, not to be taken as an excuse for complacency or a turning away from the sinful world that surrounded the colony. For one thing many people in Nova Scotia did not participate in the revival and it was the duty of those in the revivalist camp to expose these recalcitrants as "barren and unfruitful" and to jolt them from their "pernicious courses."[55] Not only must strenuous efforts be made to achieve the complete internal reformation of the colony but the followers of Alline realized that "the whole earth" with "all the inhabitants of it," desperately required the purifying effects of a "Work of Grace" in these times.[56] As the one Christian corner of the world that was being nurtured by God the people were to be prepared to serve as examples to the rest of mankind.

While complacency was to be consciously excluded from the emotions of the revival followers, there was every reason to be happy and confident that they had been chosen by God. In the songs that Alline composed and delivered in public places throughout the colony he frequently dwelt on the beneficial changes God had brought to them. Even in the wilds of Nova Scotia the people could feel secure and happy if they could "enjoy God's presence." While "mortal governments roll" the revivalists sought the "substantial good" and rejoiced in their new-found sense of community. Alline quite freely expressed gratitude to God for intervening to end the misery being experienced by the people. "In the midst of all our grief," wrote Alline, "our God made known his delivering power; His arm appeared for your relief."[57] In a land "where religion was reviving" there was good reason for some degree of public confidence providing this did not lead to pride and negligence in God's cause. During the war, as the revival extended its influence, Alline encouraged his listeners to believe that

> our lines are fallen in pleasant places, and we have a goodly heritage, for we came from the loins of our predecessors to have our trial for salvation when the gospel is in its Meridian and brightness.[58]

In a colony "where the Gospel-Sun is in its Meridian" the inhabitants could feel secure in the belief that God had an "indulgent" eye on them.[59] Alline described these happy effects of the revival to the people of Liverpool,

> Jesus has not only spread the mantle of his love over the lost world in general, but over you in particular: for your villages and Families happly enjoy the droping of the sanctuary and effusions of his holy spirit.[60]

The followers of Alline were assured of "the present sweet enjoyment of God" during the years that the war swirled round the colony.[61] Alline summed up the situation in one of his many powerful phrases. In Nova Scotia, the people were "invironed [*sic*] with the arms of omnipotence."[62]

But Alline would hardly have appeared credible if he had ignored the troubles inflicted on the people by the war, whether by privateers, or impressment or enforced militia duty. Part of the attractiveness of his message lay in his ability to incorporate local problems into his discourses and explain that suffering through such trials could be an ennobling experience. Alline advised that "although you may be called through some trying scenes and sometimes afflicted with losses, crosses and disappointments of this temporal world, yet it is all but to advance your spiritual welfare . . . for all things will surely terminate in your good." Moreover, although the outsettlements of Nova Scotia felt they were experiencing hard times, Alline emphasized that compared with the world outside the colony they were living in peace and order. Apart from Nova Scotia, the whole world, even the neighbouring colonies, rang with "peals of death" and exhibited "marks of misery and tokens of despair" produced by "temporal calamities." Alline continued his description of the multitude of signs indicating the miserable state of affairs outside the colony:

> thousands soliciting the cold hand of charity, pinched with hunger, thirst and nakedness; thousands chained to the galley and others to the chain of slavery, to endure all the hardship and misery that cruelty can inflict; thousands in prisons, dungeons and places of confinement already destined to the gallows, gibbet, rack or torture.

In view of this apparently catastrophic loss of control in the world Alline asked his hearers how "can your hearts . . . but dissolve with love or break forth with thanksgiving to God for the unspeakable privileges that you are indulged with?"[63] Alline always returned to this theme. The outside world was in total collapse, Nova Scotia alone was an exception where the people had been set apart by God and endowed with unspeakable privileges.

This was the dramatic message Alline delivered to the outsettlements of Nova Scotia during the seven years of the revolutionary war. These people were to perform an exemplary and salutary role in a world sinking into general disorder. The effects of the war had confused the Nova Scotia Yankees and had introduced a pervasive feeling of insecurity into their lives. Yet Alline, by drawing an even gloomier picture of life in New England and elsewhere, reassured people on his travels throughout the colony that Nova Scotia had actually been spared from the rampant disorder of the times. Surely then, the inhabitants had "cause to love much, for you are blest in basket and in store in time and eternity." The war, along with other indicators, was a sign that God was "about to expell that hellish darkness from the poor blinded world, and has already delivered most of his people in this part of the vinyard."[64] The Nova Scotia Yankees were "a people highly favoured of God."

In concentrating on this theme of Nova Scotia's distinctiveness from the other colonies and the rest of the world, Alline was directing his rhetoric far beyond the inner groups of core supporters. He was providing the Yankee population as a whole with a new and plausible version of their twenty-year sojourn in the northern colony. He not only attempted to explain the contemporary times to the people but sought to extract a pattern running through events since the early 1760s. Even those among the inhabitants "that know not God" were "vastly indulged" and enjoyed mercies from the Divine Being "that many cannot." Thus Alline emphasized that even those in the colony who were completely outside the revivalist camp, who did not even attend his meetings, were still part of "a people highly favoured of God indeed."[65] This belief in the superior worth of Nova Scotians, no matter how unattached to the revival, arose naturally out of Alline's reading of the times and his version of Yankee history. The people, although at the time they had been unaware of any divine intervention, had been gathered out of a declining New England by God who had planted them in Nova Scotia to carry on his cause when the collapse, precipitated by the war, finally arrived. In relation to the political rhetoric of the American Patriots the Yankees of Nova Scotia could make little use of their past, having been settled on crown land at some crown expense and having taken little interest in the struggle for American liberty. But now Alline had deciphered for them a pattern and meaning in their history. Their whole movement northward was now pregnant with significance and out of what had merely been a fortuituous communal experience of emigration there emerged a myth that their migration had been ordained by God to fulfill his cosmic purposes.

The validity of Alline's account of Yankee history did not rest only on his apparent understanding of contemporary events. His version seemed all the more plausible because it incorporated elements that had been present in the Yankee mind since the 1760s. In his Hingham sermon of 1768, Ebenezer Gay had articulated the belief that the Yankee settlement of Nova Scotia was "the doing of the Lord." The following year the Baptists of Horton, Nova Scotia, explained to their Boston correspondent that one of their aims in "this infant colony" was to ensure "that the Everlasting Gospel of the Lord Jesus Christ may flourish in this Remote part, where Anti Christ once Reigned." In the same year the Congregational adherents in Cornwallis expressed their conviction that "God in his providence . . . after previously Removing our Enemies, planted us in this Infant Colony." Such views of the task facing the Yankee settlers of Nova Scotia, expressed in the late 1760s, revealed a strain within the Yankee mind that was disposed to regard their northward emigration as specifically serving God's purposes. At the time such views did not dominate the Yankee perception of their emigration but merely represented a seam of belief open to further explanation and utilization. Alline, perhaps himself subject to such illusions, exploited these partially articulated notions to the full. When he recast the history of the Yankees, interpreting their emigration as a mission on God's behalf, he brought into clear focus these hitherto dimly perceived self-perceptions.

Under the pressure of the war and its various side effects, many of the Yankees of Nova Scotia, as they listened to Alline, began to see a clear view of the world and Nova Scotia's place in it. Alline clarified, expanded and consolidated notions that had long been present, correlated them with his analysis of the times, and presented a comprehensive version of the new identity of the Nova Scotia Yankees. In a similar way to the American colonists who, as the political pressure from Britain persisted, began to see a new view of America's place in the world, so in Nova Scotia Alline, although in much narrower, more parochial and exclusively religious terms, constructed a new world view for the Yankees. He was providing them with something which, in the political and legal terms of revolutionary ideology, they did not possess — a usable past.

With what few materials were available Alline recalled the history of the settlers and constructed a coherent pattern for them to believe in, and which gave some meaning to their predicament during the war. To both the Americans and the British the Yankees of Nova Scotia appeared an unimportant collectivity scattered through the unconnected townships of the colony. But Alline helped to drive out feelings of inferiority and helplessness. "God," declared Alline, "will not reject you because you are poor and miserable."[66] Their charismatic leader made the people of the outsettlements feel that they were participating in the important task, specially given them by God, of forwarding his earthly kingdom at a time of "backsliding" and "degeneracy":

> Wherever you find the Spirit of Christ, altho' among the most poor, and despised People on earth: believe there is more done in the cause of Christ there, than in the greatest Corporations with the most strictest Discipline of the highest Orders of Men . . . if they are possessed of the least Degree of the Spirit of the meek and lovely Jesus count them as the excellent of all the Earth, a People on whom God has set his everlasting Love, guards, and esteems, as the Apple of his Eye.[67]

This, in the final analysis, was the essence of the message Alline delivered, again and again, for seven years. Although they were a poor and despised people, God had given them a mission to save the world. He had been looking to these people to perform this task long before the war broke out and the revival, occurring at the same time, was evidence and confirmation that the terms of the mission were being at least partially fulfilled. The Yankees could now consider themselves as "the excellent of all the Earth." The world was "a stage of snares" and, during the revolutionary war, it seemed the Yankees of Nova Scotia, alone among all mankind, had avoided these pitfalls, unlike New England, and were carrying the standard of the Protestant cause.[68]

The Yankees responded to this religious ideology much more spontaneously, and in far larger numbers, than they had to the revolutionary ideology in 1775 and 1776. The evangelical religious values popularized by Alline were, compared with the political rhetoric of the American Revolution, reassuringly familiar to them. Lagging several years behind the American Patriots in terms of political understanding they could not easily commit themselves to the revolutionary war against Britain. But they could understand the ideology of the revival because this was merely an exploitation and elaboration of values they had held throughout the pre-revolutionary decade. The Nova Scotia Yankees did not participate in the American Revolution but by means of the religious movement led by Alline they experienced a revolution of their own. During the revival they demonstrated that they could function independently as a society with distinct attitudes, values and goals. At the very moment they revealed their New England background, by appropriating New England's traditional "sense of mission," they had declared their independence of New England.

10

A New Sense
of Identity

Rather than being merely an outburst of religious emotionalism, the Great Awakening of Nova Scotia provided the means and the occasion for a complete reorientation in the value system of many Nova Scotia Yankees. The leader of the revival, who articulated and popularized the new religious values, reflected this change in outlook in a dramatic fashion. In March 1775, after experiencing his conversion, Alline felt he "must proceed to New England and endeavour . . . to get learning there." He regarded New England, without question, as the source of Yankee religious values. In the wilderness of Nova Scotia the Yankees looked for cultural aid to the populous New England colonies with their well-organized churches and long traditions of piety.

Over eight years later, Alline's views had completely changed. The success of the revival in Nova Scotia had convinced him that the northern colony was no longer inferior to New England. In August 1783, although in the last stages of consumption, Alline "was determined to go to New England." This time, however, he was not going as a diffident convert from the northern wilds; he intended, instead, to "proclaim my Master's name" in corrupt New England by carrying the word of God to a people desperately in need of proper religious instruction.

Alline had "preached almost all over this country [Nova Scotia]" and had witnessed the tremendous growth of the revival.[1] It was now God's time for him to articulate into existence a similar religious movement in the land of his birth. Nova Scotia was no longer conceived to be a passive receiver of New England values as had been the case throughout the pre-revolutionary period. Rather, the northern Yankees, in a remarkable transference of roles, were now seen to be in a position to transmit their superior values to New England.

Nowhere is the evidence indicating the profound value change brought about by the revival more clear than in Maugerville. This case is all the more revealing since the St. John River township had in 1776 been one of the most pro-American areas in the colony. Led by their minister, Seth Noble, and a revolutionary committee that had been dominated by church members, the settlement had indicated its willingness to "submit" to Massachusetts. Noble had fled the town in 1777 but in 1784 he once again, from Brewer in Maine, contacted the people who had formerly followed his lead. He wrote to the Congregational Church inviting the inhabitants to move from the St. John River Valley, then being inundated with Loyalists, and return to the new states. On November 10, 1784, the members of the Congregational Church replied. They declined Noble's offer and set out their reasons for doing so:

> are we to throw away the fruits of many years of painful industry and leave . . . the place where God in his providence had smiled upon us both in our spiritual and temporal affairs and, destitute of support, cast ourselves into a place where the necessaries of life are hardly to be obtained, unless we could find a place where vice and immorality did not thrive, or at least where vital piety did flourish more than here.[2]

The Maugerville settlers had sound economic reasons for remaining in the British colony. For over twenty years they had painfully built up a viable local economy and they saw no point in abandoning their farms for a doubtful future in a poor area of the United States. These economic considerations were basic forces that moulded the living patterns of the people but, as soon as they began to rationalize their preference for remaining in Maugerville, they turned to religious considerations. Whether any inducement could have tempted them to return to New England is open to question. What is clear, however, is that these Yankees informed Noble that the only circumstances that would cause them to move would be if the new area was more pious than Maugerville. They were convinced that "vital piety" flourished in their area more than it did in northern New England and they advanced this as an important reason for remaining in the British colony.

Some people in Maugerville were even able to reinterpret the history of their township in an effort to erase all memories of the "transgressions" of 1776. When Alline first visited the town in the summer of 1779 he was informed that there had been a separation within the church "on account of the greatest part holding the minister to be an unconverted man who afterwards went away."[3] The implication in such a statement was that Seth Noble had left Maugerville because he had been regarded by a large part of his congregation as an unregenerate minister. But there is no doubt that Noble fled because he had been a ringleader in organizing pro-American activities in the region and because he was quite unprepared to submit to the British authorities. Yet, only two years later, at least some of the local populace were describing the departure of Noble in religious terms. It is impossible to establish how widespread this revision of recent history was in Maugerville. But it is a revealing example of how possible it was to view the past in the terms put forward by Alline. Instead of being a settlement that had indulged in an abortive attempt at revolution, to some people at any rate, Maugerville had driven out an unconverted minister and had thereby ensured that "vital piety" would flourish. The effect of the revival at this juncture in the settlement's history was summed up by Mary Bradley, as she looked back later in life to the years of the Revolution and the revival. She described how

> the discoveries I had at that time are out of my power to write. I can only compare them to nothing more suitable than the unfolding of past, present and future events — religious and political.[4]

As Alline presented his answers to perplexing contemporary problems, people in Maugerville began to move beyond their

uncertainty and confusion. Adoption of the values of the revival, after several years of disruption in the local community,
provided a new feeling of stability and sense of purpose. Belief
in their religious purity and moral superiority came to encompass a view that the Yankees had acted rightly, and had chosen
to do so, in spurning the political Revolution that the Americans
had indulged in. Viewing events within the framework of the
revivalist ideology, with its single-meaning interpretation of
history, the Yankees saw "past, present and future events," both
religious and political, with a reassuring clarity and simplicity.

It must be emphasized, however, that the Yankees did not
regard New England with the same degree of hostility and
bitterness shown by some of the Loyalists in Nova Scotia. Their
experiences in the northern colony during the war had been
difficult and confusing. At the hands of the privateers, they had
suffered some degree of intimidation from Americans. But they
had not been driven from their homes or seen Tory sympathizers being persecuted by Patriot mobs and they could, therefore, retain at least some affection for their friends and relatives
in New England. The characteristic attitude of these pre-
Loyalist elements in Nova Scotia in the post-1783 period was a
feeling of superiority rather than one of hostility. This emerges
clearly in the case of Joseph Dimock, a Baptist minister of Chester, Nova Scotia, who visited New England in 1796. Dimock's
father had been among the first Yankee settlers in Nova Scotia,
moving from Mansfield, Connecticut, to Newport in the early
1760s. Joseph experienced a conversion in 1785 and eventually
became a leading preacher of the revival and minister of one of
the many Baptist churches which were established by Alline's
followers. The Dimock family still had relatives in Mansfield
and in 1796 Joseph set out for a visit which was to last almost
two years. During this prolonged stay in New England the
Nova Scotian Baptist travelled extensively and showed no reluctance to preach wherever he found himself. Although some
people in New England protested against Dimock, on the
grounds that he came "from that detestable place called Nova
Scotia where we sent the refugees" and accused him of being an
agent of the Loyalists attempting "to make division through
the country," he still was not disposed to take a hostile attitude
towards the New England states.[5]

In summing up his final impressions, Dimock contrasted New England with Nova Scotia:

> I find the same God here as there, the same religion but still I find none that seem to have the life of God so pure in the soul as in Nova Scotia. Much of the life and the power of religion here seem to withdraw and forms are constituted in the room thereof.

While New England, in Dimock's view, could not equal Nova Scotia's purity, the Baptist minister was prepared to concede that New England exhibited more piety than other parts of the United States. While in Boston, he wrote that "although the hand of God is too little regarded among them in general, there are but few places in the States that the Christians stand so clear in the Doctrines of the gospel . . . ." Dimock, unlike some Loyalists, had no paranoiac view of the United States as a whole but was able to make distinctions about various areas in the new nation. The New England strain in his family background was strong enough to induce him to believe that New England was still better in moral worth than the more southern states. But having come under the influence of the revival in Nova Scotia he believed strongly that Nova Scotia was far superior to New England. Such assertions about Nova Scotia's pre-eminence in the North American world could not have appeared in the late 1760s and early 1770s. Only after the revival ideology had enabled the Nova Scotia Yankees to reinterpret their history in a way that distinguished them from New Englanders could such a self-image have emerged. New England believed in the same God as Nova Scotia; but in the northern colony many of the people maintained that they were much closer to that God and that they had achieved a degree of the purity that New England had apparently discarded. The new religious ideology, first constructed by Alline in the midst of the revolutionary war, permeated Dimock's view of New England and of the United States. Dimock, quite happy to spend two years in New England, was still very close to his relatives, and even married one of them, but the Baptist minister was utterly convinced that Nova Scotians had taken over from New Englanders the exemplary role of God's "pure" people.[6]

It must be made clear that this growing sense of identity among those influenced by the revival did not create social harmony in Nova Scotia. Indeed, the disputes arising among the pro- and anti-revivalists caused many divisions throughout the townships. Surveying the Nova Scotia scene from Yarmouth, Scott was of the opinion that the revival had broken up society by promoting rival religious parties and encouraging the establishment of separate meetings. Although Scott, and other church leaders whose positions were undermined by the revival, tended to exaggerate the disruptive effects of Alline and his party, there is every indication that the religious movement did produce intense group conflicts. Alline himself was well aware of the public debate caused by the revival and concluded, typically, that such an opposition from the unregenerate was natural at a time when an important religious awakening was taking place.

Scott, and the other opponents of the revival, however, ignored the fact that religious dissension had been common in many of the townships long before Alline established a following throughout the colony. In Yarmouth itself, apart from the years between 1772 and 1776, there had never been anything approaching unanimity in the religious affairs of the townspeople. These critics were inaccurate in their implication that the revival was destroying a tradition of unity among the Yankees. What the Great Awakening did was to divide the Yankees into two parties on a colony-wide basis. Instead of religious disputes revolving exclusively around local issues, the effects of the revival became the focal point of debate in all the places visited by Alline.

When Henry Alline first went beyond his home area between Falmouth and Cornwallis to preach the gospel, he discovered that he was travelling "in a strange land."[7] Prior to the revival there had been little communication between the various isolated Nova Scotia settlements. Yet, by 1783, Alline had visited and re-visited virtually every locality and had helped to break down the barriers of parochialism. He and the revival were things that all areas could hold in common. Alline's followers and admirers from every corner of the colony were drawn together by the force of his personality, by a shared ideology, and by a similar emotional response to revival stimuli.

In reacting to Alline's success, the opponents of the revival, wherever they lived, felt compelled to organize themselves and to communicate with each other, either to offer consolation after one of Alline's many victories or to plan methods to undermine the revival. For example, the news of Alline's victory over Scott, in the remote fishing settlement of Yarmouth, "was quickly spread through the Land...which struck Consternation, Perplexity and Disappointment among sober thinking People in different and distant Parts of the Land."[8] These anti-revivalists, a vocal minority, then contacted Scott, their unofficial leader, to inform him of the progress of Alline in their areas and to consult with him on how to prevent the revival from making further progress. Although Alline's opponents may have abhorred his emotion-charged ideology, they nevertheless could not escape from the pervasive influence of the revival. They were forced, therefore, under extreme pressure, to reaffirm their belief in religious values of some kind. And they did so by insisting that they, rather than the revivalists, were the exponents of the true Christian faith.[9]

By reacting in a positive or a negative manner to Alline Yankee Nova Scotia, while sharply divided on the question of the proper norms of religious behaviour, was nevertheless becoming integrated around certain ultimate beliefs. In the process of arguing with each other, Alline's majority and Scott's small group of supporters, for the first time since their emigration, were constructing reference groups on a colony-wide basis and thereby stretching and tightening the social and cultural bonds among the scattered settlements. In societies which have already achieved some degree of cohesion around certain shared values a religious revival of such intensity as Nova Scotia's Great Awakening might be expected to undermine, if not completely destroy, the integration previously achieved. But in Nova Scotia such a degree of cohesion did not exist in 1776. The outsettlements had not, up to the time of the revival, achieved any significant degree of social integration. Most of the Yankees, it is true, had similar cultural values but a lack of communication and economic difficulties ensured that there was no articulate sense of unity or of community. The Minas Basin townships may have developed certain ties with one another but Maugerville and Yarmouth, or Liverpool and Cumberland, for example, had no shared Nova Scotia experiences until the revival brought them into the same religious movement that was stirring up all the outsettlements. Thus, paradoxically, the revival, apparently dysfunctional because it introduced some element of controversy, acted in the previously unintegrated outsettlements as a factor encouraging more social cohesion.

Alline's followers and those who were generally sympathetic to what he preached, that is probably most of the Yankees, were in the vanguard of this cohesive process. But even his Yankee enemies were unable to escape entirely from its profound consequences. In addition, some non-Yankees, especially the Yorkshire Methodists residing in the Chignecto area of the colony, found themselves during the revival suddenly with a great deal in common with the Yankees. Alline was careful in his preaching and his writing, in spite of his Yankee orientation, not to alienate these sections of the colony. Along with the theme of a providentially directed northward emigration, specifically attractive to the Yankee elements who dominated the outsettlements, Alline's ideology also contained a "sense of place" theme that appealed to other groups in Nova Scotia. According to him, even those Yankees who did not participate in the revival were still part of a highly favoured people simply because, during the war between Britain and America, they were living in Nova Scotia where a work of God was being made manifest. Similarly, the Yorkshire people were also included among "the children of God" because they too were living in this special place.[10]

Once Alline had preached successfully in Cumberland and as many Methodist, Baptist and New Light preachers began to travel through the townships of the colony, the Yankee and Yorkshire people began to participate in the same social movement. For the first time since their separate emigrations to Nova Scotia both groups openly declared their faith in evangelical religious values and joined together to extend the influence of such values. The revival was their first shared experience and from it there emerged an increased feeling of solidarity between hitherto separate social groups. The Great Awakening provided them with a complex of identical interests. Religious values, popularized by the revival, gave both groups common goals to strive for.

What further strengthened this new sense of regional aware-

ness was the prevailing antipathy felt in the various outsettlements against Halifax. For years many of the Yankees had
reacted violently against the petty political squabbling and the
graft and corruption which seemed to characterize the life of the
capital. They were also sullenly suspicious of the small clique
of Halifax merchants and office-holders who manipulated the
legislative and executive functions of government and who attempted to impose their special brand of centralized control over
the various isolated townships. The facts that the revival had
by-passed Halifax and the Haligonians were callously indifferent to Alline, their "Messiah," added to the reservoir of suspicion and antipathy. But it did more than this. When Alline
referred to the inhabitants of Halifax as being "almost as dark
and vile as in Sodom," the Yankees, whether they lived in Liverpool or in the Chignecto, heartily agreed with his analysis. This
was something else they could share in common and which also
added to their collective feeling of superiority. The revival may
be seen as helping to channel a traditional anti-Halifax feeling
into a new Nova Scotia Yankee consciousness.

This new and growing awareness, a direct result of the Great
Awakening, encouraged an emotional commitment to the geographical area in which the Yankees were then living, a place to
which they had been specially brought by the Almighty so that
they could avoid the "desolations" produced by war. In other
words, the revival increased Yankee attachment to their new
colony of Nova Scotia. Over twenty years of farming, fishing
and trading had already committed most of them, in the economic sense, to the colony. And with the revival, the economic
ties were bolstered by emotional and ideological ones.

This did not mean, however, that these former New Englanders suddenly became pro-British partisans. Alline's gospel
did not urge that a subservient posture be adopted towards the
British authorities; what it did do was to prepare the Yankees
for a basic shift in loyalty. By questioning first and then undermining their allegiance to New England, the revival made them
receptive to new commitments. The outsettlements may have retained their basic animus towards and suspicion of Halifax. But,
in spite of this, it is apparent that the revival ideology made
most of the Yankees more content citizens of the British Empire

188 A PEOPLE HIGHLY FAVOURED OF GOD

than they had been in 1775 and 1776. Commitment to Nova Scotia as a place where "vital piety flourished" necessarily embodied a commitment to a British colony.

Many Yankees may have become increasingly loyal during the Revolution but theirs was an unusual brand of loyalism. At the end of the Seven Years' War most American colonists possessed a dual loyalty to Britain as well as to their own colonies in America. In the political heat of the 1760s and early 1770s this duality, in the case of the Patriots, was gradually transformed into a single loyalty to American values and the events of the war consolidated these newly perceived loyalties to the American nation. The Tories in the American colonies, at any rate those who wrote pamphlets, began to diverge from the Patriots as the debate between Britain and the colonies persisted. Whereas the Patriots glorified colonial history and gave all the credit for the rise of the colonies to Americans, the Tory pamphleteers, as the break drew near, played down American contributions to colonial prosperity and expansion and insisted that without British aid the American colonies would never have flourished. Thus the Patriot loyalties were transformed into a new American loyalty where the Tory pamphleteers, in reaction to Patriot emphasis on "American" achievements, tended to assume an exaggerated or distorted loyalty towards Britain. Patriots wrote that the colonies had reached their present position without British help and protection; the Tories responded that without Britain the colonies would have achieved none of the security, prosperity and freedom that they then enjoyed.[11]

In pre-revolutionary Nova Scotia, the Yankees followed neither of these paths. They did not experience the transformation of the Patriots nor did they begin to exaggerate their attachment to Britain as did the Tory pamphleteers. But rather, right up to 1775, they retained their traditional dual loyalty to Britain and the colonies. When the war came, instead of a transformation or a distortion, the Yankees experienced a complete breakdown in loyalties. Their patterns of allegiance became dislocated as their familiar loyalties suddenly became incompatible. In such a predicament the Yankees had to establish new values and attachments. It is common in such situations of cultural and sociopsychological disequilibrium for new ideologies to emerge.

According to a recent study "it is a loss of orientation that most directly gives rise to ideological activity." This disorientation creates a feeling of instability in the society it affects, as in Nova Scotia during the revolutionary war, and "brings with it conceptual confusion as the established images of political order fade into irrelevance or are driven into disrepute." In these fluid circumstances new ideologies "attempt . . . to render otherwise uncomprehensible social situations meaningful, to so construe them as to make it possible to act purposefully within them." It is this attempt that "accounts both for the ideologies' highly figurative nature and for the intensity with which, once accepted, they are held."[12] In Nova Scotia the revival, with its extremely metaphorical ideology, provided meaning and direction in a period of confusion and disorientation.

From a slightly different vantage point and perspective, the Great Awakening of Nova Scotia may also be viewed as an attempt by many inhabitants to appropriate a new sense of identity. Religious enthusiasm in this context, a social movement of profound consequence in the Nova Scotia situation, was symptomatic of a collective identity crisis. Resolution of this crisis came not only when the settlers were absorbed into what they felt was a dynamic fellowship of "true believers" but also when they accepted Alline's analysis of contemporary events and his conviction that their colony was at the very centre of a crucial cosmic struggle.

Some historians, greatly influenced by social psychology, particularly the work of Erik Erikson, have employed this concept of a collective identity crisis. Darrett B. Rutman, for example, in his recent study of American Puritanism makes the case that throughout each individual's life the mind is "forever associating and rationalizing what is in it with what is entering it." In the process, the mind is constantly subjected to "crises" as it attempts to reconcile new data with previously accepted viewpoints. At certain periods, however, the crises become so acute that a major dislocation occurs. One of the most obvious periods of acute crisis takes place when the individual moves through adolescence on his journey from childhood to maturity. Ultimately, such a person must accommodate himself "as a young man to an ever-wider world as he becomes more and more aware of what is outside the family." It is at this stage of adolescent readjustment that people frequently turn to religious values to find some kind of fundamental order to what otherwise appears to be a meaningless existence.[13]

According to Professor Erikson's analysis, the constant need for identity formulation

> employs a process of simultaneous reflection and observation, a process taking place on all levels of mental functioning, by which the individual judges himself in the light of what he perceives to be the way in which others judge him in comparison to themselves . . .;

Then Erikson concludes by arguing

> that we deal with a process "located" in the core of the individual and yet also in the core of his communal culture . . . . We cannot separate personal growth and communal change, nor can we separate . . . the identity crisis of individual life and contemporary crisis in historical development because the two help to define each other and are truly relative to each other.[14]

Not only is an individual subject to such crises, within a community, but a group of individuals may, in fact, share an identical psychic experience. This collective response mirrors the individual reaction described by Erikson. This connection or interrelationship between the individual and the group response is of fundamental importance.

Normally the process of identity formulation proceeds subconsciously or automatically, "a quiet and unspectacular adjustment to self and what lies beyond self." But at certain times, either because of the "inner conditions" in the psychological make-up of the individual or group of individuals, or in "outer circumstances," a sudden and radical change in the traditional social setting, the process of identity formulation can approach "catastrophic proportions." At such times, the individual is "most susceptible to the propaganda of ideological systems which promise a new world-perspective at the price of total and cruel repudiation of an old one."[15]

Within this general context of group behaviour, the Great

Awakening of Nova Scotia appears to provide an excellent example of a major identity crisis. There was a sudden and drastic change in the outer circumstances as the revolutionary war shattered the traditional loyalties and the general social setting of the Yankees. At this time of intense disequilibrium, the Nova Scotia Yankees were especially susceptible to Henry Alline who provided them with a new world-perspective. By accepting the propaganda of Alline's ideological system and by beginning to form new churches in which social solidarity could be strengthened, the revivalist elements in the population, whether at the core or periphery of the movement, found a new stability in their relationship to the world, to New England, and to each other. The revolutionary years thus witnessed the development of a new identity and group solidarity together with a feeling of Yankee superiority and uniqueness. Nova Scotia's Great Awakening, like other similar religious movements, was instrumental in overcoming divisions and in uniting previously isolated or even hostile groups. These people found themselves involved in a dynamic movement expanding "almost as if by contagion, cross-cutting and breaking down local barriers."[16]

The Yankee mind of revolutionary Nova Scotia was profoundly affected by the religious ideology propagated by Henry Alline. This ideology, highly figurative in nature, attempted to provide meaning and coherence to a people confronting a confusing and disturbing situation. The widespread success of the revival and the enthusiasm with which Alline was received by thousands as Nova Scotia's "saviour," indicates the key role he played in enabling many Yankees to act with confidence and a sense of purpose. Alline had helped to transform, in Nova Scotia, traditional New England religious values into an ideological commitment that cut off the Yankees from the new republic.

Nova Scotia's Great Awakening was not therefore simply "a retreat from the grim realities of the world to the safety and pleasantly exciting warmth of the revival meeting,"[17] a mere defensive reflex response to perilous times. Alline, among other things, clearly perceived the new Yankee relationship to New England. As he constantly emphasized in his sermons that New England was no longer deserving either of respect or allegiance, the Yankees began to extricate themselves from the domination of New England which had placed them in such an awkward situation during the revolutionary war. Instead of being a backward off-shoot of New England on the remote, northern fringes of the continent, the Yankees of Nova Scotia could regard themselves as a people with a unique history, a distinct identity and special destiny. The revival undoubtedly did function as a social activity that provided some immediate and local relief from trying circumstances, but the ideology that emerged from the revival made the Great Awakening a social movement with much broader implications. By creating a religious ideology that was specifically geared to conditions in the northern colony, the Great Awakening began to turn the Yankees into Nova Scotians.

Epilogue

Henry Alline died peacefully in the early morning of February 2, 1784, in the home of the Reverend Mr. David McClure, a Congregational minister of Northampton, New Hampshire.[1] McClure had been born in Newport, Rhode Island, in November 1748, only five months after Alline had been brought into the world in the same New England town. Six months before Alline arrived in Northampton, McClure had delivered "an oration . . . at the opening of the Phillips Exeter Academy" in Exeter, New Hampshire, in the course of which he displayed an unbounded confidence in the future of the young United States.[2] From the first signs of war between Britain and the Thirteen Colonies, McClure had felt certain that God was watching over the American cause. As the battle on Lexington Green was being fought McClure, along with some friends, waited anxiously in a house near Cambridge for news of the outcome. When word came that the militia had driven off the British regulars, McClure concluded that "Several Circumstances in Providence appeared to be ordered for our righteous cause." Following the American victory in the revolutionary war McClure was even more convinced that the new nation was, under God's guidance and protection, fulfilling a glorious role in human history.

In the course of his 1783 oration McClure asked his hearers to contemplate the immense possibilities that were open to this continent now that independence had been won. Since the successful struggle of the Thirteen Colonies to be free there could be no doubt that great things were in store for the United States, for the Revolution had disentangled the new nation from the corrupting influence of the Old World. God, declared McClure, had reserved the vast spaces of the American continent for

> the last and most glorious displays of the divine goodness to the children of men . . . Paradise, long lost to the children of Adam, shall be found in this western world; and become the residence of the favourites of Heaven.

McClure pictured a continent filled with populous towns settled by pious and well-educated Americans and separated from each other by verdant pastures and fields of swaying wheat. "The deserts of America," he was certain, would "flourish as the garden of God."[3]

The circumstances of Alline's death, in the home of a New England minister holding such views, could hardly have been more ironic. For over seven years Alline had been impressing upon the Yankees of Nova Scotia that they were "a people highly favoured by God." He had been convinced that New England had deserted its special mission, which Nova Scotia had taken up, yet in the winter months of 1783-84 he lay dying in the bedroom of one of the thousands of New Englanders and Americans who believed that the United States, in the process of civilizing a wilderness continent, would become "the residence of the favourites of heaven." Whereas Alline had been preaching to a scattered people confined to a peninsula stretching back towards Europe, McClure was based in one of the thirteen new states firmly established along the eastern seaboard of America and with thousands of square miles of western wilderness into which they could confidently expand. In America the themes that Alline crudely articulated in Nova Scotia were open to far more subtle and more complex development as the United States became a "Redeemer Nation" and embarked on the task of making the west "the Garden of God," the rediscovered earthly paradise.[4] It was perhaps fortunate for Alline, already "afraid he should lose his reason" as the end approached, that he died before penetrating further into New England. At best, he might have been listened to as one of many evangelical preachers with unusual powers of oratory. But if he had persisted in propagating his view that Nova Scotia had taken over New England's mission on behalf of the Protestant cause he would have been regarded as a madman. Alline's ideas were relevant to the people in the outsettlements of Nova Scotia but to no-one else. Alline had been confident that "the world would take notice" of the great revival in Nova Scotia. Not even northern New England was interested.

Notes

PREFACE (*pp. ix-xiii*)

1. H. Alline, *Two Mites on Some of the Most Important and much Disputed Points of Divinity, Cast into the Treasury for the Welfare of the Poor and Needy* : . . (Halifax, 1781), p. 177.
2. *Boston Weekly News-Letter*, August 24, 1758; T.C. Haliburton, *An Historical and Statistical Account of Nova Scotia*, Vol. I (Halifax, 1829), pp. 220-223; Governor Charles Lawrence's Proclamation, Public Archives of Nova Scotia [P.A.N.S.], Mss. Docs., Vol. 211, pp. 35-37.
3. See especially A.W.H. Eaton, *The History of Kings County* (Salem, 1910), pp. 65-72.
4. E.D. Poole, *Annals of Yarmouth and Barrington in the Revolutionary War* (Yarmouth, N.S., 1899), p. 5.
5. I.F. MacKinnon, *Settlements and Churches in Nova Scotia, 1749-1776* (Montreal, 1930), pp. 24-26; J.S. Martell, "Pre-Loyalist Settlements Around Minas Basin" (unpublished M.A. thesis, Dalhousie University, 1933), pp. 62-180; A.W.H Eaton, "The Settling of Colchester County, Nova Scotia, by New England Puritans and Ulster Scotsmen," Royal Society of Canada *Transactions* (1912), Section II, pp. 221-265; C.B. Fergusson, "Pre-Loyalist Settlements in Nova Scotia," Nova Scotia Historical Society *Collections*, Vol. 37 (1970), pp. 5-22.

INTRODUCTION (*pp. xvii-xxii*)

1. B. Bailyn, ed., *Pamphlets of the American Revolution 1750-1776*, Vol. I, 1750-1765 (Cambridge, Mass., 1965); Bailyn, *The Ideological Origins of the American Revolution* (Cambridge, Mass., 1967) and *The Origins of American Politics* (New York, 1968).

2. A. Heimert, *Religion and the American Mind from the Great Awakening to the Revolution* (Cambridge, Mass., 1966).

3. R.E. Brown, *Middle-Class Democracy and the Revolution in Massachusetts, 1691-1780* (Ithaca, N.Y., 1955).

4. J. Lemisch, "Jack Tar in the Streets: Merchant Seamen in the Politics of Revolutionary America," *William and Mary Quarterly*, 3rd Ser., Vol. XXV (July 1968), pp. 371-408; also Lemisch, "The American Revolution Seen from the Bottom Up," in B.J. Bernstein, ed., *Towards a New Past: Dissenting Essays in American History* (New York, 1967), pp. 3-45.

5. J.B. Brebner, *The Neutral Yankees of Nova Scotia: A Marginal Colony During the Revolutionary Years* (New York, 1937). This book has recently been reprinted with an introduction and historiographical note by W.S. MacNutt, in the Carleton Library, No. 45 (Toronto, 1969). All references to Brebner will be to the new edition.

6. M.W. Armstrong, "Neutrality and Religion in Revolutionary Nova Scotia," *New England Quarterly*, Vol. IX (1946), pp. 50-62; reprinted in G.A. Rawlyk, ed., *Historical Essays on the Atlantic Provinces* (Toronto, 1967), pp. 33-43; M.W. Armstrong, *The Great Awakening in Nova Scotia 1776-1809* (Hartford, Conn., 1948).

7. S.D. Clark, *Movements of Political Protest in Canada 1640-1840* (Toronto, 1959), pp. 69-70. Clark had dealt with the revival in an earlier work, *Church and Sect in Canada* (Toronto, 1948), pp. 1-44. A recent brief study, J.M. Bumsted, *Henry Alline, 1748-1784* (Toronto, 1971), appeared after this volume had gone to press. Bumsted approaches Alline more in terms of his ideas than his social impact.

CHAPTER 1 (*3-23*)

1. John Adams to Hezekiah Niles, 13 February 1818, in C.F. Adams, ed., *The Works of John Adams*, Vol. X (Boston, 1856), pp. 282-283.

2. Bailyn, *Ideological Origins of the American Revolution*, p. 22.

3. J.M. Beck, *The Government of Nova Scotia* (Toronto, 1957), pp. 19-21.

4. L.H. Gipson, *The Triumphant Empire* (New York, 1967), pp. 127-130.

5. *A Letter from a Merchant in Halifax to a Merchant in Boston, Trading to Halifax* (Boston, 1757), pp. 2-3.

6. A Petition of Fernando John Paris on behalf of the Freeholders of Halifax, 27 January 1758, Public Archives of Canada (P.A.C.), Nova Scotia State Papers, Series A., Vol. 62, pp. 2-5.

7. Benjamin Franklin to Isaac Norris, 19 March 1759, in L.W. Labaree, ed., *The Papers of Benjamin Franklin*, Vol. VIII (New Haven, 1965), p. 293.

8. C. Ubbelohde, *The Vice-Admiralty Courts and the American Revolution* (Chapel Hill, N.C., 1960), pp. 5, 52-53.

9. S. Hopkins, *The Rights of the Colonies Examined* (Providence, R.I., 1764), p. 15.

10. [M. Howard Jr.], *A Letter from a Gentleman at Halifax to his Friend in Rhode Island* . . . (Newport, 1765), pp. 5-14.

11. *A Letter to the Author of the Halifax Letter* . . . (Newport, 1765), pp. 5, 8.

12. [M. Howard Jr.] *A Defence of the Letter from a Gentleman at Halifax* . . . (Newport, 1765), p. 10.

13. Benjamin Franklin to Sir Everard Parker, 27 July 1756, in Labaree, ed., *The Papers of Benjamin Franklin*, Vol. VI, pp. 472-473.

14. J. Otis, *Brief Remarks on the Defence of the Halifax Libel on the British American Colonies* (Boston, 1765), pp. 3-15.

15. L.H. Butterfield, ed., *Diary and Autobiography of John Adams: Diary 1755-1770*, Vol. I (Cambridge, Mass., 1961), p. 285.

16. A. Cluny, *The American Traveller. Containing Observations on the present State, Culture and Commerce of the British Colonies in America* . . . (Philadelphia, 1770), p. 41.

17. *An Essay on the Present State of the Province of Nova Scotia with Some Strictures on the Measures pursued by Government from its First Settlement by the English in the Year 1749* (Halifax, 1773 or 1774).

18. Butterfield, ed., *Diary and Autobiography of John Adams*, Vol. III, p. 298.

19. Instructions to Richard Jackson, 22 September 1764, in Labaree, ed., *The Papers of Benjamin Franklin*, Vol. XI, p. 351.

20. Butterfield, ed., *Diary and Autobiography of John Adams*, Vol. I, p. 283.

21. *Ibid.*

22. Memorial of the people of the townships of Horton, Cornwallis, Falmouth and Newport to the Lords of Trade and Plantations. Public Archives of Nova Scotia (P.A.N.S.), Vol. 284, No. 10.

23. Haliburton, *An Historical and Statistical Account of Nova Scotia* (Halifax, 1829), pp. 220-223.

24. Memorial of the people of the townships of Horton, Cornwallis . . . , *op. cit.*

25. Charles Morris to the Nova Scotia Council, 1 June 1760, P.A.N.S., Vol. 211, p. 125.

26. The Humble Address of the Magistrates of Principal Inhabitants of the Township of Horton, P.A.N.S., Vol. 286, No. 27.

27. Charles Lawrence to Lieut. Col. Monckton, 8 August 1755, P.A.C., Monckton Papers, VIII.

28. D.C. Harvey, "The Struggle for the New England Form of Township Government in Nova Scotia," Canadian Historical Association *Report* (1933), p. 18.

29. Council Minutes, 1 August 1761, 15 August 1761, 1 July 1762, P.A.N.S., Vol. 204, pp. 10, 50-55; Vol. 211, p. 210; Memorial of the people of the townships of Horton, Cornwallis . . . , *op. cit.*; Harvey, *op. cit.*, p. 22.

30. Memorial of the Proprietors of the Township of Liverpool, 24 July 1762. P.A.N.S., Vol. 211, p. 250.

31. *Ibid.*

32. Memorial of the People of the townships of Horton, Cornwallis . . . , *op. cit.*

33. Jonathan Belcher to Dr. Burton, 16 December 1763, Society for the Propagation of the Gospel in Foreign Parts (S.P.G.), Series B-25, Letters Received, Nova Scotia 1760-1786, No. 25 (Washington, Library of Congress).

34. Cornwallis Town Meeting, 14 [April] 1771, P.A.C., Mss. Group 9, B-9, Nova Scotia Local Records, p. 4.

35. Bailyn, *The Ideological Origins of the American Revolution*, pp. 97, 118-119, 232-233.

CHAPTER 2 (*pp. 24-44*)

1. E. Gay, *A Call to Macedonia. A Sermon preached at Hingham in New England, October 12, 1768, at the Ordination of the Reverend Mr. Caleb Garrett to the work of the Ministry and Pastoral Care of a Society of Protestant Christians in the Town of Cumberland, in the Province of Nova Scotia* (Boston, 1768), pp. 31-33.

2. G. Stourzh, *Benjamin Franklin and American Foreign Policy* (Chicago, 1953), p. 91.

3. Gay, *A Call to Macedonia*, pp. 27-28.

4. *Ibid.*, p. 29.

5. Benjamin Gerrish and Malachi Salter to Andrew Eliot, 18 January 1770, Massachusetts Historical Society *Proceedings*, Second Series, Vol. IV (1887-1889), pp. 69-71; A.W.H. Eaton, "The First Church founded by New England People in Kings County Nova Scotia," *New England Historical and Geneological Register*, Vol. XLVI (1892), pp. 219-223; The Records of the Church of Jebogue in Yarmouth . . . By Jonathan Scott . . . P.A.N.S., pp. 6, 7, 23; E. Crowell, *A History of Barrington Township* (Yarmouth, 1923), pp. 165-167; J. Hannay, "The Maugerville Settlement," New Brunswick Historical Society *Collections*, Vol. I, no. 1 (1894), pp. 67-77; MacKinnon, *Settlements and Churches*, p. 71.

6. Records of the Church of Jebogue, P.A.N.S., p. 4.

7. Peter Bishop, John Turner and Daniel Harris to John Davis, 27 October 1771, quoted in J.M. Bumsted, "The Origins of the Maritime Baptists: A New Document," *Dalhousie Review*, Vol. LIX, No. 1 (Spring 1969), pp. 190-192.

8. Cornwallis Congregational Church to Andrew Eliot, 8 November 1769, Massachusetts Historical Society, Andrew Eliot Papers, Correspondence 1720-1812, p. 103.

9. Gay, *A Call to Macedonia*, p. 29.

10. Bumsted, "The Origins of the Maritime Baptists," p. 91.

11. Cornwallis Congregational Church to Andrew Eliot, 8 November 1769, M.H.S., *op. cit.*

12. Records of the Church of Jebogue, P.A.N.S., pp. 54-55.

13. Truro Township Book 1770-1824, P.A.C. Mss. Group 9, B-9, p. 15.

14. Brebner, *The Neutral Yankees*, pp. 299-300.

15. Truro Township Book 1770-1824, *op. cit.*

16. Cornwallis Congregational Church to Andrew Eliot, 8 November 1769, M.H.S., *op. cit.*; Eaton, "The First Church . . . ," p. 219.

17. Bumsted, "The Origins of the Maritime Baptists," pp. 90-92.

18. Records of the Church at Jebogue, P.A.N.S., p. 32.

19. Cornwallis Congregational Church to Andrew Eliot, 8 November 1769, M.H.S., *op. cit.*

20. *Ibid.* and Bumsted, "The Origins of the Maritime Baptists," p. 90.

21. *A Brief State of the Circumstances of the Protestant Dissenters*, P.A.N.S., Vol. 284, No. 18.

22. Michael Franklin to Dr. Burton, 29 December 1766, S.P.G., *op. cit.*, No. 103; Jonathan Belcher to Dr. Burton, 16 December 1763, *ibid.*, No. 42.

23. Joseph Bennett to S.P.G., 14 June 1765, *ibid.*, No. 66; Eaton, "The First Church . . . ," p. 221.

24. Cornwallis Congregational Church to Andrew Eliot, 8 November 1769, M.H.S., *op. cit.*

25. *A Brief State of the Circumstances of the Protestant Dissenters*, *op. cit.*

26. Quoted in Heimert, *Religion and the American Mind*, p. 366.

27. Joseph Bennett to the S.P.G., 22 August 1767, S.P.G., *op. cit.*, No. 112.

28. D. Adair and J.A. Schutz, eds., *Peter Oliver's Origin and Progress of the American Rebellion: A Tory View* (San Marino, 1961), pp. 63-64, 106; Butterfield, ed., *Diary and Autobiography of John Adams*, Vol. I, pp. 279-280.

29. Heimert, *Religion and the American Mind*, pp. 353-354, 387.

30. Benjamin Garrish and Malachi Salter to Andrew Eliot and Samuel Cooper, 18 January 1770, M.H.S., *Proceedings*, Vol. IV, Second Series (1887-1889), pp. 69-71.

31. *Dictionary of American Biography*, Vol. VII (New York, 1931), pp. 194-195.

32. Hannay, "The Maugerville Settlement," pp. 69-70.

33. Records of the Church of Jebogue in Yarmouth, P.A.N.S., pp. 81-82.

34. M.W. Armstrong, "Elder Moulton and the Nova Scotia Baptists," *Dalhousie Review*, Vol. XXIV (October 1944), pp. 320-325.

35. Eaton, "The First Church . . . ," p. 223.

36. Crowell, *A History of Barrington Township*, pp. 79, 94-96, 165-167.

37. Rev. M. Thomas Wood to Richard Bulkeley, 29 July 1769. S.P.G., *op. cit.*, No. 140.

38. B.E. Steiner, "New England Anglicanism: A Genteel Faith?" *William and Mary Quarterly*, 3rd Ser., Vol. XXVII (January 1970), pp. 122-136.

39. Inhabitants of Annapolis and Granville to the Reverend Mr. Clarke, 30 September 1770, S.P.G., *op cit.*, No. 173.

40. Thomas Wood to Dr. Hind, 4 April 1775, *ibid.*, no. 187.

41. Jonathan Doggett, Robert Slocombe and others of Liverpool to John Breynton, 20 December 1766, *ibid.*, no. 102; Michael Franklin to Dr. Burton, 29 December 1766, *ibid.*, no. 103.

42. W.B. Kerr, "The Stamp Act Crisis in Nova Scotia," *New England Quarterly*, Vol. VI (September 1933), p. 558.

43. Bailyn, *The Ideological Origins of the American Revolution*, p. 22. On the secularization of the American mind during the revolutionary period see E.S. Morgan, "The American Revolution Considered as an Intellectual Movement," in A. Schlesinger and M. White, eds., *Paths of American Thought* (Boston, 1963).

CHAPTER 3 (*pp. 45-62*)

1. For a more detailed description of the Eddy rebellion see G.A. Rawlyk, "Nova Scotia and the American Revolution Reconsidered," *Dalhousie Review*, Vol. XLIII (Autumn 1963), pp. 379-394.

2. Proclamation of 19 September 1774, P.A.N.S., Vol. 212, pp. 207-208.

3. Meeting of the Freeholders of the Township of Cornwallis, 14 (April?) 1771, P.A.C., 9, B-9, p. 4.

4. Anonymous letter to George Washington, 8 February 1776, in P. Force, ed., *American Archives*, Fourth Series, Vol. V (Washington, 1844), pp. 936-938.

5. Council Minutes of 5 December 1775, P.A.N.S., Vol. 212, pp. 298-299.

6. Brown, *Middle-Class Democracy and the Revolution in Massachusetts*, pp. 209, 223-224, 255-257.

7. The Petition of Jacob Barker, Israel Perley, Phineas Nevers, Daniel Palmer, Moses Pickard . . . 21 May 1776, Massachusetts Archives, Vol. 144, pp. 147-154.

8. Anonymous letter to Washington, 8 February 1776, in Force, ed., *American Archives*, Vol. V, pp. 936-938.

9. Butterfield, ed., *Diary and Autobiography of John Adams*, Vol. 1, p. 341.

10. Butterfield, *An Essay on the Present State of . . . Nova Scotia*, pp. 18-20.

11. Crowell, *A History of Barrington Township*, p. 167.

12. Petition of the Inhabitants of Barrington, 19 October 1776, Massachusetts Archives, Vol. 211, pp. 122-123.

13. John Stanton to Governor Thomas Legge, 4 December 1775, P.A.C. A-96, p. 275.

14. C.B. Fergusson, ed., "The Life of Jonathan Scott," P.A.N.S. *Bulletin*, No. 15 (Halifax, 1960), p. 51.

15. H.A. Innis, ed., *The Diary of Simeon Perkins*, 1766-1780 (Toronto, 1948), p. 75.

16. For a general discussion of how a people in a subjugated political and constitutional position develop a "colonial mentality" by accepting normal

values of the dominant society, see Albert Memmi, *The Colonizer and the Colonized* (Boston, 1967).

17. Memorial of Josiah Throop, 27 December 1776, Massachusetts Archives, Vol. 36, p. 347.

18. The Petition of Jacob Barker, 21 May 1776, *op. cit.*, pp. 147-154.

19. *Ibid.*, pp. 149-150.

20. Memorial and Petition of John Allan of Cumberland, 19 February 1777, *ibid.*, pp. 169-171; G.H. Allan, "Sketch of Col. John Allan," *New England Historical and Genealogical Register*, Vol. XXX (1876), p. 355.

21. Memorial and Petition of John Allan of Cumberland, 19 February 1777, Massachusetts Archives, Vol. 144, p. 169.

22. *Ibid.*, pp. 169-171.

23. *Ibid.*

24. John Allan to the Massachusetts Council, 27 February 1777, *ibid.*, p. 192.

25. John Allan to the Massachusetts Council, 7 March 1777, *ibid.*, p. 175.

26. John Winthrop to the Delegates of Massachusetts at the Continental Congress, 2 August 1776, *ibid.*, Vol. 195, p. 165.

27. John Fulton to John Allan, 21 July 1780, P.A.C., Mss. Group 23, B-2, Box 2, Vol. 2.

28. J. Hannay, "The Maugerville Settlement," New Brunswick Historical Society *Collections*, Vol. 1, No. 1 (1894), pp. 74-81; F.B. Dexter, ed., *The Literary Diary of Ezra Stiles* (New York, 1901), p. 518; Isaac Winslow to John Allan, Marshfield, 5 April 1775, *New England Historical and Genealogical Register*, Vol. 30 (1876), p. 354.

29. F. Kidder, *Military Operations in Eastern Maine and Nova Scotia during the Revolution* (Albany, 1867), pp. 1-23, "Memoir of Col. John Allan"; also pp. 319-320.

30. *Ibid.*, pp. 170-173.

31. Brebner, *The Neutral Yankees*, pp. 278-279.

32. E.D. Poole, *Annals of Yarmouth and Barrington in the Revolutionary War* (Yarmouth, 1899), pp. 9, 12, 38-43, 50, 51-52, 57.

33. Memorial and Petition of John Allan of Cumberland, 19 February 1777, Massachusetts Archives, Vol. 144, p. 169.

34. Inhabitants of Maugerville to Arthur Goold, 12 May, 16 May, 1777, P.A.N.S. Vol. 409; Maugerville Committee of Safety to James Simonds, James White and James Say, 20 June 1776, Massachusetts Archives, Vol. 181, pp. 248-249.

35. W.O. Raymond, "Col. Alexander McNutt and the Pre-Loyalist Settlements of Nova Scotia," Royal Society of Canada *Transactions*, 3rd Ser., Vol. VI (May 1912) sect. ii, pp. 201-217.

36. A. McNutt to James Lovell, William Whipple and John Witherspoon, 23 December 1778, P.A.C., Mss. Group 23, B-2, Box 1, Fol. 2.

37. James Lovell to Horatio Gates, 3 June 1779, in E.C. Burnett, ed., *Letters of the Members of the Continental Congress* (Washington, 1928), Vol. IV, p. 246.

CHAPTER 4 (*pp. 63-76*)

1. John Allan to the inhabitants of Maugerville, 4 June 1777, Massachusetts Archives, Vol. 197, pp. 139-140.
2. E.S. Morgan, "The Puritan Ethic and the American Revolution, *William and Mary Quarterly*, XXIV (January 1967), pp. 3-44; Bailyn, *The Ideological Origins of the American Revolution*, pp. 139-140.
3. Maugerville Inhabitants to Arthur Goold, 16 May 1777, P.A.N.S., Vol. 409, Papers on the River St. John, pp. 764-1809.
4. Inhabitants of Barrington to the Massachusetts Congress, 19 October 1776, Massachusetts Archives, Vol. 211, pp. 122-124.
5. *Ibid.*
6. Brebner, *The Neutral Yankees*, pp. 271-275; Rawlyk, "The American Revolution and Nova Scotia Reconsidered," pp. 389-390.
7. Inhabitants of Barrington to the Massachusetts Congress, 19 October 1776, Massachusetts Archives, Vol. 211, pp. 122-124.
8. Robert Monckton to Sir Charles Hardy, 12 April 1758, P.A.C. Mss. Group 18, M, Vol. I.
9. Liverpool Third Book of Justice Records, October 1779 to May 1787, *ibid.*, Mss. Group 9, B-9, pp. 17-25.
10. Fergusson, ed., "The Life of Jonathan Scott," pp. 52-54, 62.
11. Inhabitants of Barrington to the Massachusetts Congress, 19 October 1776, Massachusetts Archives, *op. cit.*
12. *Ibid.*
13. Brebner, *The Neutral Yankees*, pp. 275-278, 289-290.
14. John Burbidge to Richard Bulkeley, 12 September, 17 September, 1778, P.A.N.S. Vol. 220, No. 52-53.
15. Memorial of Several of the principal Inhabitants of the Township of Cornwallis to Arbuthnot, n.d., *ibid.*, Vol. 222, No. 65.
16. James Lyon to the Massachusetts Council, September 1776, Massachusetts Archives, Vol. 195, pp. 219-221.
17. "Diary of Robert Foster," *New England Historical and Genealogical Register*, Vol. XLVIII, pp. 182-184.
18. Memorial . . . , 21 March 1777, P.A.N.S., Vol. 227, No. 66.
19. Deposition of John Cole, 31 October 1776, *ibid.*, Vol. 342, No. 73.
20. See, for example, the Memorial of the Committee of Safety for the County of Sunbury in Nova Scotia, 24 September 1776, Massachusetts Archives, Vol. 181, p. 247.
21. Fergusson, ed., "The Life of Jonathan Scott," p. 57; Henry Alline, *The Life and Journal of the Rev. Mr. Henry Alline* (Boston, 1806), p. 123.
22. Brebner, *The Neutral Yankees*, p. 275; Clark, *Movements of Political Protest in Canada*, pp. 69-70.
23. See J.B. Brebner, *New England's Outpost: Acadia before the Conquest of Canada* (New York, 1927), passim; Proceedings of the Assembly and

Council of Massachusetts, 1755-1759, on the Acadians deported from Nova Scotia, P.A.C., Mss. Group 18, F-15.

24. Memorial of the Inhabitants of Yarmouth, 8 December 1775, P.A.C. Series A, Vol. 94, p. 300.

25. Inhabitants of Cumberland to Governor Legge, 23 December 1775, quoted in G.A. Rawlyk, *Revolution Rejected, 1775-1776* (Toronto, 1968), p. 28.

26. See J.H. Ahlin, *Maine Rubicon: Downeast Settlers during the American Revolution* (Calais, Me., 1966).

27. Joseph Tufts to Massachusetts Council, November 1775, Massachusetts Archives, Vol. 180, p. 240.

28. "Report of Col. Allan's Journey to Frenchman's Bay etc.," 17 March 1781, in Kidder, *Military Operations in Eastern Maine and Nova Scotia*, pp. 288-291.

29. Petition of Jacob Barker, . . . 21 May 1776, Massachusetts Archives, *op. cit.*

30. *Ibid.*

31. Maugerville Committee of Safety to James Simonds, James White and James Say, 20 June 1776, Massachusetts Archives, Vol. 181, pp. 248-249.

32. John Allan to Massachusetts Council, 18 and 20 June 1777, *ibid.*, Vol. 197, pp. 164-165.

33. Fergusson, ed., "The Life of Jonathan Scott," pp. 51, 62.

34. Massachusetts Committee of Safety to the Massachusetts Council, 27 November 1776, Massachusetts Archives, Vol. 195, p. 338.

35. Inhabitants of Barrington to the Massachusetts Congress, 19 October 1776, Massachusetts Archives, *op. cit.*

36. Innis, ed., *The Diary of Simeon Perkins, 1766-1780*, pp. 152, 165.

37. Letters from Joseph Winniet and Thomas Williams to the Nova Scotia Council, P.A.N.S., Vol. 212, pp. 254, 280.

38. Thomas Wood to Dr. Hind, 26 June 1777, S.P.G., *op. cit.*, No. 216.

39. J. Wingate Weeks to S.P.G., *ibid.*, No. 247.

40. Peter de la Roche to Dr. Hind, 15 December 1778, *ibid.*, No. 220.

41. William Ellis to S.P.G., *ibid.*, No. 208.

42. "Extract of a Letter from John Allan," 22 September 1777, and "Report of John Allan," 17 August 1778, in Kidder, *Military Operations in Eastern Maine and Nova Scotia*, pp. 228-231, 253-255.

CHAPTER 5 (*pp. 79-97*)

1. M.W. Armstrong, "Henry Alline's Spiritual Hymns and Songs," *Dalhousie Review*, Vol. XXXIV (1954-5), pp. 418-425. For a fuller analysis of Alline's religious thought, particularly its English sources, see Armstrong, *The Great Awakening in Nova Scotia*, pp. 93-104; for a brief account of Law's work and influence see F.L. Cross, ed., *The Oxford Dictionary of the Christian Church* (London, 1957), p. 791.

2. Alline, *Life and Journal*, pp. 7-40, 43-49.

3. J. Scott, *A Brief View of the Religious Tenets And Sentiments Lately Published And Spread in the Province of Nova Scotia* (Halifax, 1784); and Fergusson, ed., "The Life of Jonathan Scott," pp. 17-18, 22-24; Records of the Church of Jebogue in Yarmouth, P.A.N.S., pp. 82-89, 94, 132-157.

4. For example, I.E. Bill, *Fifty Years with the Baptist Ministers in the Maritime Provinces* (Saint John, 1880), p. 14, described Alline's ideas as confused and M. Richey, *A Memoir of the late Rev. William Black . . .* (Halifax, 1839), p. 45, stated that Alline's religious tenets were "fragments of different systems . . . without any mutual relation or dependence." The Reverend Mr. James Macgregor, a pioneer of Nova Scotia Presbyterians, felt that Alline's thought was "a mixture of Calvinism, Antinomianism and Enthusiasm." See G. Patterson, *Memoir of the Rev. James Macgregor* (Philadelphia, 1859), p. 351.

5. Armstrong, *The Great Awakening in Nova Scotia*, pp. 88-107.

6. Alline, *The Anti-Traditionist* (Halifax, 1783), pp. 20-22; Alline, *Two Mites on Some of the Most Important and Much Disputed Points of Divinity . . .* pp. 40-45, 221; William Law, *Works* (London, 1762), Vol. VI, pp. 2-8; Vol. VII, pp. 55 ff; Vol. VI, pp. 58, 132, 158.

7. W. Law, *An Extract from a treatise by William Law* (Philadelphia, 1766), pp. 16, 29, 36; Alline, *Two Mites*, pp. 18, 121; Alline, *A Gospel Call to Sinners . . .* (Newburyport, 1795), p. 16.

8. Armstrong, *The Great Awakening in Nova Scotia*, pp. 95-97.

9. John Wesley to William Black, London, 13 July 1783, in J. Telford, ed., *The Letters of the Rev. John Wesley*, Vol. VII (London, 1931), pp. 182-183.

10. Alline, *Two Mites*, preface.

11. C. Black, *Historical Record of the Posterity of William Black who settled in this County in the year 1775* (Amherst, N.S., 1885), p. 31; Records of the Church of Jebogue in Yarmouth, P.A.N.S., pp. 134-135; Alline, *Life and Journal*, pp. 138-141.

12. Scott, *A Brief View*, p. 208; D.C. Harvey, ed., *Diary of Simeon Perkins, 1780-1789* (Toronto, 1958), p. 177.

13. Scott, *A Brief View*, pp. 81, 193, 201, 209, 211, 263-265, 301, 319-321.

14. Alline, *Life and Journal*, pp. 3-7, 20, 24, 30, 40-42.

15. *Ibid.*, pp. 24, 30, 43.

16. Scott, *A Brief View*, p. 209.

17. E.W. Baker, *A Herald of the Evangelical Revival. A Critical Inquiry into the Relation of William Law to John Wesley and the beginnings of Methodism* (London, 1948), pp. 43, 73-74.

18. Alline, *Two Mites*, pp. 33-34, 234-237, 251, 325, 339-340.

19. Scott, *A Brief View*, p. 207.

20. Alline, *A Sermon preached at Pt. Medway, February 19, 1783* (n.p., n.d.), pp. 19, 40; Alline, *The Anti-Traditionist*, p. 40; Alline, *A Gospel*

Call to Sinners, pp. 13, 33. Edwards, in his *Sinners in the Hands of an Angry God* (1741), had used the simile of a spider suspended by a thread over a fire to instil into his hearers the necessary sense of urgency about conversion. See Heimert, *Religion and the American Mind*, pp. 39-40, where he argues that "terror" sermons were not typical of evangelicals and that to regard them as such "is to distort the character of the entire evangelical impulse."

21. Alline, *A Sermon preached at Pt. Medway*, pp. 19-20.
22. Quoted in Heimert, *Religion and the American Mind*, p. 337.
23. Alline, *A Sermon preached at Pt. Medway*, pp. 19-20; Alline, *A Gospel Call to Sinners*, p. 20; Records of the Church of Jebogue in Yarmouth, P.A.N.S., pp. 144-145.
24. Alline, *Two Mites*, pp. 267-268.
25. Alline, *The Anti-Traditionist*, pp. 63-65; see also Armstrong, *The Great Awakening in Nova Scotia*, pp. 101-103.
26. Alline, *Two Mites*, pp. 264, 128, 84.
27. Alline, *A Gospel Call to Sinners*, pp. 25-26; Alline, *A Sermon Preached . . . at Liverpool . . . on the 21st November, 1782* (Halifax, n.d.), pp. 8, 25-26, 38; Alline, *Two Mites*, pp. 130, 175; Alline, *Life and Journal*, pp. 34-35, 59.
28. Alline, *Two Mites*, pp. 339-340, 251.
29. Scott, *A Brief View*, pp. 144-147, 209.
30. Alline, *Life and Journal*, pp. 51, 59-60; Alline, *Two Mites*, pp. 159, 161, 153-154, 177.
31. Heimert, *Religion and the American Mind*, pp. 41-42.
32. Alline, *A Gospel Call to Sinners*, pp. 25-26; Alline, *Life and Journal*, pp. 34-35.
33. Scott, *A Brief View*, p. 167.
34. Alline, *Life and Journal*, p. 22.
35. Records of the Church of Jebogue in Yarmouth, P.A.N.S., pp. 138, 147.
36. Alline, *Life and Journal*, pp. 40-47.
37. Manuscript New Brunswick History, by the Rev. Joseph Crandall, p. 2, Acadia University Archives.
38. Alline, *A Sermon preached at Pt. Medway*, pp. 43-44.
39. Harvey, ed., *Diary of Simeon Perkins, 1780-1789*, p. 177.
40. Heimert, *Religion and the American Mind*, p. 159.
41. Records of the Church of Jebogue in Yarmouth, P.A.N.S., p. 140.

CHAPTER 6 (*pp. 98-120*)

1. During the revolutionary war period there were two main areas of settlement within Yarmouth Township — Chebogue (or Jebogue) and Cape Forchu. This chapter deals with the Congregational church organized at

"Jebogue in Yarmouth" and for convenience it is referred to as the "Yarmouth Church." Jebogue was the most populous part of the region; no churches were formally organized in Cape Forchu or nearby Argyle in the pre-revolutionary period.

2. Records of the Church of Jebogue in Yarmouth, P.A.N.S., pp. 9-10, 14-17.

3. *Ibid.*, pp. 19-21, 36; Fergusson, ed., "The Life of Jonathan Scott," pp. 29-34.

4. Records of the Church of Jebogue in Yarmouth, pp. 20-21; C.K. Shipton, *Sibley's Harvard Graduates* (Boston, 1960), Vol. XI, pp. 568-569.

5. Records of the Church of Jebogue in Yarmouth, p. 23.

6. *Ibid.*, pp. 9-10, 21.

7. *Ibid.*, pp. 23-24.

8. M. Armstrong, "Elder Moulton and the Nova Scotia Baptists," *op. cit.*, pp. 320-325.

9. Records of the Church of Jebogue in Yarmouth, pp. 24, 27.

10. *Ibid.*, pp. 28-30.

11. *Ibid.*, pp. 37, 45; Fergusson, ed., "The Life of Jonathan Scott," pp. 28-30, 34.

12. *Ibid.*, pp. 18, 20-21.

13. *Ibid.*, pp. 17-18, 26, 30.

14. Records of the Church of Jebogue in Yarmouth, pp. 20-21, 29-30.

15. Fergusson, ed., "The Life of Jonathan Scott," pp. 30-33.

16. *Ibid.*, pp. 17-21, 29.

17. C.C. Goen, *Revivalism and Separatism in New England, 1740-1800* (New Haven, 1962), p. 218, 222n; Publications of the Colonial Society of Massachusetts. *Collections*, Vol. XII, Plymouth Church Records, 1620-1859, Vol. I, Part I, pp. xxv-xxxvi, xxxix.

18. Records of the Church of Jebogue in Yarmouth, p. 37.

19. Scott, *A Brief View*, pp. 285, 145, 158, 294, 320, 147.

20. Scott to the Church and Congregation of Liverpool, 20 November 1782, Records of the Church of Jebogue in Yarmouth, pp. 157-159.

21. Fergusson, ed., "The Life of Jonathan Scott," p. 24; Records of the Church of Jebogue in Yarmouth, p. 138.

22. Records of the Church of Jebogue in Yarmouth, p. 107.

23. Fergusson, ed., "The Life of Jonathan Scott," p. 31.

24. *Ibid.*, pp. 60, 62; Records of the Church of Jebogue in Yarmouth, pp. 138-139.

25. Records of the Church of Jebogue in Yarmouth, pp. 136-139, 147, 150.

26. *Ibid.*, pp. 133, 140, 151-153. See also Scott, *A Brief View*, vi-vii.

27. Records of the Church of Jebogue in Yarmouth, p. 133.

28. Scott, *A Brief View*, pp. 276-277.

29. Records of the Church of Jebogue in Yarmouth, p. 146.

30. *Ibid.*

31. *Ibid.*

32. Scott, *A Brief View*, p. 208.
33. Records of the Church of Jebogue in Yarmouth, pp. 133-134.
34. *Ibid.*, pp. 134-135; Scott, *A Brief View*, pp. 225, 276-277.
35. Records of the Church of Jebogue in Yarmouth, p. 135.
36. *Ibid.*, p. 135; Alline, *Life and Journal*, pp. 147-151; Harvey, ed., *The Diary of Simeon Perkins*, 1780-1789, pp. 103, 108-109.
37. Records of the Church of Jebogue in Yarmouth, pp. 135-136.
38. Alline, *Life and Journal*, p. 70; Scott, *A Brief View*, pp. 266-269.
39. Records of the Church of Jebogue in Yarmouth, p. 134.
40. *Ibid.*, p. 137.
41. Fergusson, ed., "The Life of Jonathan Scott," p. 25.
42. Scott, *A Brief View*, p. 285.
43. *Ibid.*, pp. 285-287, 293, 301.
44. Records of the Church of Jebogue in Yarmouth, pp. 92-93, 97-98, 138-139.
45. *Ibid.*, pp. 138-139.
46. J. Johnson, *Zion's Memorial of the Present Work of God* (n.p., 1765), pp. 49-50.
47. *Ibid.*, pp. 58-60.
48. See Heimert, *Religion and the American Mind*, pp. 131-133.
49. Johnson, *Zion's Memorial*, p. 59.
50. Records of the Church of Jebogue in Yarmouth, p. 136.
51. *Ibid.*, p. 143.
52. Fergusson, ed., "The Life of Jonathan Scott," p. 20.
53. Alline, *Life and Journal*, pp. 155-156.
54. Scott, *A Brief View*, pp. 252, 333.
55. Records of the Church of Jebogue in Yarmouth, p. 144.
56. *Ibid.*, pp. 132-157.
57. *Ibid.*, pp. 82-83, 89, 92-93, 95, 98, 100-101, 156-157, 182-183, 186-187.

CHAPTER 7 (*pp. 121-139*)

1. Records of the Church of Jebogue in Yarmouth, pp. 133-140,142-143.
2. Mary Bradley, *A Narrative of the Life and Christian Experience of Mrs. Mary Bradley of St. John, New Brunswick* (Boston, 1849), p. 16.
3. Harvey, ed., *The Diary of Simeon Perkins*, 1780-1789, p. 177.
4. Alline, *Life and Journal*, pp. 57, 66-70.
5. Records of the Church of Jebogue in Yarmouth, pp. 136, 153.
6. Harvey, ed., *The Diary of Simeon Perkins*, pp. xxii, 1n, 102, 108-109.
7. Alline, *Life and Journal*, p. 138.
8. *Ibid.*, pp. 98, 117, 131-133, 145, 158, 168; Records of the Church of Jebogue in Yarmouth, p. 133.

9. Compare for example Alline, *Life and Journal*, pp. 147, 151-152, with Records of the Church of Jebogue in Yarmouth, pp. 132-136.

10. Alline, *Life and Journal*, pp. 49-165; Harvey, ed., *The Diary of Simeon Perkins*, pp. 103, 108-109, 113, 117; Records of the Church of Jebogue in Yarmouth, pp. 82-187; Scott, *A Brief View*, pp. vi, 205-208, 212-216, 219-222, 257, 266-270.

11. *Ibid.*, pp. 206, 219-221.

12. Harvey, ed., *The Diary of Simeon Perkins*, pp. 103, 108-109, 113, 177; Alline, *Life and Journal*, p. 149.

13. *Ibid.*, pp. 166-167.

14. *Ibid.*, p. 148; Harvey, ed., *The Diary of Simeon Perkins*, p. 103.

15. Alline, *Life and Journal*, pp. 148, 167.

16. Records of the Church of Jebogue in Yarmouth, p. 132.

17. Alline, *Life and Journal*, pp. 70-71; Hannay, "The Maugerville Settlement," pp. 63-88.

18. Bradley, *A Narrative*, pp. 17-18.

19. Alline, *Life and Journal*, pp. 47-51; Records of the Church of Jebogue in Yarmouth, p. 100.

20. William Ellis to S.P.G., S.P.G., *op. cit.*, No. 208.

21. Records of the Church of Jebogue in Yarmouth, pp. 143, 153.

22. Alline, *Life and Journal*, pp. 54, 60, 135, 138, 140, 145; Scott, *A Brief View*, p. 219.

23. Alline, *Life and Journal*, pp. 160-162.

24. *Ibid.*, p. 134.

25. Alline, *A Sermon Preached at Pt. Medway*, p. 3.

26. Records of the Church of Jebogue in Yarmouth, p. 135.

27. Alline, *A Sermon Preached at Liverpool, 21 November*, p. 38.

28. Alline, *Two Mites*, pp. 154, 175. For another view of the issue see S.F. Wise's "God's Peculiar Peoples," in W.L. Morton, ed., *The Shield of Achilles* (Toronto, 1968), pp. 38-40.

29. Alline, *A Sermon Preached at Liverpool, 21 November*, pp. 6, 25-57.

30. *Ibid.*, p. 26. J.M. Bumsted, in a recent study, sees the revival, as did S.D. Clark and others, as a revolt of the outsettlements against the Nova Scotia "establishment." See for example, J.M. Bumsted, "Henry Alline and the Counterculture of Maritime Canada," pp. 20-22, a paper prepared for delivery on June 3, 1971, at the Annual Meeting of the Canadian Historical Association at St. John's, Newfoundland.

31. C.B. Fergusson, "Early Liverpool and its Diarist," P.A.N.S. *Bulletin*, no. 16 (Halifax, 1961), pp. 20-29, 39, 50-53.

32. Alline, *Life and Journal*, p. 123.

33. Records of the Church of Jebogue in Yarmouth, pp. 136, 138.

34. A Return of the Settlers with their Stock of the Township of Yarmouth, June 1764, P.A.N.S. Vol. 222, No. 23.

35. Fergusson, ed., "The Life of Jonathan Scott," p. 24n.

36. Records of the Church of Jebogue in Yarmouth, pp. 137-138.

37. *Ibid.*, p. 132; Scott, *A Brief View*, pp. 223, 227.

38. William Ellis to the S.P.G., S.P.G., *op. cit.*, No. 208.

39. Alline, *Life and Journal*, pp. 119, 123.

40. *Ibid.*, p. 138.

41. Scott, *A Brief View*, pp. 208, 213-214; Alline, *Life and Journal*, p. 138; Records of the Church at Jebogue in Yarmouth, pp. 133-134.

42. Scott, *A Brief View*, pp. 210-216.

43. It appears from the limited evidence available that age rather than economic status may have been a critical factor in the revival. Alline constantly referred to the "young people" or people in the "prime of life" who were his most enthusiastic supporters. Many of his followers were drawn primarily from the age group 15-40, that is, people who had been born since 1740 who were either young children when the emigration to Nova Scotia occurred or who were actually born in the northern colony. This might be one of the major reasons why Alline's confused ideas had such an appeal. See Alline, *Life and Journal*, pp. 17, 49-50, 55, 58, 78, 112, 120-122, 137-140.

44. W.A. Sloan, "Halifax During the American Revolution: The Role of the Inarticulate?" (Unpublished paper, Queen's University, December 1969).

45. Y. Talmon, "Pursuit of the Millenium," in B. McLaughlin, ed., *Studies in Social Movements. A Social Psychological Perspective* (Toronto, 1969), p. 419.

CHAPTER 8 (*pp. 140-153*)

1. C. Ake, "Charismatic Legitimation and Political Integration," *Comparative Studies in Society and History*, Vol. IX, No. 1 (October 1966), pp. 4, 12.

2. Max Weber, *The Theory of Social and Economic Organization* (New York, 1947), and S.N. Eisenstadt, ed., *Max Weber on Charisma and Institutional Building: Selected Papers* (Chicago, 1968).

3. Ake, "Charismatic Legitimation," pp. 7-10.

4. Weber, *The Theory of Social and Economic Organization*, pp. 329, 358-359.

5. Ake, "Charismatic Legitimation," p. 10.

6. Alline, *Life and Journal*, pp. 36-37.

7. Alline, *A Gospel Call to Sinners*, p. 29.

8. *Ibid.*, p. 5.

9. Alline, *Life and Journal*, pp. 110, 134, 139, 147-150, 164-165.

10. *Ibid.*, pp. 17, 47-48.

11. *Ibid.*, pp. 48, 57, 67, 77, 80, 84, 97, 101.

12. *Ibid.*, pp. 58, 63, 74, 134, 139, 153.

13. *Ibid.*, p. 69.

14. *Ibid.*, p. 163.

15. *Ibid.*, p. 164.
16. *Ibid.*, p. 53.
17. *Ibid.*
18. W.H. Friedland, "For a Sociological Concept of Charisma," *Social Forces*, Vol. 43, No. 1 (October 1964), pp. 18-26.
19. Alline, *Life and Journal*, pp. 119, 123, 159.
20. Fergusson, ed., "The Life of Jonathan Scott," pp. 56-60.
21. Alline, *Life and Journal*, pp. 82, 143, 148-149, 151, 171.
22. *Ibid.*, p. 132.
23. *Ibid.*, p. 133.
24. *Ibid.*
25. *Ibid.*, pp. 137-141; Records of the Church of Jebogue in Yarmouth, p. 143.
26. Alline, *Life and Journal*, pp. 140-141, 161.
27. Records of the Church of Jebogue in Yarmouth, p. 143.
28. Scott, *A Brief View*, pp. 235-236.
29. Alline, *Life and Journal*, pp. 109, 124.
30. Records of the Church of Jebogue in Yarmouth, pp. 138, 151.
31. Alline, *Life and Journal*, pp. 61-62.
32. Records of the Church of Jebogue in Yarmouth, p. 136.
33. *Ibid.*, p. 138.

CHAPTER 9 (*pp. 154-178*)

1. Friedland, "For a Sociological Concept of Charisma," p. 25.
2. Heimert, *Religion and the American Mind*, pp. 62-67.
3. Alline, *A Sermon Preached at Liverpool, 21st November*, p. 9; Alline, *A Sermon Preached at Pt. Medway*, p. 15; Alline, *The Anti-Traditionist*, pp. 7-9, 63-67, 70; Alline, *Hymns and Spiritual Songs* (Dover, N.H., 1797), p. 87.
4. Alline, *The Anti-Traditionist*, p. 24.
5. Alline, *Life and Journal*, p. 85.
6. Alline, *Two Mites*, p. 264.
7. For example, Johnson, *Zion's Memorial*, pp. 12, 65, 67.
8. W. Law and A. Benezet, *Thoughts on the nature of war and its repugnancy to the Christian Life* (Philadelphia, 1766), p. 14.
9. Alline, *Two Mites*, pp. 9, 24-25.
10. Alline, *A Sermon Preached at Liverpool, 21 November*, pp. 22-24.
11. See for example S. Sherwood, *The Church's Flight into the Wilderness . . .* (New York, 1776), p. 18.
12. S. Conant, *An Anniversary Sermon Preached at Plymouth, December 23, 1776 . . .* (Boston, 1777), p. 27.
13. Sherwood, *The Church's Flight*, p. 43.
14. Heimert, *Religion and the American Mind*, pp. 470-473, 481-490.

15. Alline, *A Sermon Preached at Liverpool, 21 November*, pp. 22-24; Alline, *The Anti-Traditionist*, pp. 9, 24-25; Alline, *Life and Journal*, p. 85; Alline, *Two Mites*, pp. 261-262; Conant, *An Anniversary Sermon*, pp. 74-80; Sherwood, *The Church's Flight*, pp. 17, 48-49.

16. Alline, *A Sermon Preached at Liverpool, 21 November*, pp. 21-22.

17. Alline, *Two Mites*, pp. 264-269.

18. *Ibid.*, p. 265.

19. There were small British garrisons posted at Liverpool, Windsor, Cornwallis, Cumberland, and at Fort Howe at the mouth of the St. John River. Apart from Cumberland and Windsor, most of the troops had arrived after 1777.

20. John Starr to John Allan, May 1779, P.A.C. 23, B-2, Box 2, Fol. 1; Council Minutes, 15 July 1775, P.A.N.S., Vol. 212, p. 254.

21. Fergusson, ed., "The Life of Jonathan Scott," p. 60.

22. Alline, *Life and Journal*, pp. 143, 148; Samuel Adams to James Warren, Philadelphia, 26 June 1776, in Burnett, ed., *Letters of the Members of the Continental Congress*, Vol. 1 (Washington, D.C., 1921) No. 684.

23. Alline, *A Sermon Preached at Liverpool, 21 November*, p. 23.

24. Alline, *Two Mites*, pp. 237-238, 261-262.

25. *Ibid.*, p. 238-239.

26. *Ibid.*, p. 197.

27. Scott, *A Brief View*, p. 147.

28. Records of the Church of Jebogue in Yarmouth, pp. 157-159.

29. Alline, *Life and Journal*, p. 68.

30. Alline, *Two Mites*, pp. 325, 339-340.

31. Alline, *A Gospel Call to Sinners*, p. 23; Alline, *A Sermon Preached at Pt. Medway*, pp. 27-28.

32. Alline, *Two Mites*, pp. 111-112.

33. Alline, *The Anti-Traditionist*, p. 9.

34. Alline, *A Sermon Preached at Pt. Medway*, p. 29.

35. Alline, *A Sermon Preached in Liverpool, 19 November*, pp. 27-28.

36. Alline, *Life and Journal*, pp. 64, 72.

37. *Ibid.*, p. 72.

38. Alline, *Two Mites*, p. 210; Alline, *A Sermon Preached in Liverpool, 19 November*, pp. 22, 27-28.

39. Alline, *Two Mites*, p. 233.

40. Alline, *Life and Journal*, pp. 49, 59, 68, 98.

41. Alline, *Two Mites*, pp. 33-34.

42. Alline, *Life and Journal*, p. 168.

43. Johnson, *Zion's Memorial*, p. 5.

44. Alline, *A Sermon Preached at Liverpool, 21 November*, pp. 28-29.

45. *Ibid.*, pp. 21-22.

46. See for example Sherwood, *The Church's Flight*; Conant, *An Anniversary Sermon*; and Nicholas Street, *The American States Acting Over the Part of the Children of Israel in the Wilderness* . . . (New Haven, 1777).

47. Conant, *An Anniversary Sermon*, p. 21; Sherwood, *The Church's Flight*, p. 18; Nicholas Street, *The American States Acting Over the Part of the Children of Israel in the Wilderness* (New Haven, 1777), pp. 28, 34.

48. Heimert, *Religion and the American Mind*, pp. 488-489, 497-498, 520, 532-534; Goen, *Revivalism and Separatism in New England*, pp. 68-90.

49. *The Ministers of the County of Windham to the People in their Charge* (Norwich, 1780), pp. 3-4, 8.

50. I. Backus, *A History of New England with Particular Reference to the Denomination of Christians Called Baptists* (Newton, 1871), Vol. II, pp. 265-266.

51. Conant, *An Anniversary Sermon*, pp. 22-23, 27; Sherwood, *The Church's Flight into the Wilderness*, dedication.

52. Backus, *A History of New England*, Vol. II, pp. 265-266.

53. Alline, *A Sermon Preached at Liverpool, 21 November*, pp. 22, 29.

54. Alline, *Life and Journal*, p. 60.

55. Alline, *A Sermon Preached at Liverpool, 21 November*, pp. 29-30.

56. Alline, *Life and Journal*, pp. 66-67, 171.

57. Alline, *Hymns and Spiritual Songs*, pp. 4-5, 160-161, 224.

58. Alline, *A Sermon Preached at Liverpool, 21 November*, p. 21.

59. Alline, *Two Mites*, pp. 50, 53.

60. Alline, *A Sermon Preached at Liverpool, 21 November*, p. 15.

61. Alline, *Life and Journal*, p. 64.

62. Alline, *A Sermon Preached at Liverpool, 21 November*, p. 22.

63. *Ibid.*, pp. 23-24.

64. *Ibid.*, pp. 9, 23.

65. *Ibid.*, pp. 23, 24.

66. Alline, *A Gospel Call to Sinners*, p. 29. Sections in the previous paragraphs paraphrase Bailyn, *The Ideological Origins*, pp. 22-23.

67. Alline, *Two Mites*, p. 234.

68. Alline, *A Sermon Preached at Liverpool, 21 November*, p. 12.

CHAPTER 10 (*pp. 179-192*)

1. Alline, *Life and Journal*, p. 171.

2. Hannay, "The Maugerville Settlement," pp. 84-86.

3. Alline, *Life and Journal*, pp. 70-71.

4. Bradley, *A Narrative*, p. 40.

5. G.E. Levy, "Diary of the Rev. Joseph Dimock," Nova Scotia Historical Society *Collections*, Vol. 28 (1949), pp. 62-63, 65-67.

6. *Ibid.*, pp. 66, 68.

7. Alline, *Life and Journal*, p. 54; Alline, *Two Mites*, pp. 309, 333.

8. Records of the Church of Jebogue in Yarmouth, p. 146.

9. *Ibid.*, pp. 82, 92-103, 132-159, 182-185.

10. Black, *Historical Record of the Posterity of William Black*, p. 31.

11. For examples of Tories' exaggerated loyalty towards Britain see Henry Barry, *The Advantages which America Derives* (Boston, 1775); Joseph Galloway, *A Candid Examination of the Mutual Claims of Great Britain and the Colonies* (New York, 1775); Charles Inglis, *The True Interests of America Impartially Stated* (Philadelphia, 1776); Thomas B. Chandler, *The Strictures on the Friendly Address Examined* (New York, 1775); and Samuel Seabury, *A View of the Controversy Between Great Britain and Her Colonies* (New York, 1774). On the emergence of American nationalism after the Seven Years' War see Paul A. Varg, "The Advent of Nationalism," *American Quarterly*, Vol. XVI (1964), pp. 160-181. See also J. Potter, "The Lost Alternative: Loyalist Ideology and the American Revolution," (unpublished M.A. thesis, Queen's University, 1970).

12. G. Geertz, "Ideology as a Cultural System," in D. Apter, ed., *Ideology and Discontent* (Chicago, 1964), pp. 52-66; on dual loyalties, multiple loyalties and breakdown of loyalties, see Harold Guetzkow, *Multiple Loyalties: A Theoretical Approach to a Problem in International Organization* (Princeton, 1955). Also Richard Merritt, *Symbols of American Community 1735-1775* (New Haven, 1966), pp. 119-122.

13. D.B. Rutman, *American Puritanism* (Philadelphia, 1969), pp. 114-115.

14. Erik Erikson, *Identity, Youth and Crisis* (New York, 1968), pp. 22-23.

15. Rutman, *American Puritanism*, pp. 116-17; Erikson, *Young Man Luther* (New York, 1958) p. 41.

16. Talmon, "Pursuit of the Millenium," in McLaughlin, ed., *Studies in Social Movements*, p. 419.

17. Armstrong, "Neutrality and Religion in Revolutionary Nova Scotia," in Rawlyk, ed., *Historical Essays on the Atlantic Provinces*, p. 40.

EPILOGUE (*pp. 193-195*)

1. F.B. Dexter, ed., *The Diary of David McClure, Doctor of Divinity, 1748-1820* (New York, 1899), Introduction.

2. D. McClure, *An Oration on the Advantages of an early education . . .* (Exeter, 1783).

3. *Ibid.*, pp. 15-18.

4. E.L. Tuveson, *Redeemer Nation: The Idea of America's Millenial Role* (Chicago, 1968); H.N. Smith, *Virgin Land: The American West as Symbol and Myth* (Cambridge, Mass., 1950); R.W.B. Lewis, *The American Adam: Innocence, Tragedy and Tradition in the Nineteenth Century* (Chicago, 1955); C.L. Sanford, *The Quest for Paradise: Europe and the American Moral Imagination* (Urbana, 1961).

Index

215